To Dad with all our love,
Dot, Malcolm
and children
Christmas 1993.
x

WILLIAM HEATH ROBINSON

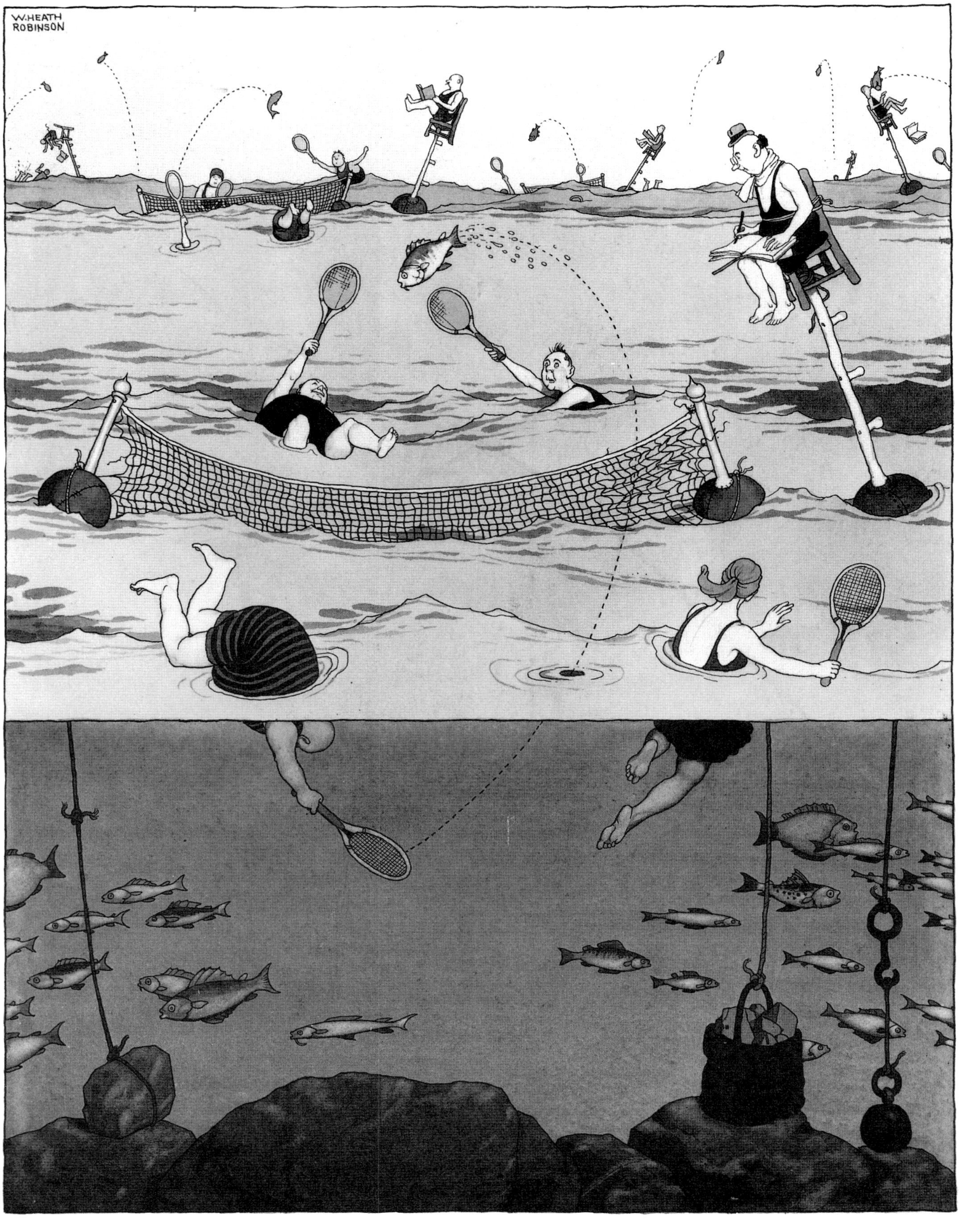
W. HEATH
ROBINSON

WILLIAM HEATH ROBINSON

James Hamilton

PAVILION

For

THOMAS and ELINOR

and to the memory of
DOM BASIL ROBINSON O.S.B.
1909–1992

The author would like to thank The Authors' Foundation for their generous contribution to the costs of research for this book.

First published in Great Britain in 1992 by
PAVILION BOOKS LIMITED
196 Shaftesbury Avenue, London WC2H 8JL

Designed by David Heath Fordham

The moral right of the author has been asserted

A CIP catalogue record for this book is available from the British Library.

ISBN 1 85145 719 4 (hbk)
ISBN 1 85793 030 4 (pbk)

Printed and bound in England by Butler and Tanner

2 4 6 8 10 9 7 5 3 1

Frontispiece: Fish Tennis: A Thrilling New Water Game
Pen and ink and wash, 1931
From *The Humorist*
Victoria and Albert Museum, London

Title page illustration: William Heath Robinson (1872–1944)
Photograph by Harrods, *c.* 1938
The Joan Brinsmead Trust

CONTENTS

ACKNOWLEDGEMENTS

As a young curator at Portsmouth City Museum and Art Gallery in the early 1970s I spent a memorable afternoon selecting an exhibition to be held at the Art Gallery with William Heath Robinson's widow, Mrs Josephine Robinson, and their daughter, Mrs Joan Brinsmead. Instead of the houseful of gadgets that I had expected unimaginatively to find, I met the friendly and generous Joan Brinsmead and her 95 year old mother, in a house that was disappointingly normal.

Josephine Robinson sat in the corner by the fire in a wing chair, smiling and nodding at me and asking me to speak up. I told her how much I admired her husband's work, and how his machines had preserved my sanity and raised my spirits when I spent a miserable term at Manchester University in 1966 as a first year Mechanical Engineering undergraduate. Had my tutors seen the sense in Heath Robinson's inventions, I thought, we might all be having a considerably happier time. Instead, the talk at Manchester was of big-ends and gyroscopes, and I was lost. I switched as quickly as I decently could to the History of Art.

This book is written in belated thanks for the enjoyment that Heath Robinson's drawings have given to me for many years, and for the generosity of spirit of William Heath Robinson and his family. Both Josephine Robinson and Joan Brinsmead have died, but the support I had from them has been amply renewed by Will and Josephine's surviving sons Oliver, Tom and Alan, now Dom Basil Robinson OSB. Other members of Will's family, including Dennis Brinsmead, Mrs Joyce Cooper, Mrs Alison Greenwood, Peter Higginson, Sir John Latey, the late Miss Christine Robinson, Guy Robinson, Helen Robinson, Toby Robinson and the late Mrs Madeleine Stevenson, answered my questions patiently and much more fully than perhaps the questions deserved.

If I have gained any new insight into my subject, a man whose elusive image strengthened and faded and changed in my mind as the book was being written, this is largely because of the many conversations I had with Will and Josephine's third child, Dom Basil, who was able to talk about his father with affection and detachment. The insight that Dom Basil gave me made up handsomely for the fact that Heath Robinson's surviving papers had left the family's possession and I did not have access to all of them. Those papers which have found their way to the security of public and university libraries in Britain and the United States were generously made available to me.

Many other people have been generous with information, encouragement and with their time: Barbara Arnold, Kathy Arrington, C. J. Ball, Celia Bannerman, Bernard Bergonzi, Michele Biety, Michael Bott, Jonathan Brown, Mike Butler, Donald Cameron, Andrea Cantrell, Terry Charman, Liz Corcoran, Vivian Cox, Annetta Crane, D. D. Dunkley, J. F. Earle, Rodney Engen, Anne Escott, Michael Farr, Michael Felmingham, Alex Freeman, Sally Goldsmith, Anne Goodchild, Caroline Goodfellow, Derek Graves, Andrew Greg, Patrick and Caroline Hamilton, Thomas and Elinor Hamilton, Vada Hart, Colin Harris, Christine Hawkins, Michael Heath, Simon Heneage, Cathy Henderson, Michael Heseltine, David and Shirley Hines, George Hoare, Ann Hobbs, Anthony Hussey, Father Peter Jackson, Ray Kelly, Valerie Kettley, Andrew Kirk, Michael G. Knapp, Lionel Lambourne, Zena Lawrence, Mark LeFanu, Christopher Lloyd, Kenneth Lohf, E. Longbottom, Ian Lowe, Stephen Lyons, Barry Mann, Suzanne Mann, Monty Moss, Carol Moulson, Heather Munro, George Musk, Lt Col Clayton R. Newell, Maureen C. O'Brien, Caroline Oliphant, John Palmer, Gerald Pollinger, Kate Pool, Ian Rogerson, Jean Rose, Richard Ryder, Peyton Skipwith, Gyongyi Smee, Karen C. Smith, Joanna Swinnerton, Neil Somerville, Wynne and Diana Thomas, Martin Tupper, Angela Weight, Colin White, Pam Williams, David Wilmore, Michael Winner, Christopher and Michael Wood and Peter Wright. I should also like to thank the library staff at the Universities of Birmingham and Warwick and at the Birmingham and Midland Institute, and the ever-cheerful trolley-pushers of the Newspaper Library at Colindale who brought me one load of magazines after another.

At Pavilion Russell Ash, Julie Davis, Steve Dobell, David Fordham, Karin Hills and Angelo Hornak have been patient, helpful and inventive, while Colin Webb, who first proposed this book, has been dogged in pursuing it to publication, after a difficult and long drawn out gestation.

I should also like to thank the trustees of the Estate of Mrs J. C. Robinson for giving me permission to quote from the writings of William Heath Robinson, and for his work to be reproduced in this book. Thanks too are due for the following permissions to quote: to Mary Fedden, from the writings of her husband, the late Julian Trevelyan; to Norman Hunter and The Bodley Head, from *The Incredible Adventures of Professor Branestawm*; to Mrs Laura Huxley and Chatto and Windus, from Aldous Huxley; and to A. P. Watt Ltd on behalf of the Literary Executors of the Estate of H. G. Wells. I should like too to thank the following libraries for permission to quote from papers or reproduce paintings and drawings in their possession: University of Reading Library; Rider Haggard Collection, Butler Library, University of Columbia, New York; University of Illinois Library at Urbana-Champaign; University of Arkansas Libraries, Fayetteville; Harry Ransom Humanities Research Center, University of Austin at Texas. And finally, my wife Kate, who has been living with this book for longer than she or I would care to remember.

JAMES HAMILTON Warwick, February 1992

HIS LINE OF LIFE

WILLIAM HEATH ROBINSON'S name is said to have begun its passage into the English language in the House of Commons a few years before the First World War, when an MP described an Austrian air display as being performed by 'Heath Robinson contraptions'.[1] Since then, Heath Robinson has joined an exclusive club, of which Hooligan, Titian and Wellington are fellow members, by becoming, posthumously, the root of an adjective in the *Oxford English Dictionary*.[2]

Heath Robinson was not, however, merely an adjective with a technical bent, but a subtle and sensitive painter and illustrator of books for adults and children, a story-teller, a magazine illustrator, a cartoonist of both gentle and acid wit, and an accomplished and successful artist for advertising.

Magnetic apparatus for putting square pegs into round holes
Pen and ink, c. 1943
Private Collection

His contraptions, however, constantly demand our attention, and it is they that have made him unique. The essential quality of a Heath Robinson machine is that it has its own inexorable interior logic. Each movement unerringly dictates the next, until the task for which the machine was built has been satisfactorily completed, whether it be the testing of golf clubs or the putting of square pegs into round holes. The paradox, however, is that a Heath Robinson machine does not test the golf clubs, or whatever it may be – quite the reverse, in fact. The driving of the golf ball is itself the test for the *machine*. When each time the machine shows that it works, it justifies its own existence, and the jobs of the huge numbers of staff required to operate it.

Heath Robinson's name has a soothing effect on the word 'contraption', which has a derogatory meaning when used alone, being a scornful description of a new-fangled gadget or contrivance. Kipling used the word in

1898, and there are other nineteenth century instances, but it seems first to have been used in the west of England, where the word had been listed as obsolete in 1825.[3] How very appropriate this is – like the materials Heath Robinson used to build his contraptions, the word itself has been picked up off a scrap-heap and tied into place to describe the works of the Master of the Genre.

Even his name sounds as if, like his contraptions, it has been knotted together out of disparate parts: Robinson – secure, suburban, well-to-do, and undoubtedly insured to the full; Heath – raw-mannered and graceless, but practical. Robinson suggests a man of status, while Heath knows his place. Of the men (for they are, invariably, men) who staff his contraptions, the Robinsons are the managers, while the Heaths do the work.[4]

Heath Robinson's contraptions are constructed variously out of recycled bits of wood, knotted string, reused nails, repaired football bladders and old ironwork, made as if by enthusiasts in a suburban back yard, or by a boffin in a workshop obsessed by his discovery of a mechanical solution to his problem. Indeed, a quick glance at the contraptions will show that most component parts are of human scale, and that there are few that could not have been built by one man and an assistant working together.

As well as being jokes at the expense of modern manufacturing processes, the contraptions demonstrate how cod-Victorian levels of industrial manning could happily survive into the twentieth century – on the assumption that money was not a problem. The process for tipping matches with phosphorus, for example, is operated by four men and two boys and overseen by a man from the HM Excise Department. If the workmen are paid £4 an hour, the boys £2 and the Excise man £10, the match tipping plant would cost £30 an hour to run in labour alone. If it manages to tip 600 matches an hour, a generous estimate given the fact that the machine seems

Testing Golf Drivers

The driving of the golf ball is itself the test for Will's machine. When each time the machine shows that it works it justifies its own existence and the jobs of the staff required to operate it. It is not the machine that would fail, but the economics.

prone to breakdown, it would put nearly five pence on to the price of each match – let's say £2.50 on to the price of an ordinary box of fifty. And that's just to tip them. The cost of the wood, the boxes, the fish, the rent and the overheads, of course, come extra. This patent absurdity finally makes the machines believable, because it is not they that would fail, but the economics.

The latest machine for tipping matches with phosphorus (amorphous, or non-poisonous)
Pen and ink, published 1920
Photograph: Christies

Another category of Heath Robinson's inventions includes the neat gadget which is not a contraption in the sense that we use the word here, but improvements on existing objects, tools or implements aimed at making life just that little bit easier. There is the extended tennis net designed to enable thirty or forty people to play tennis together on one court; the machine for rationing tea and sugar at elegant wartime tea parties; and the L-shaped cricket bat, that the cautious Heath Robinson suggested might make for a safer game of cricket. Each of these pieces of equipment is shown finely made, undoubtedly by craftsmen who would scorn the slipshod arrangement of a Heath Robinson contraption. If this is another paradox, it is one that is eternal, and is central to Heath Robinson's work.

Some of his humorous drawings, particularly those which date from before the First World War, have an element of the macabre, and reveal an acidly satirical side to Heath Robinson's nature. *Remarkable Case of Absence of Mind in a Dutch Restaurant* (1912), for example, depicts a savant, engrossed in his magazine, taking a slice from the bald head of his sleeping neighbour instead of from the nearby round red Edam cheese.

Many of Heath Robinson's drawings have become prophetic. This is perhaps not due to any particularly ingenious streak on his part, but because, like many inventors, he has simply pointed out the obvious, and fashion and the manufacturers lag behind. The protective barrels and extended pads worn by the middle-aged

The Wimbledon Serving Tube – for practise in tackling the most difficult service and acquiring true Wimbledon form
Pen and ink and wash, 1929. From *Piccadilly.* Private Collection

When tea as well as sugar is rationed. An elegant contraption for all occasions
Pen and ink and wash, 1940
From *The Sketch*
Photograph: Christies

players of *Safety First Cricket* are merely precursors of the helmets and body armour worn by Test cricketers today, and *Afternoon at a Whitebait Factory* anticipates the manufacturing process for Fish Fingers. The *Walking Dragline*, devised by Heath Robinson in the 1930s for removing mountains, directly prefigures the massive opencast mining machines with which a British civil engineer proposed to extinguish Kuwait's burning oil wells after the Gulf War of 1991 – by lowering an enormous bell-bucket over them, and snuffing them out like candles.[5]

In his illustrations of works of classic literature, such as *The Poems of Edgar Allan Poe* (1900), and *Twelfth Night* (1908), Heath Robinson put his sense of humour aside. His professional detachment enabled him to keep a completely straight face, and produce a group of moving and emotive works which reflect the depth of his feeling for the texts. As an

Exeunt Bottom, Quince, Flute, Snug, Starveling and Snout
Pen and ink, 1914
From *A Midsummer Night's Dream*

Remarkable case of absence of mind in a Dutch restaurant
Pen and ink and wash, 1912
From *The Sketch*
British Library, Colindale

illustrator of these and other works, such as *Don Quixote* (1902) and *A Midsummer Night's Dream* (1914), Heath Robinson had some tough competition. Arthur Rackham and Edmund Dulac were in the publishing market against him, fighting for commissions and recognition. In a contest in which subtlety of line or limpidity of colour were to be judged, Heath Robinson would probably not win the main prize. In composition, characterization and merriment, however, his work is barely rivalled.

As a young man, Heath Robinson drew from antique casts in the Royal Academy Schools, called himself Titian in playful boasting with his brothers, and daydreamed of painting the Himalayas. If as an art student he had been able to see the way his career would progress, he might have been perplexed. Disappointments, financial disaster and the urgent need to earn his living pushed him away from the traditional world of fine art and into the one in which he made the name that now trips off the tongue more lightly than does the name of Titian.

CHAPTER ONE

MY STORY IS A PLAIN ONE 1872–1887

WILLIAM HEATH ROBINSON, known to his family as Will, was born on 31 May 1872 at 25 Ennis Road, Stroud Green,[1] the third child of Thomas Robinson (1838–1902), an engraver, and his wife Eliza Heath (1849–1921), the daughter of an innkeeper.

At the time of his birth this area of North London – Highgate, Islington, Holloway and Hornsey – had, within living memory, been four neighbouring but distinct country villages, with distant views from high ground south to the City of London, and north to Alexandra Palace. By the 1870s, however, the villages had become so threaded by railway tracks, so bruised by road widening, and so riddled by lines of new terraced housing, that they and the City of London were already bound inseparably together.

Islington, like the three other former villages nearby, had become a thriving suburb, buoyant and busy, and changed beyond recognition from Islington of the 1820s in which the writer Charles Lamb had lived. Describing his house in Colebrooke Row, Lamb wrote that the New River 'runs, if a moderate walking pace can be so termed, close to the foot of the house, and behind is a spacious garden with vines, peas, strawberries, parsnips, leeks, carrots and cabbages to delight the heart of old Alcinous.'[2] So urban had Islington become, indeed, that by 1870 its population was approaching 250,000, and 249 miles of sewers and pipe-drains had been constructed in the Borough.[3]

On the day that Will Heath Robinson was born, 31 May 1872, the Metropolitan Board Works Committee met to consider improving the drainage still further with a 9,400 foot long replacement for the overflowing Fleet Sewer, and that evening the Barnsbury Literary Institute heard a performance of Mendelssohn's operetta *Son and Stranger* in Islington's Myddelton Hall.[4] For Will Heath Robinson, who came to love amateur music-making, and whose life's work poked fun at the labours of officialdom, this was a very well organized arrival into the world.

The past of Islington was bound into its future. In 1877, for example, twenty-six cowkeepers and dairymen and sixteen corn merchants still found employment in the greater area of Islington alone. While their numbers were shrinking annually, other trades, supported by the growing middle classes, were strengthening. Twenty-one grocers were in business in Islington in 1877, while thirty-eight linen-drapers, thirteen professors of music and nineteen undertakers attended to their gentility, entertainment and obsequies.[5]

By the 1880s, the new residents of the area had become so much of a type that they were rich material

Thomas Robinson (1806–1885), Will's grandfather, drawn by Will's uncle, Charles Robinson (1840–1881)
Pencil, 1858
Robinson Papers, University of Reading Library

Will made his own version of this drawing (left) to illustrate My Line of Life.

for the satire of George and Weedon Grossmith in *The Diary of a Nobody*. 'We have a little front garden;' writes the Grossmiths' central character, Charles Pooter of The Laurels, Brickfield Terrace, Holloway,

> ... and there is a flight of ten steps up to the front door, which, by-the-by, we keep locked with the chain up. ... We have a nice little back garden which runs down to the railway. We were rather afraid of the noise of the trains at first, but the landlord said we should not notice them after a bit, and took £2 off the rent ... beyond the cracking of the garden wall at the bottom, we have suffered no inconvenience.[6]

Lamb's evocation of his garden in Colebrooke Row and, sixty years later, Pooter's proud marking out of his boundaries, signal the extent of the social change that the Industrial and Commercial Revolution of the mid nineteenth century had brought to north London. William Heath Robinson, whose work came to satirize Victorian ingenuity, and to re-invent its mechanical excesses, was born as this change was in progress.

The fullest source of information we have for Will's early life is his autobiography *My Line of Life* (1938), which was drawn from what Will remembered at the age of sixty, and was prepared to tell. 'My story is a plain one,'[7] he writes disarmingly, and by devoting six of the book's sixteen chapters to his childhood, he indicates how important this period was to him. The anecdotal tone of the book reveals, however, that his characteristically romantic attitude to life and his sense of humour and fantasy were rooted at an early age. It also reflects his tendency to mask himself from the world, whether it be in play-acting, day-dreaming, the telling of elaborate and ingenious stories, or in developing his absurd inventions. Will Heath Robinson only rarely deceived himself, but he did, effectively, disguise himself from others, to the extent that *My Line of Life* is long on anecdote, but short on insight. The Cheshire Cat left Alice with his smile hanging in the air. Unless we are prepared to dig around *him*, Will Heath Robinson might follow the example of the Cheshire Cat and leave us with just his smile.

The practice of commercial art for the printing and publishing industries was long established in the Robinson family. Will's father had trained as a wood-engraver, but, by the 1870s, was employed by the *Penny Illustrated Paper* to make drawings of current events for other craftsmen to engrave.[8] His paternal grandfather, another Thomas Robinson (1806–85), had been born in County Durham,[9] and had begun his career as a bookbinder in Newcastle-on-Tyne. Will records that he bound books both for the wood-engraver Thomas Bewick (1753–1828) and for the railway engineer George Stevenson (1781–1848). His relationship with Bewick, however, would have been a youthful one, as Robinson

Wood engraving attributed to Thomas Robinson, Will's grandfather. (Much enlarged.)
Robinson Papers, University of Reading Library

was only 22 when Bewick died aged 75. As his bookbinder, or perhaps more likely as apprentice to his bookbinder, the young man is certain to have met some of Bewick's pupils in his workshop, and seen and discussed the work being done there.

A number of Bewick's pupils moved to London in the early years of the nineteenth century to seek employment as illustrators to the rapidly growing publishing trade. Bewick had already spotted the crucial importance that wood-engraving was to have in the nineteenth century as a means of disseminating visual information, and knew that his pupils would be in constant demand. He encouraged them to go to London, knowing, as he wrote in his *Memoir*, 'that the use of wood-cuts will know no end ... so long as the importance of printing is duly appreciated and the liberty of the press held sacred.'[10] The rôle of the wood-engraving was as important to the spread of knowledge in the nineteenth century as was the microchip revolution in the twentieth.

Bewick himself lists his brother John as having migrated to the capital, as well as some of his pupils, including Charlton Nesbit, Edward Willis, Henry White and Luke Clennell.[11] Thomas Robinson is not known to have been a pupil of Bewick, but it is likely that as he, too, chose to go to London he was following in the footsteps of Bewick's young men. By 1834 he had settled at Cold Bath Fields, Clerkenwell,[12] and married Harriet Dinah Atkins, from Cripplegate.[13] They had moved by 1838 to 1 Upper Grove Cottages, Holloway,[14] and soon prospered, Thomas becoming an engraver of works for reproduction in magazines such as *The London Journal*, *Good Words* and *London Society*.

The quiet, reflective, rural magic that Charles Lamb evoked in the 1820s was by the 1840s and 50s being replaced by a magic of another kind and one which might have influenced the choice of the elder Thomas Robinson to settle in north London. Islington and Holloway had a busy printing industry, which generated the growth in the area of firms of trade wood-engravers, artist craftsmen who cut illustrations for the hundreds of magazines and newspapers published to cater for the demands of the new enquiring classes. Ebenezer Landells (1808–1860), a founder of *Punch* and the *Illustrated London News*, was, like Robinson, born on Tyneside and trained there by Thomas Bewick. He attracted other younger artists, including Edmund Evans and Myles Birket Foster, to work with him at his studio in Thornhill Road, Islington. The leading artist businessmen in the field, however, were the brothers George (1815–1902) and Edward (1817–1905) Dalziel. They, too, were Tynesiders, and ran a highly efficient and organized studio workshop at 110 High Street, Camden Town, where they produced engravings for the mass reproduction of drawings by Burne-Jones, Millais, Rossetti, Houghton, Poynter and most of the great artist illustrators of the nineteenth century. The strong Newcastle connection in the area may even have contributed to the naming of streets. Benwell Road, built *c.*1864–5, in which both Thomas Robinsons eventually lived, is thought locally to have been named after a district on the River Tyne.[15] Wood-engraving was an unhealthy and highly pressurized occupation, as the Brothers Dalziel tell us with a marked unconcern: '... for while any strain might be put upon the engraver, no excuse was permissible for keeping the printing machine waiting a single hour.'[16]

Thomas and Harriet Robinson had two sons and four daughters: the second child, named Thomas after his father, was born in Upper Grove Cottages in 1838.[17] Young Thomas became apprenticed to a watchmaker, before following in his father's footsteps and becoming a

News illustration drawn by Thomas Robinson (1838–1902), Will's father, to be engraved for *The Penny Illustrated Paper*, January 21st 1882
British Library, Colindale

wood-engraver. He married in 1868, the nineteen-year-old Eliza Heath, daughter of an inn-keeper William James Heath and his wife Mary. Their first child, Thomas Heath Robinson, was born the following year, and a second son, Charles, followed in 1870.[18]

The family settled first at 29 Benwell Road, Holloway, sharing part of the house with Sarah Ashley, Thomas' sister, and her husband William, the manager of an isinglass warehouse,[19] and by May 1872 they had moved the short distance north to 25 Ennis Road. In this rented end-of-terrace house, in a secluded crescent, Will Heath Robinson was born.[20]

Will recalls that his father had given up wood-engraving, probably in the early 1870s, to become an illustrator.[21] In effect, this means that Thomas Robinson had risen from the ranks of the 'peckers', as the trade wood-engravers were known, to the position of Staff Artist on the *Illustrated London News* and the *Penny Illustrated Paper*. His job was to interpret the news with descriptive and emotive drawings made from on-the-spot sketches at trials, scenes of crimes and accidents, or from written descriptions sent by special correspondents.[22] Thomas Robinson described himself on Will's birth certificate as an 'Engraver', while in 1874, perhaps marking his change from engraver to illustrator, he chose the more elevated title of 'Artist on Wood' on his first daughter Mary's birth certificate. In 1879 he was sufficiently established to take on an apprentice for a six-year term,[23] and by 1890 was diversifying his work as a journalist, entering that year into a contract with Henry Sells to spend three days a week making drawings for advertising.[24]

Thomas Robinson and his family moved back to Benwell Road in 1878.[25] They now occupied an entire terraced house, number 51, in this suburban street half a mile north-west of Highbury Fields. The house, which still stands, has two upper storeys over a ground floor and basement. It was large enough to accommodate the family which, by the time the 1881 Census was taken, had grown to five children, Mary having been born in 1874 and George in 1879. A sixth child, Florence, was born in 1883.[26] With them lived Eliza Robinson's 23-year-old brother George, a manufacturer's clerk, and her 21-year-old unmarried sister, Lizzie, who had been living with them for ten years at least.[27] They kept one young general servant, Esther Randall. Until their deaths in 1885 and 1886 respectively, the children's grandparents and their aunt, Harriet Robinson, also lived in Benwell Road, first at number 19, and then, from 1878, at number 37.

Esther

The physical closeness of the family, with parents, children, grandparents, uncle and aunts all living together hugger-mugger like rabbits in Benwell Road, suggests contentment. Though Will suspected that they were always living to the top of his father's income, the family budget was 'so nicely balanced that the younger members never realized how close to the door was the wolf'. The keel of the family was Will's mother, whom her son described lovingly:

Silhouette portraits of Will's mother, Eliza Robinson (top), and her brother and sister, George and Lizzie. Cut *c.* 1870 by Will's father Thomas Robinson
The Joan Brinsmead Trust

Perhaps in depicting our household, its contentments, the fortitude with which its troubles were borne, and the smooth running of the wheels of our daily life in spite of the occasional roughness of the road, I shall best describe the mother of our family. Quiet in the background, directing, organizing, placating, she was responsible for all of these.[28]

Most movingly, however, he describes his mother standing beside the body of a baby, probably her daughter Mabel who died in infancy: 'I remember indistinctly in my early childhood seeing a baby lying all robed in white and surrounded by flowers. My young mother stood by its side, very still.'[29]

As a relief from the household, Will and his two elder brothers played in the street with their friends, who included the children of two neighbouring mariners,[30] or went on long walks. Calling themselves the Three Musketeers, Tom, Charles and Will took themselves off on Saturday mornings, aiming to walk as far as they could go along the Great North Road in the direction of High Barnet, St Albans, York and Scotland. 'These enchanted places could be reached by simply walking straight along the road that passed near our home, if only you were able to keep going long enough.'[31] They remembered as they walked that they were following in the footsteps of Dick Wittington, Dick Turpin, Oliver Twist and the Artful Dodger, and this gave them a boyish sense of history.

Their modest destination, however, would be High Barnet and Hadley Church, with the beacon in its tower. 'We might even get a glimpse of the man on watch, who, we liked to think, was ever ready with match in hand to ignite the fuel at a moment's notice.' Past Holloway Road Market they went, past the knife-board buses which each working day carried their father to his studio at Dane's Inn, under Highgate Archway and out into the

country. This began at Shepherds Hill, and as their journey progressed into the afternoon they would straggle into Finchley, which was about as far as they ever got.

Active, imaginative and resourceful, Will's childhood was an ideal and apparently undeprived episode. We might compare the character, energy and the inventiveness of the Robinson 'Three Musketeers' with William and the Outlaws or the Swallows and Amazons of later generations of children, or even with A. A. Milne and his

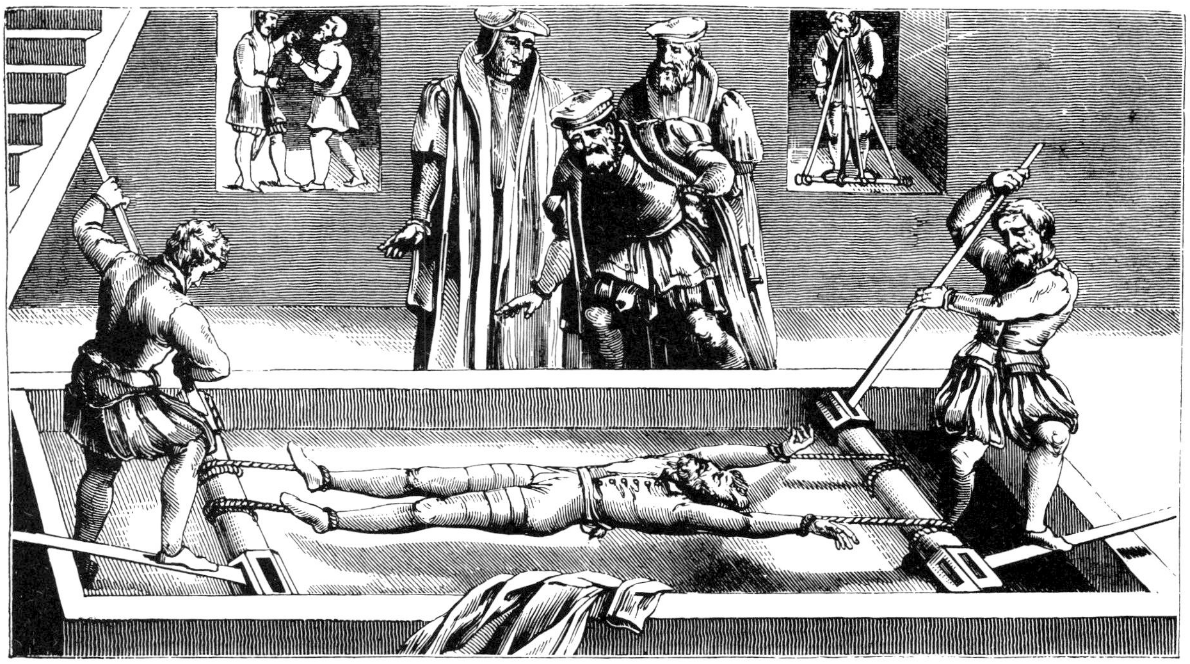

brother Ken, who, in 1897, eventually achieved their ambition of cycling a hundred miles in one day.[32] As further food for the imagination, Will and his brothers read voraciously. They put nursery tales and fairy stories aside at an early age, and instead read *Robinson Crusoe*, and books by Captain Marryat, Harrison Ainsworth, J. Fenimore Cooper and Sir Walter Scott. They also fed upon the gore and *gravitas* of Foxe's *Book of Martyrs*.[33]

Their father constantly encouraged Will and his brothers and sisters in their creativity, in collecting, story-telling and toy making, and Tom, indeed, had his own museum of shells. They were encouraged to use their imaginations continually and at every turn, so that quite naturally drawing became a necessity and a normal means of expression.[34] Among Will's favourite subjects were battles and siege machines.[35] From drawing on slates and in sketchbooks, their explorations led them to the making of model theatres, and to the staging of home and street pageants. 'I think that in such early imaginative play probably lurked the germ which developed into the imaginative work of my maturer years, for what it is worth,' Will wrote in 1925.[36] A letter from Tom to his parents and brothers proposes one of these pageants, though we have no way of knowing if it actually took place. Tom was recovering at home from Scarlet Fever on Christmas Day 1882, while the rest of the family crowded into 37 Benwell Road for a Christmas Feast with their grandparents. Becoming bored with his convalescence, Tom wanted entertainment. Scarlet Fever had not blunted *his* imagination:

Dear Charlie [he wrote to his brother],

You might ask Grandma, Grandpa and all the residents of 37 Benwell Rd to form a procession on the other side of the road, I should be very pleased to see you do it, it would not only please us, but all the inhabitants of Benwell Road. Now then Miss Polly I can set you a task in the Royal Procession. Take your perambulator and set Grandma & Grandpa in it and push them along in the Procession, and the People will think that it is the Lord & Lady Mayoress. Auntie Harriet will pass as Mistress of the Robes. Charlie as a Policeman. Edie as the tin, I mean brass band. Aunty Lizzie can hire a costermongers barrow and put the Piano in it while Fred and Willy can pull it along. Auntie Sarah can sit on the top of the Piano with the toasting fork and will pass as Britannia. The two Uncles will form an escort of Life Guards. They can hunt up any of Willie's horse and they will do fine. Now you have the Procession, you had better start from the house, march past our window, and you will be saluted, then proceed down Queensland Road and then home, and you will see in the Papers next morning a good account of the Procession. For banners the pudding cloth will do very well. Hurrah! Hurrah!! Hurrah!!![37]

Domestic theatricals of this sort were nothing new in Islington, and indeed the district supplied the world with one of the most vivid means available to stimulate children's imaginations. Islington was not only the home of theatres such as Sadlers Wells, famous for its epics and spectacular transformation scenes, but also of the toy theatre trade in which the three worlds of the theatre, engraving and printing were linked. Its products were exported throughout Britain and abroad to America and the Colonies. Toy theatres, with scripts of their own, and casts and scenery to colour and cut out, were written, drawn and engraved by local publishing entrepreneurs such as W. G. Webb, Redington and Benjamin Pollock. Amidst scissors and glue-pots, on thousands of family tables, some of the most lurid and poignant of Victorian dramas came to life.

Left: The Racking and Cruel Handling of Cuthbert Symson in the Tower
From Foxe's *Book of Martyrs*, 1839 edition

The Robinson family owned a copy of this book with its gory illustrations of early mechanical devices at work. Will and his brothers studied it avidly.

Right: The stage at the Drury Lane Theatre, showing the hydraulic bridges in action
Photograph, 1898
The Theatre Museum, London

Theatrical machinery was an early source of inspiration for Will's inventions.

The young Charles Dickens and his friends created their own dining table theatricals,[38] and one child who was addicted in particular to the theatrical products of Islington was Robert Louis Stevenson (1850–1894). Stevenson described the passion with which he, as a child living far away in Edinburgh, seized the opportunity to possess *The Red Rover*, *The Forest of Bondy* and *Three-Fingered Jack, the Terror of Jamaica*:

> In the Leith Walk window, all the year round, there stood displayed a theatre in working order, with a 'forest set', a 'combat', and a few 'robbers carousing' in the slides; and below and about ... the plays themselves, those budgets of romance, lay tumbled one upon another. ... I cannot deny that joy attended the illumination. ... With Crimson Lake and Prussian Blue a certain purple is to be compounded which, for cloaks especially, Titian could not equal.[39]

How much stronger might this passion have been in the Robinson household, which was so full of children who could press their noses against the actual glass windows of the Webbs' and the Pollocks' shops. In the event, however, the children soon outgrew these 'Temples of Nursery Dramatic Art',[40] and graduated to making their own much more elaborate toy theatres. 'A wider field was found for our imaginations when we made our own stage,' writes Will:

> This was larger and permitted much more ambitious effects than were to be obtained in the ordinary stages bought in shops. The standardized materials we formerly relied upon were of no use to us now. We had to write our own plays, and design our own characters and scenes to fit the new theatre. Our pantomime would take weeks to prepare. There was the lighting with little candles to be arranged. There were trap-doors for the sudden appearance and disappearance of demons and fairies, and many other striking effects. They all had to be tested and rehearsed many times. Our first night was a great occasion, and if our audience was not quite so enthusiastic as we had hoped, we certainly enjoyed it ourselves. We were in a privileged position; we were behind the scenes.[41]

On one particular occasion, as Will told his parents: 'We enjoyed ourselves very much on Charley's birthday. ... We acted Richard the First. We hung the flag in the passage. Auntie Tiddles made some tarts.'[42]

Once a year, every year, Will and his brothers and sisters were taken to the theatre. This was a treat that thrilled them for weeks in advance: they might be taken to the Eagle in City Road, the Standard in Hoxton or a Drury Lane theatre. In his Christmas Day letter, written when the boys were thirteen, twelve and ten respectively, Tom also revealed their father's plan to take them all to the Drury Lane pantomime: '... and we are going in a private box. The Pantomime is called Sinbad the Sailor which I suppose you have read in my Arabian Nights. I think it is the best Pantomime in London. There is [*sic*] 2 giants 50 feet high and can only come across the stage a half at a time.'[43]

At other times, when they were recovering from illnesses, or to get them out of the way for the birth of a brother or sister, the children were sent to Brighton to

stay with a distant relation,[44] the widow Mrs Bradley who, with her children, kept a lodging-house at 16 Atlingworth Street. This was a small street full of other lodging-houses leading off Marine Parade at the east end of the town. 'You could smell the sea in every room in the house,' Will wrote. Letters home from Brighton tell of April Fool pranks, of playing in the sand on the beach and going to the Tivoli Gardens, a popular pleasure-ground on the outskirts of the town.

Will himself was at Atlingworth Street recovering from an illness with Charles over one April Fool's Day, and sent a sketch of himself to his mother, showing a swollen-cheeked boy (was it mumps?), enigmatically inscribed 'I AM GETTING'.[45] When the news of the birth of their youngest sister, Florence, their parents' final child, reached them, they wrote home excitedly: 'When we received your letter this morning stating we have a new sister we were so overjoyed that we nearly jumped out of our clothes.' In the middle of the letter Tom has sketched himself and his brothers reacting to the news of their sister's birth. Tom and Charles are jumping with joy – but all the enthusiasm Will can muster consists of the speech-bubble words 'Another misery'.[46]

More often than not, when they were in Brighton it was the winter or early spring, but this did not detract from the fascination that the Chain Pier held for the children. 'Walking between the little kiosk at the bases of the great stanchions that supported the chains was like walking the deck of a ship. In windy weather it sways like a ship at sea.' Will was entranced by the engineering below the pier:

> ... a forest of wooden piles and iron ties, encrusted with shells and hung with seaweed ... To enter this weird underworld, you descended the mere skeleton of a stairway ... Another iron stairway led from here without any compromise straight down into the depths of the water. I never believed the story of the silk-hatted gentleman who was said to have come up these stairs from out of the sea and walked calmly away.[47]

Right: Deeds of Kindness: Heroic conduct of an engine driver in sacrificing his reputation for punctuality to save the life of a stranded eel
Pen and ink and wash, 1925
Private Collection
In drawing the railway bridge, Will may be recalling his childhood fascination with the ironwork beneath Brighton Pier.

A self portrait with mumps: the earliest known drawing by Will, decorating a letter written to his parents *c.* 1880, when he was 6 or 7
Robinson Papers, University of Reading Library

It is clear from stories such as this that Will was fascinated from the beginning by the bizarre and the breathtaking: the man who walked out of the sea, their annual visits to the theatre, intricate experiments with model theatres, and stories of adventure.

One of the most revealing passages in *My Line of Life* comes, however, when Will describes a visit to Alexandra Palace. He admits to knowing how Jack must have felt on climbing up the giant's beanstalk:

> One Sunday evening in summer, I mounted with my mother and father the stairs to old Holloway station and stepped upon the platform. Here, to my young eyes, was magic; a wide track of country high up in the sky, of which we had never dreamed in the every-day streets just below. As we waited for our train, a Scottish express roared along this great highway to the wide world beyond.[48]

Even from his youngest days, Will was enchanted with the modern world, and in his imagination mixed it inextricably with fantasy and story-telling.

The rebuke

Tip-cat

The schoolmaster

Home was always the centre of the activities of Will and his brothers and sisters. Their schooling was local, and for Will it was partial. With one exception, his teachers left him unsatisfied, without giving him the foundation he needed to learn. He did single out, however, the work of one school-mistress who had, Will felt, a genius for teaching electricity and magnetism. She took her pupils step by step through the subject, and gave Will a confidence in it that, from the age of ten or eleven, he never lost. The school, Holloway College, specialized in science – physiology, chemistry, electricity and magnetism – and Will remembered how the laboratory was impressively equipped with retorts, Leyden jars, batteries, magnets and various kinds of electrical machines. 'Interesting and odiferous experiments were carried out,' and in one of perhaps a number of scientific lectures, the headmaster, Dr William Roston Bourke, accurately prophesied to the class that some day telegrams would be sent without wires.[49]

The benefit and understanding that Will's science teacher, whose name is unknown, brought to him can be compared with the insight that Alice Gostick gave to the young Henry Moore (1898–1986) at Castleford Grammar School.[50] The teaching of Miss Gostick opened Moore's eyes to Italian and English sculpture, and ignited his desire to become a sculptor. In their turn, Will's science teacher and his headmaster provided the spark that lit the candle that set fire to the fuse that, spitting and guttering but always staying alive, led their pupil eventually to invention and to fame. It was through their early encouragement and care that William Heath Robinson became perhaps the greatest inventor who yet showed not the slightest desire of ever seeing his inventions in operation.

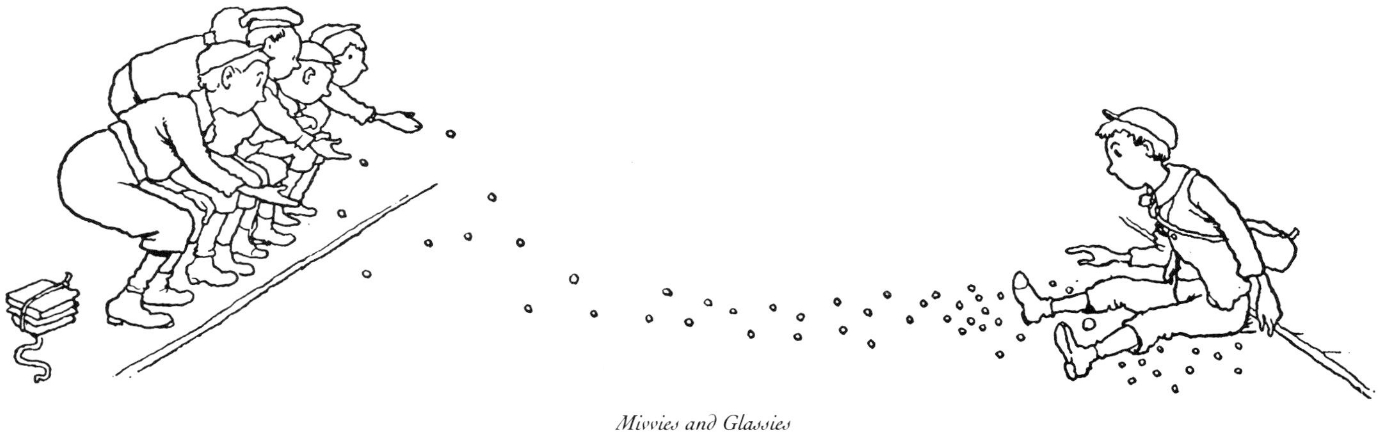

Mivvies and Glassies

CHAPTER TWO

DISAPPOINTMENT IN THE BALLS POND ROAD 1887–1902

DESPITE THE LURE of the science laboratories, Will's parents decided in 1887 that he had learnt just about as much at school as he ever would. He had moved by now to the Islington Proprietary High School, and, as he wanted to be nothing else but an artist, his parents sent him at the age of fifteen to Islington School of Art.[1]

There was no limit to Will's ambition as he began work at Islington. 'Not that I told myself I should rival Velasquez or Rembrandt, but there was at that stage of my artistic career a pleasing indefiniteness as to my future development.' Fifty years later he recalled this charming but naïve enthusiasm:

> My ideas of an artist's life were taken from the lives of the great masters which I loved to read. It was only a matter of choosing whether I should paint frescoes in cathedrals or monasteries, or whether I should wander all over the world painting mountain scenery or old cities, and, on an occasional visit to my own country, the woods and fields of England. The last seemed to me the ideal life.[2]

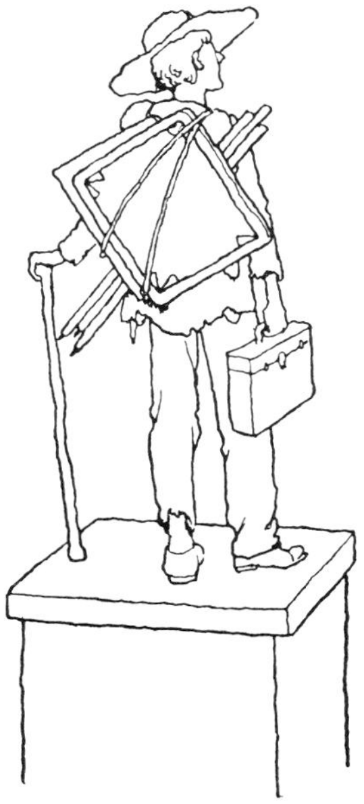

The ideal landscape painter

It takes a rich imagination to develop such a heated caricature of an artist's existence. Will is describing a way of life of a kind culled from the pages of Vasari's *Lives*, and from artists' biographies such as Crowe and Cavalcaselle's *Life of Titian* (1881). In imagining himself to be a wandering landscape painter, Will was dreaming of a mid-Victorian art world that was gradually ceasing to exist, and he was bound to be disappointed.

> I pictured myself tramping the country roads without a care and returning from some painting expedition in the Austrian Alps or the Bay of Baiae. My clothes were worn almost to rags, but by Turner and by Constable, what did that matter to one who despised the vanity of the neatly clothed townsman and held as naught his approval! My face was a rich brown by exposure to the weather and my hair was blowing in the wind. Upon my back was strapped my paintbox, some few works of art destined for the National Gallery via the Royal Academy, and my scanty baggage.[3]

At Islington Will was taught by Henri Bosdet,[4]

> ... a real artist if ever there was one. He couldn't be mistaken for anything else. He wore a black velvet coat and an artistic tie. His head was that of a pale young Moses adorned with a long silky beard, moustache and waving hair. The finishing touch to this artistic personality was the gold-rimmed monocle which continually dropped from his eye and was replaced as he took a broader or closer view of your drawings.

Out of perversity, and to Bosdet's annoyance, the male students anglicized his name to 'Bozzdett', while the ladies, swooning over him, competed to pronounce his name elegantly in the French manner.

Will's cheery teasing of his teacher disguised a determination and an enthusiasm to reach a sufficient standard to gain admission to the Royal Academy Schools. He and his colleagues drew from plaster casts of the classical statues that stood in the studio, or were hung up in fragments on the walls. 'We became so accustomed to drawing fragments, that we were inclined to prefer figures in a state of mutilation to the commonplace examples with a normal number of limbs.' Tedious though he may have found it, Will knew that he had to pass through a period of training in academic drawing to

Right: **Hampstead Heath**
Oil and panel, 1897
147 × 224 mm
The Joan Brinsmead Trust

Left: Nude Study
Pencil, in a student sketch book of the 1890s
The Joan Brinsmead Trust

achieve his ambition of becoming no less than a *great* landscape painter.

One of his fellow students at Islington was Percy Billinghurst (active 1898–1906), a close friend who later became a collaborator. Billinghurst, who lived with his parents at 7, Highbury Place,[5] about ten minutes' walk from Benwell Road, also had a family connection with the Robinsons, as Will's Uncle Charles had married a Miss Billinghurst.

To improve his drawing and win a place at the Royal Academy Schools, Will regularly visited the British Museum, where he drew directly from the Elgin Marbles.[6] This was the 'marble stage' of Will's art education, as he described it. 'Too much plaster, after a while, has a tendency to enter the soul and check its expansion.' His natural light-heartedness resisted this, although it might have been his undoing when he was caught by the Principal Librarian whistling 'Little Dolly Daydream' under the statue of Diana of Ephesus, and threatened with permanent expulsion from the Museum.

Will gained admission to the Painting Schools of the Royal Academy at his second attempt in January 1892. Percy Billinghurst was admitted too. He was now, to his great joy, able to combine his studies from the antique with painting and drawing from life. He did not, however, achieve the success of some of the contemporaries whom he lists in *My Line of Life*, and whom he particularly remembered. Charles Sims (1873–1928) won the Landseer Scholarship in 1895, Harold Speed (1872–1957) the Gold Medal in Painting in 1893, and the sculptors Paul Montford (1868–1938) and Francis Derwent Wood (1871–1926) won the Gold Medals in Sculpture in 1891 and 1895 respectively.[7] The Professor of Painting, John Evan Hodgson RA (1831–1895) was a painter of highly detailed but pedantic historical and genre subjects in the manner of Frith, Crofts or O'Neill, and was not the sort of artist likely to encourage his students in the study of modern trends in art.[8]

Will recalled that his attendance at the Royal Academy Schools was never very regular, and he did not enter into the student social life. It is likely that the pull of the Robinsons was too strong for him to overcome. He lived at home, and Sunday lunch with the family was a

feast that it was impossible to avoid, as was church-going. 'Our mother, who took charge of our religious welfare, only insisted that we should attend one service every Sunday.'[9] Will's teasing of 'Bozzdett' also perhaps concealed a xenophobic streak which prevented Will from turning his imaginative travels into fact. While many of his contemporaries made the journey to Paris in the 1880s and 90s to experience Impressionism at first hand and to study in the open classes of the Académie Julien, Will (and his brothers) stayed firmly at home. He did not, indeed, leave England until he was forty-six, when he made a well-protected visit to Northern France as a guest of the American Army in 1918.

Will's studentship at the Royal Academy lasted until January 1897, when the necessity of earning his living became acute. In the later months of his studentship Will submitted illustrations for publication in magazines, his work being accepted by *The Sunday Magazine* and *Little Folks* in 1896. He saw the possibilities now open to him to be as follows: portrait painting, 'a lucrative living, but so few people wanted their portraits painted'; church decoration, 'congenial work, but nearly all the churches were already decorated'; theatre or house decoration and book or magazine illustration, 'commissioners unresponsive to my overtures'; subject or landscape painting, ditto; scene painting, 'unsuccessful in convincing scene painters of the value of the help I could give them.' All Will's options seemed negative, but he was never daunted and decided to take one of these branches of his profession and persevere with it. The branch he chose was landscape painting: '... to be hardened to all weathers, heat, cold and all climates. To be equally at home in raging storms and under the dazzling sun of the desert. To be unfettered by the restraints and conventions of life in town. That was the way to live.' Quite clearly, the kind of landscape painter Will pictured himself to be was a Romantic, walking in the Alps, the Himalayas, Tibet, Greece, Rome and Egypt, as Turner, David Roberts, Edward Lear, Holman Hunt and the German Romantics had done. Making no serious attempt to turn this dream into a reality, however, Will contented himself with painting on Parliament Hill Fields, Highgate Ponds and Hampstead Heath in the afterglow of John Constable, who had painted on the Heath seventy years earlier.

In the bright summer of 1897, Will Heath Robinson became one of a curious little group of landscape painters, 'a picturesque band ... stray artists and, belonging to no particular school, mostly self-taught. Art galleries rarely saw their work, and collectors ignored it.' One small panel painting of *Hampstead Heath* survives, in

Figure and Tree
Gouache, *c.* 1900
140 × 126 mm
The Joan Brinsmead Trust

which Will shows a watery sunset seen over a green scarred sandy hillock. It shows him to be struggling with freely moving brushstrokes to liberate himself from the nineteenth-century tradition that still racked the Royal Academy Schools, and to paint a landscape of the senses rather than one of anecdote.

Towards the end of this Hampstead summer, Will took a group of his paintings to a dealer in the Balls Pond Road.

'How long have you been painting?' the dealer asked.

'About four or five years,' Will replied.

'Have you ever sold a painting before?'

'No.'

'Have you got to depend upon your own earnings for a living?'

Will explained to the dealer that this was certainly how he was placed.

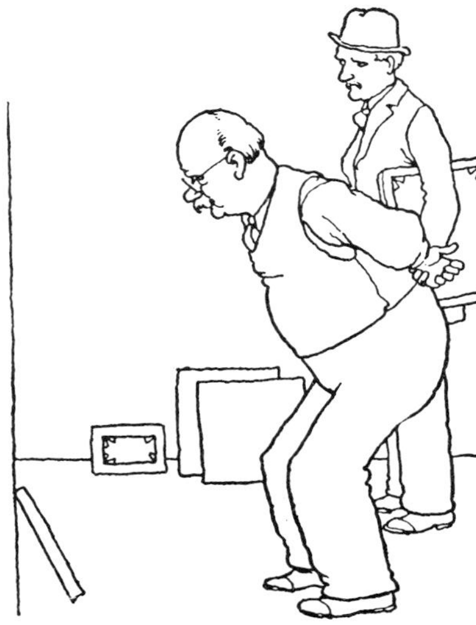

'Well in that case,' said the dealer, 'I should try something else.'[10]

Will did not, however, allow this unwarranted discouragement to overwhelm him, and instead travelled for a painting holiday to Cornwall, where he shared a cottage with Francis Black RBA (d. 1939), the Principal of the Camden School of Arts and Crafts. Black introduced Will to Alfred East (1849–1913), a much travelled and successful landscape painter about twenty years his senior who had worked in France, Africa, the Far East and America. All Will records of this meeting was that East 'advised me about my work'. He is remarkably silent on the kind of advice he was given, and indeed on the whole subject of meeting an artist who was, to all appearances, living just the sort of life to which Will himself professed to aspire.

Will was now within a tantalizingly short distance, geographically and emotionally, of the artists working at Newlyn in the company of Stanhope Forbes (1857–1947). Given the right encouragement he might have persevered further, and persevered too with showing his work to his contemporaries and to art dealers. In the light of the intimate and enchanting study in green and white gouache of a figure beside a tree, painted with the square-ended brush that was favoured by the Newlyn artists, it is clear just what William Heath Robinson could have achieved as a landscape painter. Had he taken his landscape paintings to the Fine Art Society or the Grosvenor Galleries, for example, rather than to a dealer in the Balls Pond Road, he might have received more encouraging advice. In that summer of 1897, however, Will sold only one picture – and that to a friend, to help him pay for his trip to Cornwall. Believing the writing to be on the wall, he decided that landscape painting was not going to be a living.

Instead, at a spare table in his father's studio in Dane's Inn, Will submitted to Robinson family tradition, and continued to work from his imagination on a portfolio of black and white drawings to show to publishers and art editors. His two elder brothers were successfully doing the same thing, and beginning to make a living by selling drawings for reproduction in books and magazines. If his dream of becoming a painter of the landscapes of the world was beginning to fade, Will's imagination and the sense of pantomime that tended to influence his way of life replaced that fantasy with another. Having grown out of pretending to be the Three Musketeers, Tom, Charles and Will now called themselves Michelangelo, Raphael and Titian respectively.[11]

In the spirit of the dashing adventures of the Three Musketeers of his boyhood, however, Will, sometimes accompanied by his brothers, concocted campaigns by which he would win commissions from publishers. He wrote of 'deeply laid schemes' to overcome publishers; of 'bold attacks'; of 'sallies against their western wing'; and of concentration on 'the enemy's centre' in Covent Garden. In Leicester Square, Grant Richards was 'strongly entrenched', and in Bedford Street were Heinemann and 'the castle of the venerable Dent'. Isbister's, too, was 'attacked'. This was all stirring stuff, the novels of Dumas, Captain Marryat and G. A. Henty lived to the full. If Will's approach was adversarial, it was always good-humoured, and no bones were broken. From the venerable Dent, Will this time received a paternal blessing; later, he would win a commission.

The author Frank Swinnerton (1884–1982), then an office boy with Dent, remembered one of the Robinson boys' attacks:

> Tom, rather small and sedate, first; Will, very thin and taller than the others, in an overcoat which was so closely buttoned that he looked thinner than ever, in the middle; and Charles, always freer and more jaunty in his movements than the others, last. They would stand talking with me while they waited ... soon afterwards they would come clattering down like schoolboys, always very much amused at what had happened above.[12]

Will moved out of his father's studio into one of his own in 1897. With Percy Billinghurst, who had begun to specialize in illustrations of animal subjects,[13] he rented a small square room, constructed of match-boarding, with a top light but no side windows, in Howland Street, off Tottenham Court Road, conveniently near the publishing heartland of London. It was built over a stable, and after only a few months, the smell of horse became so strong that he and Billinghurst were driven out. They found replacement accommodation only a few hundred yards away at 115 Gower Street, in a wooden extension high up on the roof. The studio was open to the winds, and 'here we were more healthily situated,' wrote Will. In a storm the walls shook and creaked, and the pair pictured themselves being blown from their moorings, and sailing gaily over London. This physical insecurity

... and sailing gaily over London

did not daunt them. They saw it, indeed, as an advantage to be able to float over the city, the more easily to alight on the roof of some publishing house, and attack the publisher from above. 'Covering him with a revolver we would demand a commission to illustrate the whole of Shakespeare's works, the *Encyclopaedia Britannica*, and a few little things like that.'[14]

By 1897, when *The Giant Crab and Other Tales from Old India* was published by David Nutt with Will's illustrations, another book publisher had fallen to his assaults. In that year Bliss, Sands published *Danish Fairy Tales and Legends of Hans Andersen*, and *Don Quixote*, while Sands & Co published his illustrated edition of *The Pilgrim's Progress*. Soon, other publishers succumbed: Archibald Constable & Co (*The Queen's Story Book*, 1898), and, breaching at last the castle of the venerable Dent, Will's illustrations to *The Talking Thrush and Other Tales from India* appeared under J. M. Dent's imprint in 1899. If Will was gradually being noticed, so were all three of the Robinson Brothers, seen now as a group who might be marketed together. Seizing this idea, Dent commissioned Tom, Charles and Will Heath Robinson to provide 112 illustrations to *Fairy Tales from Hans Christian Andersen* in 1899.

The edition of *The Arabian Night's Entertainment*, published by George Newnes in the same year, consolidated Will's audience. His drawings shared the pages with the work of four other illustrators, Helen Stratton (active 1892–1925), Arthur McCormick (1860–1943), A. L. Davis (active 1899–1925) and Edwin Norbury (1849–1918). As an indication that publishers' interest in him had now gone beyond the casual, Will's name is first on the title page, and one of his drawings is reproduced on the cover. Will's work, too, occupies the first 93 pages, as well as two further sections within the book. Of the full-page drawings, Will contributed the majority – 18 out of 39.

Although his illustrations show a strong debt to Aubrey Beardsley (1872–1898), for example in his drawing of the sumptuously robed Grand Vizier, *'Remember that I impatiently await your return ...'*, Will is beginning to show the individuality and the humour that mark his illustrations out from those of his contemporaries. In a manner derived from Beardsley's illustrations in *The Yellow Book* and *The Savoy*, the Grand Vizier is set high in the picture with a wide area of blank space below him. In drawings such as *'Made a low obeisance to him'*, and *'Brought out thence upon his head ten basins'*, Will is developing his use of the heavily shadowed figure, sometimes characteristically in back view, while the menacing quality of *'He took me under his protection'* foreshadows his *Rabelais* illustrations.

Another of the characteristics Will develops in this *Arabian Nights* edition is his use of hatching and cross-hatching, often in the background, or where depicting areas of dappled sunlight. This is particularly successful in *'A small stream which I crossed'*, in which the figure wades through shallow water towards the distant mountains.

Where the Beardsleyesque line in *'Remember that I impatiently await your return ...'* uses all the potential of the zinc block in reproducing black line on white, Will's manner of hatching suggests the effect of wood-engraving. Having been brought up in a wood-engraver's family, this manner of rendering shadow came as second nature to him. The cliff background to *'A very large winged serpent coming towards me'* is also suggested in a manner that apes wood-engraving, the white spaces between the black ink lines suggesting the path of the engraving tool.

Although he is unlikely to have learned the now old-fashioned craft of reproductive wood-engraving, any more than a schoolboy with an electronic calculator would bother with a slide-rule, the residual influence of the medium in which his grandfather and father were expert lasted throughout his life. Illustrations to *A Midsummer Night's Dream* (1914) still reveal this influence, as does the drawing for the rotund and wrinkled circus elephant that Will made for *The Radio Times* as late as 1937.[15]

All the artists in the 1899 *Arabian Night's Entertainment* show to some degree the influence of wood-engraving. It took a graphic genius of the scale of Beardsley to break fully with the manner of the old craft, and show the way

Right: 'A very large winged serpent coming towards me'
Pen and ink, 1899
From *The Arabian Nights Entertainments*

Left: Radio Times *cover design, 31 December 1937, announcing the radio broadcast of circus performances from London.*

In both of these drawings, made 38 years apart, the graphic influence of wood-engraving is apparent

to others. As if he knew the extent of his prowess, however, Will's illustrations are all boldly signed W. H. ROBINSON or W.H.R. in a much more obvious manner than those of his colleagues in the book.[16]

There seem, at least during his early career, to have been two Will Heath Robinsons. There is the imaginative, fantasizing Will, a precursory Walter Mitty character daydreaming of the life of a landscape painter, or of subjecting publishers to military assault. There is also, however, another Heath Robinson, for whom it was *not* always playtime, and to whom the obtaining of commissions was a serious business, to be undertaken firmly and professionally. If in *My Line of Life* Will prefers to present the former to the world, the latter, the real, the ambitious Heath Robinson, lay behind the mask.

The ambitious Heath Robinson had a further mask which endeared him to his artist friends, but which might have given publishers, had they known, cause to reflect. His proposals and his illustrations were created in his studio amongst a welter of old sketches, piles of books, rolls of drawing paper, and a mass of flotsam and the unfileable, unsortable matter that attracts itself to untidy offices and is left on one side to wait. He often had to borrow drawing and painting material from friends, not because he did not have his own, but because he could never quite put his hands on his pens or pencils the moment they were needed. His studios never saw a broom, still less a duster, and if the smell of horse had not driven him and Billinghurst out of Howland Street first, the lack of having anywhere left to put anything might have done the trick instead. Will was not really a man to lend a book to. The lender would eventually get it back, but not until it had been to the top and bottom of his piles once or twice. His hospitality, however, was generous and unbounded. He might find a crust of bread and a piece of rancid butter in his cupboard, toss the bread on the fire and when it was well alight, retrieve it and say with a grand gesture to a visiting artist: 'You take toast, I suppose? Draw up, and don't spare the viands.'[17]

When he was at work, however, Will's concentration was intense. Visits from friends did not disturb him, he just sat in rapt attention to his work, with his feet curled around the leg of his chair, as they talked, and he drew. Though always good company, Will rarely dressed up for an occasion. 'Oh damn,' he said to another friend as he failed to remove a long smudge of ink from the side of his face before going out. 'Anyhow, it doesn't matter; anyone can see it's an accident and that I'm not really dirty.' He might forget to put on his dress trousers before a formal dinner, arriving in a working blue serge pair: 'I don't see that it mattered. My legs were under the dinner table all the time.' And a spot of blood, dropped on his shirt front when shaving fully dressed, might be covered up by a lick of Chinese white.

This mild asperity concealed a shyness that his charades helped him to overcome, but he could probably not have maintained such a front indefinitely. Fortunately for him, a woman soon appeared in his life. Josephine Latey, six years younger than Will, was a mettlesome creature, with long fair hair, pronounced cheekbones and lively eyes. She had been educated at the North London Collegiate School for Ladies, but her

Right: Thomas Robinson (1838–1902), Will's father
Photograph, 1890s
Robinson Papers, University of Reading Library

Above: William Heath Robinson, possibly a self portrait
Pencil, in a student sketch book of the 1890s
The Joan Brinsmead Trust

parents were advised by the headmistress, Miss Buss, to take her away when she stood up against an injustice.[18] Josephine was the daughter of John Latey (1842–1902), the author and journalist who had written for the *Penny Illustrated Paper* since its inception in 1861, and for the *Illustrated London News*.[19] Latey became Editor of the former and Assistant Editor of the latter, and in both these posts was a close colleague of Thomas Robinson, whose drawings he commissioned. Latey and Robinson could rely upon each other, and in the pressurized world of journalism they became close friends. Their families met regularly.

Josephine was attracted to Will's steady hazel eyes[20] and his reserved manner. Among friends and good company this warmed into a boyish, flippant humour, a tonic for any party. Will never seemed to be in despair, and had a quiet and reassuring determination to succeed. If he felt more at home in his lived-in tweed working suit than in his party clothes, and had tousled hair and a permanent scum of Indian ink under his finger-nails, he was as affectionate as a spaniel pup, a man with possibilities, who only needed dusting down, tidying up and organizing. Will and Josephine became engaged in 1899.

The Robinsons were a happy, patriotic family, who sang songs together at the piano, were content in the comfortable but unfashionable suburbia of Stroud Green, who dressed their best, and ate roast beef on Sundays. Though enthusiastic and warm in their friendships, they were naturally clannish, limiting their circle to the extended families of the Heaths, the Lateys and the Billinghursts, and to long-standing professional friends such as the journalist Walter Jerrold and his family, and former school friends Fred Barnard Smith and the musician Richard Walthew. Their prosperity was still only skin-deep. Thomas Robinson, though successful and well respected in his profession, lived to the limit of his small income. 'Other than his own resources he had little to depend on except the ravens.'[21] A photograph taken of him at his drawing-board, probably in the 1890s, shows a slim man with bright enquiring eyes, a well-tended handlebar moustache, and oiled grey hair combed back over his head. His tie is held by a jewelled pin, his cuffs are white and firmly starched, and his jacket, trimmed with velvet, has a sharp, fashionable cut to its lapel. On his right hand is a bulky gold ring; in his left he holds his pipe. If this man spent his life drawing for the press, he might also, to all appearances, have been a successful portrait painter, playwright, novelist or musician. 'No doubt his life was an adventure,' Will supposed, 'which I am glad to think he enjoyed.' Thomas Robinson, in direct contrast to his son, expressed his joy through his clothes and through what Will described as a modest display of jewellery, 'of which he was a little proud'.

Eliza Robinson ran the family house, which, from 1895, was Glenhurst, a stone terraced house, 1 Granville Road, Stroud Green. Will remembers his mother as one who expressed her kindness through good meals, 'and there was only one way to respond, and that was by consuming them.' Eliza Robinson was a natural, conscientious hostess, for whom (in her son's view) Sunday lunch was the grand achievement of the week. 'It was a work of art, a symphony in roast beef, baked potatoes and pudding. The first, second and third movements were so nicely adjusted that they did not detract one from another.'

Will's eldest niece, Edith 'Bay' Robinson, the daughter of his brother Charles, recalled the kitchen of Glenhurst, its 'walls aglow with the light of the kitch-

Above: Edith 'Bay' Robinson, Will's niece, to whom he dedicated *The Adventures of Uncle Lubin* in 1902
Photograph, *c.* 1901
Robinson Papers, University of Reading Library

Left: Eliza Robinson (1849–1921), Will's mother
Photograph, *c.* 1890
Robinson Papers, University of Reading Library

ener. The maid, Sarah, wore a cap with long starched strings and she goffered all the frills on cap and apron.'[22] The pictures that Will and Bay draw of the household at Glenhurst overlap remarkably, despite the fact that one was seen through the sophisticated eyes of an adult, and the other with the subjective responses of a child. Will remembered the curly-limbed chairs of the drawing-room, the sweet smell of old rose petals from a china bowl on the table, and the summer shadows cast by an old chestnut tree across the little suburban lawn. Bay, aged three, sitting with her grandmother behind the white lace curtains of the drawing-room, played with odd cards, dominoes and halma men kept in the sideboard, and watched people going to church on Sunday evenings. 'There was an aspidistra on the little round table, whose leaves were kept bright and shining by my dear aunts.'

Photographed in about 1890, Eliza is a dark, curly-haired woman in her early forties, with full cheeks and smiling eyes. Hard work, anxiety and extended motherhood have brought her a premature double chin and bags under her eyes. Eliza was a very young mother, and when Will described his childhood memory of her as 'quiet in the background, directing, organizing, placating', he was writing of a woman of 28 or 29, who had already become the keel and counsellor of a large extended family.

Tom, Charles and Will lived at home until their marriages. Their working lives may have been a chaotic stew of drawings and deadlines, but Sunday lunch at Glenhurst was a formal gathering at which the family came together. Suits were worn, and hands were washed – even as grown men, Tom and Will might be sent away from table by Eliza to go and wash their hands.[23] After lunch,

> ... those who were to be married departed gloriously in silk hats and frock-coats to meet their fiancées, and to bring them home, where we gathered for tea.... The young men ... were resplendent with luxurious growth of hair and heavy but well trimmed moustaches. They were rather uncomfortable in their high stiff collars and clothes that must not be creased. The girls were charming in high coiffures, blouses with wide leg-of-mutton sleeves, and flounced skirts that rustled on the ground as they walked. After a little polite persuasion, a young lady, with becoming reluctance, would oblige by playing on the piano. Then perhaps the strains of Mendelssohn's Spring Song would float through the room, tempering our gaiety with sentimental thoughts.[24]

Will's good notices, and the regular exposure of his work in the bookshops, were strengthened by his unbounded enthusiasm and the support of his family and fiancée. He was now beginning to vary his approach to publishers, adopting the more professional course of sending a hand-written letter. A few examples survive, and between them they draw a picture of a young man who would not easily be dissuaded from his path. In February 1898, he was in touch with the publisher Edward Bell about an unnamed group of drawings then in course of production.[25] Nearly two years later, Bell approached Will asking him for ideas for titles he would like to illustrate, to which Will offered *The Ingoldsby Legends* ('I think my style would suit this, and I should delight in illustrating it'); *Don Quixote*, which Will had already illustrated once; and Edgar Allan Poe's *Poems*. Of this title, Will wrote, 'This particularly would give me immense scope.'[26] After Christmas, the two men met, and by 2 January Bell had commissioned Will to make 70 drawings for a forthcoming edition of the poems of Poe for a fee of £50.[27]

Poe's *Poems* was the fifth title in the *Endymion Series*, which Bell had launched with *Poems by John Keats* and *Poems by Robert Browning* in 1897. The drawings, which occupied Will for the first six months of 1900,[28] show

W. HEATH. ROBINSON

'The night's Plutonian shore'
Pen and ink, 1900
From 'The Raven', *The Poems of Edgar Allan Poe*

him at the age of 28 to be capable of portraying deep, sonorous feeling. *The Night's Plutonian Shore*, from 'The Raven', is a double-page spread in two bordered images which reflect the lingering influences of the book design of William Morris. The treatment of the background reflects Will's wood-engraving heritage, making a further connection with Morris and his work. The Gothic mood of the subject, however, its low-slung design and the lurking, unspecific, shadow of the raven, carry a strong emotional charge that rises to the challenge of the symbolism in Poe's text:

'Prophet!' said I, 'thing of evil! – prophet still, if bird or devil! –
By that heaven that bends above us – by that God we both adore –
Tell this soul with sorrow laden if, within the distant Aidenn,
It shall clasp a sainted maiden whom the angels name Lenore.'
Quoth the Raven, 'Nevermore.'

Other illustrations in this collection, such as *A Dream within a Dream* or *To One in Paradise* seem overworked and clogged with ink. Though he launched himself with zeal into the Poe commission, Will did not fully find his voice there, producing an uneven, halting interpretation of the poems.

During one of their meetings, Bell lent Will an edition of Dante, no doubt suggesting in conversation that Will consider illustrating it for the *Endymion Series*, to join editions illustrated by Anning Bell, Byam Shaw and Garth Jones. 'I have been reading the edition of Dante you lent me and needless to say feel all the more desirous of illustrating it. I learnt a lot in illustrating Poe's *Poems* and feel that now I could do much better work of this kind. I think too that this work would lend itself more readily to decorative line drawing.'[29]

Left: Count von Hoogan Haagen (whose offer of a life-long devotion has just been rejected by the Marquise de Boulogne): 'Hang it all, this is a bit off, next time I commit suicide, I'll bring a lead-line'
Pen and ink, *c.* 1907/08
Private Collection

The tone of this correspondence shows Will to be an assertive young man, fully in command of his powers as an illustrator, and above all rightly certain of them. In retrospect, though the *Dante* was never commissioned, it looks as if Will was now poised to become one of the classic illustrators of his generation. His work has the assurance that Arthur Rackham's early illustration was showing at this time – *Ingoldsby Legends* (1898); *Grimm's Fairy Tales* (1900) – and the sense of design of which the young Edmund J. Sullivan (1869–1933) had shown himself capable in Carlyle's *Sartor Resartus* (1898). The main influences on Will, however, were his brother Charles, whose illustrations to R. L. Stevenson's *A Child's Garden of Verses* had appeared in 1895, Walter Crane (1845–1915), Sidney Sime (1867–1941), Robert Anning Bell (1863–1933), Garth Jones (1872–*c.*1930) and the revolutionary Aubrey Beardsley. Beardsley's bold invention of a pure, open line which danced and swept across the page, immediately pushed the newly-developed zinc printing block to the limits of its capability, and created with it a new way of thinking. His contemporaries were not long in following his example. Now, the image was no longer to be cut in white out of the solid black of the wood block, but instead printed with a metal plate in black on to the white page.

In 1899 Will took studios in New Court, Carey Street, behind Lincoln's Inn.[30] This was a red-brick block of chambers, now demolished, designed by Alfred Waterhouse RA, and completed in 1884 to house apartments for artists, architects and, principally, members of the manifold branches of the legal profession. Freed from the distracting smell of horse seeping up through the floorboards, and from the danger of being wafted across London whenever the wind blew, Will was now firmly accommodated in a solid studio, albeit up in the eaves,[31] from which a solid professional career could be managed.

A few weeks after making a strong proposal to Edward Bell that he, with Percy Billinghurst, should illustrate *Gay's Fables*, Will made another proposition to another publisher. The former idea fell on stony ground; the latter certainly did not.

'May I ask your consideration of the following idea for a child's picture book,' Will wrote in March 1902 to the young and already controversial publisher Grant Richards (1872–1948). With his letter Will enclosed four sample drawings and a group of sketches to illustrate his idea. He explained the subject of the drawings, and outlined the character and adventures of a figure called Schnitzel.

In the first of these [drawings] Schnitzel loses his little brother, in the last he finds him in the nest of the bag bill bird. The other are of adventures he meets with while searching for the stolen child. There would be twelve adventures having an average of about 4 or 5 page drawings and a corresponding number of slighter drawings to face them, artistically arranged in the letterpress, thus making a book of about 130 pages exclusive of the introductory pages.

Apart from the change of name from Schnitzel to Uncle Lubin, nothing of the plot or the character of the earnest little saintly man was altered between Will's first conception of it and the book's publication.

Though I have chosen a humorous subject, I hope you will not think that I intend to make merely a sketchy nonsense book as my intention is to make a book full of most careful and highly finished work. Each picture, though as humorous as I can possibly make it, will at the same time be very seriously carried out and in this way greatly increasing the humour. Schnitzel is not a mere puppet of a nonsense book, but in his quaint way quite a personality as I think you would admit on seeing the completed work and my hope is that he may become very popular among children as 'Shock Headed Peter' [*Strewwelpeter*] has become before him. I think at any rate that you will find the humour of this subject to be entirely my own and that the book would be quite unique in every way. It would almost be like a travesty on grown-up books of adventure, though not only this but a series of very simply told tales with absurdly obvious conclusions, easily understood and appreciated by children. In order that there may not be too much of Schnitzel, I have introduced one or two simple little tales told by persons he meets on his travels ... thus following the methods used in Don Quixote, Arabian Nights &c, &c.

Schnitzel will prove himself to be very courageous ... very ingenious ... very kind and sympathetic ... and in all of them very bland and chivalrous. The adventure of the Iceberg which I have carried out shows too that he is capable of righteous indignation. He is very simple, very patient & always bearing up well against his misfortunes and ever resourceful when fresh difficulties turn up during his travels. At times, though the situations will always be absurdly humorous, there will be a vein of humorous pathos and sadness. He might almost be like a child's Quixote, except that he will be quite in keeping with his surroundings.[32]

Right: 'They found him sitting up in bed'
Pen and ink, 1902

From *The Adventures of Don Quixote of La Mancha.*

Left: '*All* that we see or seem is but a dream within a dream.'
Pen and ink, 1900
From *The Poems of Edgar Allan Poe*

Will's clear exposition of Uncle Lubin's gestation, when the idea was fresh in his mind, is much more direct and revealing than the over-sentimentalized, retrospective picture of Lubin that he draws nearly forty years later in *My Line of Life*. In the later account, Will complicated the issue by musing that Lubin must have wandered long in Alice's Wonderland, and that the only book he seems to have read was Gilbert's *Bab Ballads*. This is all hindsight, and it is likely that in 1902 Will was thinking no such thing, but beginning to develop his character as a contribution to children's literature that would be 'quite unique in every way'.

In describing Lubin in his proposal to Grant Richards as 'a child's Quixote', Will is disarmingly stating his character's literary forebear. *Don Quixote* was very much in Will's mind at the time, as in 1902 Dent's edition of this classic was published with 45 of his illustrations. This suggests that in *My Line of Life* he was indulging in some convenient revisionism by omitting the fact that Lubin had started life with a Germanic name, and that he had originally conceived his 'strange little genius' as having a great work of Spanish literature as its source. Instead, in 1938, when the Nazi party was fully in control of Germany and the Fascists ran Spain, Will concealed Uncle Lubin's German and Spanish heritage, choosing patriotically to associate him with the more comfortable English authors Lewis Carroll and W. S. Gilbert.

Grant Richards saw the commercial possibilities of the proposal, and two weeks after his initial approach, Will was returning a signed contract to the publisher.[33] The proposed title for the book, *Schnitzeliana*, was soon dumped, and six months later it appeared as *The Adventures of Uncle Lubin*. In thanking Richards, Will, enterprising as ever, warns his publisher that he hopes to submit 'another idea of mine which I have been developing lately'.[34]

Will's father died in May 1902, five months before *Uncle Lubin* was published, but not too soon to be fully aware of his three elder sons' successes as artists. Bay Robinson, to whom *Uncle Lubin* was dedicated, remembers the last time she saw her grandfather, and how she was taken up the long staircase to his bedroom, and lifted up.

> The old man took my hand in his. Daddy lowered me to kiss him. The eyes lighted for me and after a brief moment I was hurried away downstairs ... I had thought as I looked at him in his beautifully draped four-poster bed with starched curtains, flounces and counterpanes, that he must be very tired, lying in bed so early in the day.[35]

Will and Josephine were married after an engagement lasting four and a half years in the spring of 1903. Their fathers had both now died, John Latey's death coming in September 1902. Eliza never fully recovered from the loss of her husband, emotionally or financially, and to balance her weekly budget now that all her sons had left home she was forced to take in paying guests.[36]

Will and Josephine's first home together was a furnished top-floor flat on the Holloway Road, next door to the Empire Theatre. The sound of cheering and applause filtering through the wall enlivened their evenings, and turned a dinner party into a theatrical event. 'It was disconcerting when, in the polite pause following a guest's declining a second helping, a burst of clapping intervened.'[37]

Applause, too, was now greeting the published work of Will Heath Robinson. *The Studio* welcomed his *Poe's Poems* as the work of 'a most worthy disciple of the modern school of penmen'.[38] 'Clever cuts' was *The Athenaeum*'s verdict on his 1902 illustrations to *Don Quixote*,[39] while the influential critic R. E. D. Sketchley wrote in 1903 of the 'wilder and more intense fancy' of his work.[40] Will's struggles to overcome his disappointment in the Balls Pond Road and to achieve recognition as an illustrator had, it seems, been successful. He and his wife moved within a year the few streets south from the Holloway Road to unfurnished rooms in Cathcart Hill, off Junction Road, Tufnell Park. Here their first child, Joan, was born.

British Sports and Pastimes: Netting Wild Rabbits on the Berkshire Downs
From *The Sketch*, 1906 British Library, Colindale

The earliest published drawing to feature a recognisable Heath Robinson 'contraption'.

CHAPTER THREE

A STRANGE LITTLE GENIUS 1902–1914

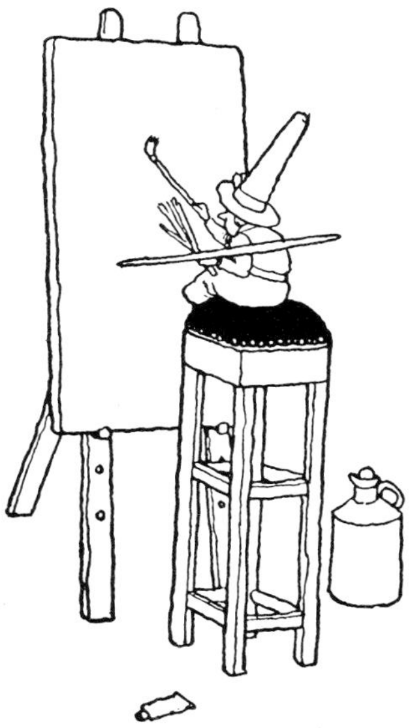

THE ADVENTURES OF UNCLE LUBIN, published by Grant Richards on 4 October 1902,[1] was the first of Will's books to reveal his delight in contraptions. Uncle Lubin's pioneer spirit impells him to build an airship, the *Phoenix,* a boat, the *Kraken,* and a submarine. Charmingly inventive though these craft are, their sources are a mixture of the science fiction writings of Poe and Verne, and 'Penny Dreadfuls'. The central theme of the stories, however, is not the craft but Uncle Lubin and his dogged insistence and determination to succeed in his task.

Each page of the text, laid out in columns, pyramids and zigzags of type opposite the illustrations, suggests the influence of the typography of *Alice in Wonderland.* Keeping in step with the page design of *Alice,* Will has dispensed with the decorative borders with which he

JUST look at the beautiful boat Uncle Lubin built in order that he might search the seas for little Peter. In this boat little Peter's uncle sailed and sailed for many months, till he came to an island in the very middle of the sea.

24

Double page from *The Adventures of Uncle Lubin,* 1902

Lubin sets sail in search of his nephew, but encounters Vammerdopper.

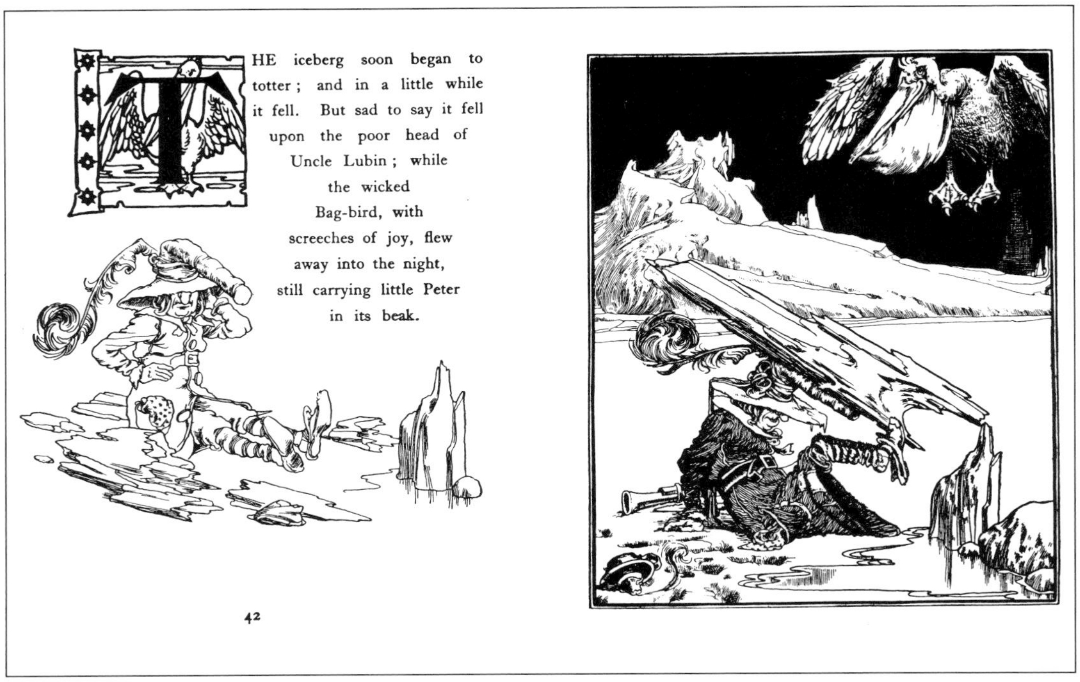
THE iceberg soon began to totter; and in a little while it fell. But sad to say it fell upon the poor head of Uncle Lubin; while the wicked Bag-bird, with screeches of joy, flew away into the night, still carrying little Peter in its beak.

42

'The iceberg soon began to totter'
Pen and ink, 1902
From *The Adventures of Uncle Lubin*

gave a studied, fashionable air to the pages of his *Poe*, and has contained his *Lubin* illustrations within a simple double ruled line. There is a new sense of control in the *Lubin* illustrations, too, the areas of solid black being contained within rigorous boundaries, and balanced artfully with areas of white. Will's enthusiasm for stagecraft is evident in his depiction of Vammerdopper and the giant, and particularly in the Bag-Bird (a Pelican), which hangs from the top of one of the illustrations like a pantomime bird suspended on wires.

Will's particular achievement in *Uncle Lubin* was to bring a light, anarchic humour to the worthy world of children's books, and with it to vanquish the tight-lipped and hidebound nannies of Kate Greenaway. Here was a vulnerable little innocent, in his seventeenth-century Germanic traveller's costume, overcoming one bitter disappointment after another to triumph amidst a colliding collection of anachronisms. Lubin carries a sword, fires a blunderbuss, travels to the bottom of the sea in a submarine and sweeps to the moon in a balloon which he fills from his domestic gas supply. Will's humour extends even as far as creating in the illustration *Uncle Lubin's Dream of Little Peter* a parody of the *Midsummer Night's Dream* paintings of Sir Joseph Noel Paton (1821–1901), the Limner for Scotland to HM the King. Paton's Memorial Exhibition, which included five drawings for *A Midsummer Night's Dream*, was being held at the Fine Art Society in London in July 1902, even as Will was preparing his *Lubin* illustrations for publication.

Will tells in his autobiography of how Lubin came into his life, describing him as a strange little genius with not a shred of humour, who could do wonderful things with a piece of knotted string.[2] Will thought that he might have been haunted by Lubin for years before he recognized the fact, and gives Lubin the credit for introducing him to new friends and reviving old friendships that were almost forgotten. He even gives Lubin the credit for introducing him to Grant Richards.

Influenced as he may have been by *Don Quixote*, *The Arabian Nights*, Gilbert's *Bab Ballads* and *Alice*, Lubin was

BUT when Uncle Lubin did get to the top his heart was filled with a great joy. For there, amid the tender young leaves, was the nest of the wicked Bag-bird, and in it, quite warm and cosy and safe and sound among the little bag-chicks, was his dear nephew, little Peter. Of course Uncle Lubin kissed little Peter with all his might, and in a very few moments he had him out of the Bag-bird's nest and was running home with him as hard as ever he could. I am pleased to say that they got home quite safely and lived happily ever after.

114

Uncle Lubin Discovers Little Peter
Pen and ink, 1902
From *The Adventures of Uncle Lubin*

Will's own creation, his own parody of adult adventure stories. Lubin is in the long tradition of other-worldly literary inventions with magical powers of one sort or another, who are able to distort logic and re-invent reality as the story-teller wishes. These started with Homer's gods; Shakespeare's Puck is another example, as are Rabelais's Gargantua and Pantagruel. Characters who follow after Lubin include Kipling's Puck of Pook's Hill and P. L. Travers's Mary Poppins. Will, however, must be one of the very few whose authors have allowed themselves to be deluded by their own creations.

Grant Richards, to whom, as Will insisted, he was introduced by Uncle Lubin, was five months younger than Will. Like Will, too, he had embarked on his career in 1897, starting his publishing business at the age of twenty-four on 1 January that year. By 1902, when they first came together in business, they should perhaps have both begun to lose their first innocence. Will's launch in 1897 had been as successful as he might have dared to hope, while Grant Richards's launch as a publisher in the same year was less auspicious, as he himself admitted. Richards soon discovered that to commission books was one thing, but to produce them quite another.[3]

Richards's ambition was to publish books of the standard of production that Macmillan, Heinemann and John Lane had achieved, an undertaking that required a very high financial backing and more experience than at his age he could possibly have had. Though in his first few years he made some money on books by E. V. Lucas, Vernon Lee, A. E. Housman and Richard le Gallienne, Richards had too much of his capital tied up in them and in slower-selling books. He lost money on Maeterlinck, on William Rothenstein's *English Portraits* and Laurence Binyon's *Porphyrion*. In his second book of autobiography, *Author Hunting*, Richards is remarkably frank about these difficulties, though stops short of going into detail. His list reflects his literary sympathies which, in the aftermath of the Aesthetic Movement, were with Walter Pater's notion of 'art for art's sake', and with the anti-academic Grosvenor Gallery artists and writers

whom W. S. Gilbert lampooned in his libretto for *Patience*. Richards was an early patron of Charles Conder and J. Q. Pringle,[4] and when the *Savoy* magazine was about to close after its brief appearance in 1896, it was Richards who was approached, though unsuccessfully, to save it.[5]

If it was Uncle Lubin who led Will to Grant Richards, it turned out to be a very bad move indeed. Grant Richards, described as 'the best dressed publisher in London, and he wears an eyeglass',[6] was generous and always ready to help a friend. 'He might not be able to cash a cheque for twenty pounds,' Alec Waugh remembered, 'but he would always sign a bill for fifty pounds. And he looked so sleek, so prosperous; his manner was so assured, so reassuring that it was impossible not to believe that the situation was sound at base.' Richards, however, criticized himself for giving too generous terms to authors and artists, adding 'it was not to be wondered at that by the time I had been a publisher for two years I had made intimate acquaintance with anxiety.'[7]

Uncle Lubin was a moderate success, selling over half its first printing of 4,000 copies in three months.[8] This led to Will and Richards making a further agreement, that Will rewrite for children and illustrate a group of stories from *The Arabian Nights*.[9] In the same letter in which this agreement was confirmed, Will spoke of 'Lubin's successor', a further idea he had had, and which he was now urging Richards to commission: '... as I would much rather you published it than another, perhaps we may come to some arrangement.' This was *The Works of Rabelais*, in the unexpurgated translation by Urquhart and Motteaux (1653), the book with which Will was 'ambitious to make himself famous'. Richards made this claim in a letter to the American publisher J. P. Lippincott, with whom he somewhat half-heartedly attempted to make a pre-publication deal in 1903.[10]

Will's illustrations to *Rabelais* were the largest body of work that he had attempted for a single title, before the projected Cape *Shakespeare* of 1921–2.[11] In subject-matter and intended audience it could not be further from *Uncle Lubin*, and this suggests that Will was making a conscious and highly ambitious effort to launch himself as a leading illustrator of serious, if fantastical, books for adults.

In total, Will made 254 black and white illustrations for *Rabelais*,[12] of which two are reproduced as frontispieces in photogravure, and 98 are full-page line drawings. The rest are character heads and small vignettes interspersed within the text. The title of the book reflects its invention and prolixity: *The Works of Mr. Francis Rabelais Doctor in Physick. Containing Five Books of the Lives, Heroick Deeds and Sayings of Gargantua and his Sonne Pantagruel. Together with the Pantagrueline Prognostication, the Oracle of the Divine Bacbuc, and response of the bottle.*

François Rabelais (*c.*1494–*c.*1553) was a French physician, humorist and satirist, whose monumental, abundant and carnal work, translated into English in 1653 and 1693–4, brought the word 'Rabelaisian' into the language, and had a profound influence on such writers as Jonathan Swift, Laurence Sterne and James Joyce. It characterizes the essence of Renaissance energy, abundance, realism and fecundity, and recognizes and celebrates all the physical functions that flesh is heir to.

Grant Richards (1872–1948) *c.* 1900
Publisher

Richards' bankruptcy before the publication of Rabelais *was the cause of the rift with Will.*

With an encyclopaedic vocabulary and the most voracious intellectual curiosity, Rabelais tells the story of the giants Gargantua and his son Pantagruel. Gargantua was born from his mother's left ear after a twelve-month gestation, and immediately shouted out 'with a high, sturdy and big voice ... "Some drink, some drink, some drink."' Gargantua was no ordinary baby giant and needed 17,913 cows

> ... to furnish him with milk in ordinary, for it was impossible to find a nurse sufficient for him in all the country ... He was worth the seeing; for he was a fine boy, had a burly physiognomie, and almost ten chins; he cried very little, but beshit himself every hour: for to speak truely of him, he was wonderfully phlegmatick in his posteriors, both by reason of his natural complexion, and ... his much quaffing of the septembral juyce.[13]

The story progresses in this fantastic and earthy vein, piling wonder upon wonder, dimension upon dimension. At the age of 'four hundred, fourscore fourty and four years', Gargantua fathered his son Pantagruel, who was 'so wonderfully great and lumpish' that the child's mother suffocated in childbirth.[14] Pantagruel, the image of his father, grew to such vast dimensions that one character lived for six months amongst the cities, mountains and valleys inside Pantagruel's mouth.

'... and wherewith didst thou live? what didst thou drink?' Pantagruel asked his little visitor when he emerged.

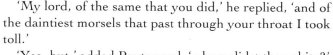

'My lord, of the same that you did,' he replied, 'and of the daintiest morsels that past through your throat I took toll.'

'Yea, but,' added Pantagruel, 'where didst thou shite?'

'In your throat, my Lord.'

'Ha ha thou art a merry fellow.'[15]

Jauntily describing the most intimate of bodily parts and functions Rabelais finds a string of no fewer than 809 adjectives to describe the scrotum of Pantagruel's side-kick Panurge,[16] and a further 295 to list the qualities of their Fool, Triboulet.[17] Dimensions and comparisons, and enormities of scale and behaviour flood Rabelais's pages, and overwhelm, too, the capacity, daring and imagination of Heath Robinson as an illustrator. Prolific though they are, his illustrations underestimate the book. Will misses opportunities and seems to be approaching the subject as if he were tackling the knockabout nonsenses of *The Ingoldsby Legends*, rather than one of the inspirations for *Gulliver* or *Tristram Shandy*.

Gargantua
Pen and ink, 1904
From *The Works of Mr Francis Rabelais*

This, however, was as much a reflection of the restrictive *mores* of the time as of any prudishness on Will's part. In his profile of Heath Robinson, published in 1913 in the *Brush, Pen and Pencil* series, Will's agent A. E. Johnson writes defensively: 'Rabelais presents obvious difficulties to the would-be illustrator. It needs courage, in the first place, to tackle such a colossus: and if the artist begins by rejoicing in the wealth of the material which is offered to him, it is more than likely that its superabundance will presently be his despair.'[18] Touching on Rabelais's coarseness, Johnson continues: 'Moreover, when such initial misgivings are overcome and ignored, the difficult problem arises of where to draw the line. ... It is at least probable that a too sympathetic interpretation would cause commotion in the modern lending libraries!'

Johnson tiptoed round the fact that he believed Rabelais's text to be just too scatological and pornographic for early Edwardian public taste. Richards, however, had identified a market for it:

Of course the character of Rabelais's work is accountable for a good deal of interest of a grosser kind, and there is no reason why we should not take this into consideration when estimating sales, although my own interest in the production is limited to my admiration of Mr. Heath Robinson's work and my anxiety to give him this chance of producing what I think will be a really fine monument, for I never could read Rabelais and I don't suppose I ever shall be able to.[19]

To succeed as a commercial venture, Heath Robinson's *Rabelais* had to ride two horses, as Richards realized. It had to appeal to the 'interest of a grosser kind', and win the approval of the moral majority whose outrage at the decadence of the 1890s had found a focus in public outcries against the drawings of Aubrey Beardsley. Beardsley, who was sacked from the staff of *The Yellow Book* in the wake of Oscar Wilde's arrest and trial in 1895, remained a touchy subject, and continued to create divisions in the art world.[20] This is evident even as late as 1916. Malcolm Salaman, writing in that year about the work of Will's brother Charles, speaks of his early influences: 'Although Mr. [Charles] Robinson began as an illustrator about the same time as Aubrey Beardsley, he was nevertheless influenced early in his career by that remarkable artist, *not, of course, in subject matter* [my italics] ... but in the decorative significance of his fine rhythmic line and the balance of black and white masses.'[21]

'She's kind and ever did admire a well-fed monk'
Pen and ink, 1904
From *The Works of Mr Francis Rabelais*

Rabelais, however, represented a different kind of decadence to the perceived decadence of Wilde and Beardsley, with drinking, defecating and wenching in abundance, but comfortably little sign of buggery there. If Heath Robinson manages to keep his inspiration under control, one can almost hear Richards say, the text

Rondibilis
Pen and ink, 1904
From *The Works of Mr Francis Rabelais*

is so densely written in seventeenth-century English that who will read it and be offended?

The adversarial spirit that Will displayed when he was chasing publishers for commissions did not cease once he had won a contract. He was persistently assertive towards Richards in the years 1902–4, to the extent that Richards came to betray an understandable exasperation. Will badgered Richards to use a brass printing plate for the cover of *Uncle Lubin* in the interests of quality;[22] pressed, not unreasonably, for payment of his fees for his illustrations to *Baron Munchausen*,[23] *Uncle Lubin*[24] and *The Child's Arabian Nights*;[25] and made clear his disappointment at Richards's proposal to cut down the number of photogravure illustrations in *Rabelais*.[26] There was a terse exchange of letters, too, concerning a complaint that Will was reported to have made about the quality of reproduction of his *Rabelais* drawings, a complaint that Will denied ever making.[27]

After nearly eight years in publishing, Grant Richards's costs had got out of hand, and in November 1904 he was declared bankrupt.[28] The expenditure on *Rabelais* was probably the last straw,[29] as 1,000 copies and an *edition de luxe* of 25 had already been printed and bound. The title, with the bankrupt business, was sold to Alexander Moring,[30] and Richards immediately set up in business again, trading under his wife's name. Although Richards led Will to believe that Moring would not sell the print run of *Rabelais* back to him, it is clear that Richards resisted Moring's approaches, and refused to buy the stock back when it was offered in 1905.[31] A contributory factor to this commercial decision may have been the publication by Methuen in December 1905 of an expurgated edition of *Rabelais*.

Richards mentions neither *Uncle Lubin* nor *Rabelais* in his autobiography, nor does he write about Will. He does, however, say with candour that 'I lost small sums on many other books, but they are not books the names of which anyone will now remember.'[32] Richards may have wanted to forget Heath Robinson and *Rabelais*, both contributory factors to his failure, but posterity, nevertheless, has remembered them.

Will's *Rabelais* illustrations divide themselves broadly into three categories. The first, such as *Rondibilis* or *Triboulet*, contains single figures set right up into the foreground, generally cropped at the knees or the head, and variously having a horizon line and perhaps subsidiary figures in the distance. They are reminiscent of the portraits of William Nicholson, or the works of popular caricaturists of the day such as 'Spy', and have a pantomime, posed quality, as if they are portraits of actors in character.

The second group contains darkly brooding images, with strong diagonals in the composition, and dramatic effects of light and darkness to reinforce the horror of subjects such as *'When my Lords the Devils had a Minde to Recreate Themselves upon the Water'* and *'Exceeding Odious and Hateful to Thieves and Robbers'*, an uncompromisingly horrific image of a bound corpse hanging from a tree, with two waiting vultures. These are influenced particularly by some of Arthur Rackham's illustrations to *Ingoldsby Legends* (1898) or *Grimm's Fairy Tales* (1900), and by the work of others of the contemporary Gothic school of illustrators, such as Sidney Sime and Edmund J. Sullivan. A third category includes *'They Fell down before him like hay before a Mower'* and *'Burned with Ling'ring Fire'*, which have a more open line, as if etched, and drawn in the manner of Garth Jones or Laurence Housman (1865–1959). Their complicated and often crowded compositions are ultimately derived from Italian or Flemish baroque paintings and prints. In the physiog-

Right: 'She's taking tired people to the Islands of the Blest!'
Pen and ink and watercolour, 1909
Illustration to *The Three-Decker* by Rudyard Kipling, from *A Song of the English*
National Gallery of Canada, Ottawa

Young man with gaping mouth
Pencil, in a student sketch book of the 1890s
The Joan Brinsmead Trust

nomy of some of the grotesque character heads in the margins of the book, the influence of the drawings of Leonardo da Vinci is apparent, some of whose grotesque heads had been widely known through engravings since the 1780s.

A characteristic that recurs again and again in Will's *Rabelais* illustrations is the wide open mouth, either in laughter, song, terror or feasting. He practised the image in his sketchbooks, and developed it as his symbol of the book as a whole, which reflects the human being *in extremis* of mirth, pain, happiness and misery. Unlike, for example, the plays of Shakespeare, Hans Andersen's *Tales* or *The Arabian Nights*, *Rabelais* is not a work that had a long history of illustration. The only edition Will may have been aware of is that illustrated by Gustave Doré, published in France in 1858 and in England in 1871.[33] If Will did not truly succeed in giving expression to the depths of horror, mirth, lust and scatology of the stories, or even convey an adequate sense of the scale of the eponymous giants, he did at least bring to public notice once again stories of a European significance that rank with those of Bocaccio, Chaucer, Swift and Sterne.

When the edition came onto the market under Alexander Moring's imprint in 1912, its illustrations had left Will's drawing-board eight years earlier. In the meantime, his *Twelfth Night* (1908) and *A Song of the English* (1909) had been published, and *Bill the Minder* (1912) shared the bookshops with *Rabelais*. The critic of *The Athenaeum* welcomed *Rabelais*, finding the drawings to be 'as good as any Mr. Robinson has done'.[34] While the *Times Literary Supplement* muttered that the *Rabelais* illustrations were 'weird and clever',[35] it was clear to *The Athenaeum*'s critic that Will had tackled a text that was almost impossible to illustrate:

> ... if [Heath Robinson's drawings] appear a somewhat inadequate commentary on the text, we must remember that the latter is to the ordinary reader such a thick-set hedge of mystification that any attempt to illustrate it must be either inadequate or obscure. ... The larger drawings are too grammatically articulate – make too much pretence at an impossible clarity of subject matter to be quite satisfactory.

Rabelais writes his own Apologia at the end of the Second Book, absolving his readers and suggesting a sympathy, indeed, for his illustrator:

> If you say to me ... it would seem that you were not very wise in writing these flimflam stories, and pleasant fooleries: I answer you, that you are not much wiser to spend your time in reading them: neverthelesse, if you read them to make your selves merry, as in manner of pastime I wrote them, you and I both are far more worthy of pardon, than a great rabble of squint-minded fellows, dissembling and counterfeit Saints, demure lookers, hypocrites, pretended zealots, tough Friars, buskin-Monks, and other such sects of men, who disguise themselves like Maskers to deceive the World.

Grant Richards's bankruptcy came only a few weeks before Will and Josie were to spend their first Christmas together with their baby. One of Will's main sources of income for that year had been removed in Grant Richards's financial collapse, and although he had already received an advance payment,[36] he later claimed that he was still owed money by Richards. Christmas 1904, then, was a grim time, and it may be this particular Christmas that Will was remembering when, in 1909, he was asked as one of a number of celebrated literati to tell the readers of *The Bookman* how he spent Christmas: 'Alas!', he writes, 'I have principally one impression of Christmas, an impression so sad and overpowering as to nearly obliterate others from my memory. It grieves me therefore very deeply, to have to tell you that I feel hardly qualified to answer the questions you put to me.'[37]

Printed beside Will's paragraph in the magazine is an

W. HEATH
ROBINSON

'Follow after – we are waiting by the trails that we lost'
Watercolour, 1909 Frontispiece to *A Song of the English*
Private Collection

Inscribed to Will's agent, A. E. Johnson, the author of the first book to be written about his work, 1913.

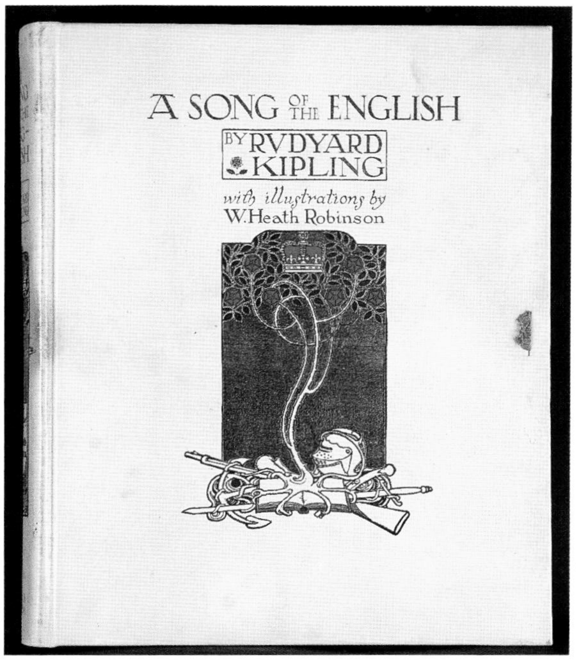

Cover for the vellum bound de luxe edition of ***A Song of the English,*** published by Hodder and Stoughton, 1909
The Joan Brinsmead Trust

ink drawing by him captioned 'Mr. W. Heath Robinson taking his Christmas cheer.' But this is not a self-portrait of Will. The figure has a beaky nose, which Will had not, a high-domed balding head – not Will's. The single figure sits tucking into an enormous Christmas dinner. So is Will imagining the Christmas dinner others may have had in 1904, when his own was so meagre, or is he being merely playful, hiding behind his pantomime mask, and keeping the extended Robinson family's riotous Christmas romps as private as they should properly be?

After the *Rabelais* disaster, Will had to find a publisher who would guarantee him a regular income as a matter of urgency. Before 1905, his work for newspapers and magazines had been spasmodic, his book illustrations filling so much of his time. Now, however, he began to concentrate his efforts on comic drawings and on quickly finding outlets for them. The comic drawings caused some consternation among magazine art editors, and in presenting them for publication Will suffered his share of disappointments.

Mr W. Heath Robinson taking his Christmas Cheer

'These drawings are very interesting and show careful work,' one art editor told him. 'But what we are looking for is something really funny, you understand, something to make our readers laugh.'

'But,' Will remonstrated, 'they are meant to be funny ...'.

'Then do you do any what you would call serious work?'

'Oh yes.'

'Well,' the art editor said, 'if this work is humorous, your serious work must be very serious indeed.'[38]

Will did eventually find some sympathetic, even enthusiastic, art editors. One was Clement Shorter (1857–1926), of *The Tatler*, who published his cartoons in 1905 and 1906, and another was Bruce Ingram (1877–1963), the young editor of both the *Illustrated London News* and *The Sketch*. Will particularly compliments Ingram in *My Line of Life*, by saying that it was largely due to him that 'I was fairly launched on my career as a humorous artist.'[39] Ingram published Will's drawings in *The Sketch* without a break from 1906 to 1919, and it was here, and in *The Strand Magazine* and *The Bystander*, that his great reputation was forged.

The Bystander published Will's cartoons from February 1905, beginning with a series of eight under the general title *The Whimsicalities of William Heath Robinson*. These drawings, with titles such as *The Tiff*, *Philosophy* and *Love*, are soupily sentimental, and, if they have a humour, it tends to escape us now. In this series, however, Will is earnestly searching for a new style with the immediate popular appeal that *Rabelais* lacked. He chose to carry his humour on the back of the design of Japanese prints, with their wide areas of flat colour, their strong diagonals and compositions that defy Western traditions of perspective. *Japonisme* was at its height in Europe in the wake of Art Nouveau, *The Mikado* (1885) and Puccini's new opera *Madame Butterfly* (1904); and the collection of Japanese art at the Victoria and Albert Museum was by this time already one of the greatest in the West. Will's signature on his cartoons in *The Bystander* reflects his Japanese influences – it is placed vertically, with ragged intermingling letters vaguely in the manner of Japanese characters. He even puts a Japanese spirit into the sequence of cartoons that followed *The Whimsicalities*, his interpretations of the 'Seven Ages of Man' from Shakespeare's *As You Like It*. Perhaps this was the time that Will acquired the group of Japanese prints that hung on his drawing-room walls throughout his married life, and which were a constant source of enjoyment and inspiration to him.

Will's pre-war *Sketch* cartoons have a far stronger bite than those drawn for *The Bystander*. They begin with a series of nine full-page drawings, *The Gentle Art of Catching Things* (March–May 1906). One of these, *Angling for Alligators*,[40] showing two black babies being used as alligator bait, would procure no laughs now. In the subsequent series, *British Sports and Pastimes* (July–September 1906), the first inklings of Will's machinery can be seen making a cautious début in the cartoon *Netting Rabbits in the Berkshire Downs*.[41] Other early *Sketch* cartoons, such as the two series anticipating a German invasion of England in 1910,[42] are topical, even political, in their message.

At the same time as he was building up a new reputation as an illustrative journalist, Will strengthened his contacts with book publishers. T. C. & E. C. Jack, who published his illustrations to *Stories from Chaucer* in 1905, commissioned Will to illustrate their subsequent editions of *Stories from the Iliad* and *Stories from the Odyssey* (1906). In his Everyman series, J. M. Dent reissued the three Robinson brothers' illustrations to *Hans Andersen* in 1906.

Right: Blasting limpets on the Barbary Coast
Pen and ink and watercolour, 1906
Sheffield City Art Galleries

A most elegantly, even poetically, composed cartoon, reminiscent of Japanese art. Will had a collection of Japanese prints from which he drew inspiration. Even the figures seem to be a translation of the humorous and gentle men and women who populate Hokusai's prints of Japanese daily life.

Warm hearted old soul disguised as a merman endeavouring to lure a mermaid from her native element
Pen and ink and wash, mid 1920s
Private Collection

GUNPOWDER
PARAFFIN
W. HEATH
ROBINSON

Right: Sport in the Wild West: Trapping clothes moths in the wilds of Idaho
Pen and ink and watercolour, 1906
Private Collection

Left: Bombing tunny in the lagoons of Bude
Pen and ink and wash, 1906
Private Collection

When Hodder and Stoughton commissioned Will to provide forty illustrations to Shakespeare's *Twelfth Night* (1908), it was as part of a concerted challenge by Hodder to the success that their rival publishers Heinemann had been having with their leading illustrator Arthur Rackham.[43] Alongside Will's *Twelfth Night*, Hodder published Edmund Dulac's edition of *The Tempest*, both sumptuous gift books coinciding with Heinemann's publication of Rackham's illustrated edition of *A Midsummer Night's Dream*. The autumn of 1908, then, was a blockbuster season for Shakespeare. *The Times Literary Supplement* reviewed the books together, giving a balanced critical opinion of the three leading British book illustrators. Dulac, the paper's critic believed, had a 'feeling for the pretty and attractive. ... Curious blend of influences ... [of] the art of Persia and Japan.' Will's illustrations were 'more obvious in fancy, and hardly attempt to realize or illuminate character. They are effective as stage scenery by Mr. Harker or Mr. Telbin is effective, but the effects are not very appropriate to book illustration. The setting counts for more than the figures; and the whole atmosphere is that of the theatre, and of the costume play.' The critic found Arthur Rackham, on the other hand, to be 'an artist of finer fibre; but he is becoming mannered ...'[44]

The reviewer pinpoints the weakness of *Twelfth Night*, in which Will Heath Robinson creates an atmosphere that suggests he is illustrating a stage production of the play, with the characters speaking the lines, rather than illustrating the action. This is underlined by his choice of

W. HEATH ROBINSON

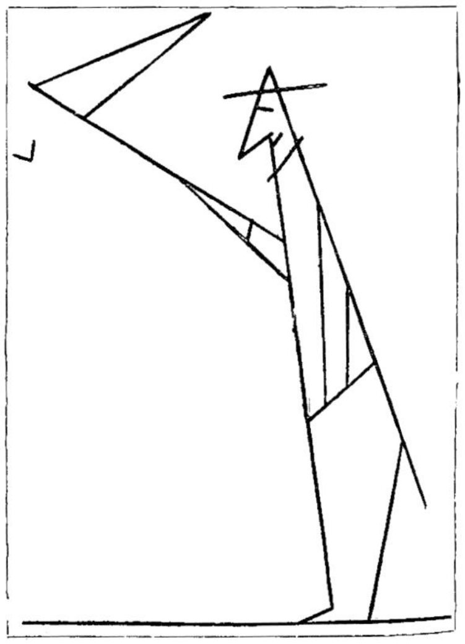

Above: The Lepidopterist
A straight-line drawing from *The Strand Magazine*, 1913.

Olivia: 'Blame not this haste of mine'
Pen and ink and watercolour, 1908
From *Twelfth Night*, Act IV, sc iii
Private Collection

architectural settings, and also by the fact that, reflecting his love of singing, eleven of the illustrations feature songs.

The palette Will has used in *Twelfth Night* is heavily restricted. Deep blues, greens and greys predominate in the moody night scenes, except where relieved by the reds and oranges of sunset. Will's reading of the play is overcast, and even the relatively few day scenes are in a heavily dappled or otherwise subdued light, leading the reader to forget that the play is, in fact, a comedy. This betrays Will's uncertainty about his rôle in the book: many of his illustrations are painterly, even scumbled, a technique that was not suited to clear reproduction by the pre-war four-colour method. With traces of the influence of Watteau, Turner, Pettie and Clausen, we are perhaps witnessing the painter in Will Heath Robinson struggling in *Twelfth Night* to be free of the illustrator's bonds.

The first profile of Heath Robinson as an artist, an article which introduced him as a public personality, appeared in *The Strand Magazine* in July 1908. This almost certainly came as a result of Will's decision in 1908 to appoint A. E. Johnson as his agent. In making this decision, Will was withdrawing himself from the business side of his activities, something he now found he had neither the time nor the inclination to deal with. By appointing an agent, Will was expressing his awareness of the new variety in the nature of his work, and the different markets to which it now appealed. He was at once a comic magazine illustrator with a popular weekly following, an illustrator of classic titles, and an author and illustrator of his own work. He was also becoming a celebrity, being portrayed on stage by René Koval as 'Mr Ascot Heath Robinson' in the Alhambra Theatre production of George Grossmith's revue *Kill That Fly* (1913). His career, now, needed to be carefully handled.

Viola: 'What country, friends, is this?
Captain: 'This is Illyria, lady'
Pen and ink and watercolour, 1908
From *Twelfth Night*, Act I, sc ii
Sheffield City Art Galleries

The profile of Will and his work in the *Strand* immediately followed the issue in which he made his début in the magazine with a group of comic drawings under the title *Why I am Not a Criminal*. Will is described in the profile as 'a very earnest gentleman and accomplished painter, who is as much absorbed in his elaborate absurdities as a Senior Wrangler might be in the differential calculus.' The anonymous article, perhaps written by the *Strand*'s art editor, W. J. K. Boot, also noted the level of Will's popularity in Europe, referring to the fact that his drawings were now making not England alone, but all Europe laugh. The writer points out that President Fallières of France was so amused by one of Will's drawings in the series *The Gentle Art of Catching Things* in *The Sketch*, that he passed it round the table at an Elysée Palace luncheon, 'causing, we are told, many of the guests to nearly choke with laughter'.[45]

Will confessed in the article for the first time that he had misjudged the best market for his humour; and went on to define his own contentious view of children's humour:

> I suppose I have been what you call funny a great many years; only I made the common mistake of dosing children with humour instead of giving it to 'grown ups' ... I hadn't then found out that children, although extremely humorous to others, have very little sense of humour of their own, but are very, very matter-of-fact little people. A book for them, I feel, should take them most seriously. *Strewwelpeter* to a child is real earnest, and is consequently, I believe, the most successful book with children. The humour that it has is accidental, and is for us 'grown ups' alone.

This view helps to explain the sobriety of *Uncle Lubin*. Lubin's adventures are not in themselves particularly funny, and his humourless earnestness in pursuit of his quarry is endearing rather than amusing. The laughs, and macabre laughs at that, come as a result of Lubin's or other characters' actions – for example the death of

Bubbulozoon, from 'The Descent of Man'
Pen and ink and wash, 1907
From *The Sketch*
British Library, Colindale

Right: The Diver – Thank heavens it's a soft roe
Pen and ink and wash, 1920
From *The Bystander*
Private Collection

the Dragon-Snake as a result of tangling itself up during a dance to the music of Lubin's concertina, or the swallowing of the Mer-man by a big fish. This prompted an exchange that strikes us as funny because it is so priggish:

'What did you do?' asked Uncle Lubin.
'Well, we did nothing but laugh,' said the little Mer-boy.
'That was not nice of you,' said Uncle Lubin.[46]

This 1908 interview gives the impression that Will considered that he had now got beyond drawing for children. 'I liked drawing for children. It was a relief to my mind, because I didn't feel it necessary to restrict myself; I could just put down whatever came into my head, without thinking whether or not it violated the canons of probability.' Although there may be a certain casualness in the way this view is expressed, Will is revealing an irrational tendency that marks him out as an embryonic Surrealist, carrying the spirit of Edward Lear into the twentieth century.

Gradually [Will continues], I found that what was primarily meant to interest children interested their elders a good deal more. If a sketch of mine was very extravagant the youngsters turned from it in incredulity, but I observed that the boredom of the child was directly in inverse ratio to the delight of his parent.

This understanding marked the beginning of Will's humorous work as we know it now, though in the event he never entirely left the world of children's illustration. In a revealing description of his working method, he spoke of how he tried to make his drawings funny internally, that is without relying on any title or inscription. Most of his comic drawings have titles, but the titles' humour, written in the deadpan language of officialdom, is not so much explanatory, as there to provide an extra layer of enjoyment.

'I like a series – that is, a succession of adventures happening to the same person – or ramifications and applications of the same idea, because it gives me the greatest chance to let myself go and bring all the drollery out of which the notion is capable.' This led Will to 'pile up' the drawing, adding all the details and accessories that his imagination could supply.

To maintain his living, and develop his following, Will had to take careful notice of what his public wanted. He believed that the gruesome streak and cynicism in *The Descent of Man*[47] made it the least popular of his series to date. 'People want their humour to be as light as it can be, and for the time be reminded of nothing serious or heavy. Cynicism, I find, is particularly unpopular.' Will was not alone in admitting his own revisionist tendency. Dickens removed slang and indelicate passages from *Sketches by Boz* when they were reissued in 1839 after he had become famous.[48]

The *Strand* article provides a marker in the development of Will's career. Circumstances had forced him in 1905 to rely for a living on his natural talent as a comic artist, and by 1908 he had become fully established. His first appearance as an artist in the *Strand* the month before, in his series of six drawings *Why I am Not a Criminal*, is typical of the level of his achievement in draughtsmanship and design. In the off-centre composition of *Child Stealing in Highgate Woods*, another unfortunate subject which only Will's humour could make remotely funny, he creates a high horizon and a wide area of open space which shows the continuing influence of Japanese prints. *Pickpocketing in Hampstead Lane* has spiky trees and undergrowth in parody of Arthur Rackham, a Hampstead resident. Will considered Rackham to be ripe for parody, satirizing his style in a 1910 *Bystander* cartoon entitled *Too Much Christmas*.[49]

In 1908, Will, Josie and their family moved out of Tufnell Park to Hatch End, near the country village of Pinner, north of London. This move gave a new freedom to the family, and brought them a large garden, which Will was able to cultivate. It allowed him, too, to indulge his other passions, country walking and the pursuit of good ale.

With his brothers Tom, Charles and George, and a group of close friends, who included the artists Philip Pimlott (active 1893–1940), P. B. Hickling (active 1908–*c.*1960) and S. Jacobs, he formed in 1911 a walking and drinking club, The Worshipful Grandiose and Loyal Federation of Frothfinders. The Frothfinders drew up their Charter, a cod-medieval inscribed vellum scroll, which the 26 members signed at the Crown Inn at Stanmore.[50] The Charter, written out by Charles Robinson, describes the true Frothfinder in the language of the Psalms, as one 'yearning glad to the sound of the four stringed musick even to the hundred stringed instrument eager to the dance bacchanal the feast saturnal'. The types that the true Frothfinder shunned were 'gamblers, drunkards, garrotters, thugs, libellers, liars, wifebeaters, magicians, blackmailers, shoplifters, dissolute persons, dissipated debauchees, lewd pursuers, chasers of the female' and so on and so on and so on. The Frothfinders walked and drank and sang together, both by night and by day. They climbed the Downs, lost their way, stopped for lunch, made detours, fancied seeing Oberon and Titania, Bottom and Snout, sang songs that roused the inhabitants of Stanmore and generally had a

Too Much Christmas
W HEATH ROBINSON
Mrs. Ginabody: "You old rogues, how dare you—at your time of life, too"
BY HEATH ROBINSON

Too Much Christmas
Pen and ink and wash,
1910
From *The Bystander*
British Library, Colindale

A Heath Robinson parody of the style of Arthur Rackham.

noisy, energetic and thoroughly hearty time.

Without putting too fine a point on this piece of nonsense, the Frothfinders were one of the many consequences of the opening up of the countryside around London by improvements in the roads and railways. Will and his friends put on their braces and discovered the Green Belt. As he recalled when he was writing the last few, poetic lines of *My Line of Life*, 'I may not have romped with Satyrs in the woods of Arcady, but I have had some pleasant evenings in the Crown at Stanmore.'[51] Feeling comfortable in the company of artists, Will became a member, too, of the London Sketch Club and the Savage Club, two organizations that combined the serious purposes of sketching and conversation with a clownish, practical joking camaraderie.[52]

Nearly two years after coming to Hatch End, the family moved to Moy Lodge, a detached house in Moss Lane, Pinner. There were three children now, and all were beginning to demand stories and attention from their father. As a result Will wrote *Bill the Minder* (1912), the most elaborate of his fantasies, based on the bedtime stories that he wove to entertain his family. The story, which he illustrated profusely, concerns the trials of

Right: Thirst
Pencil, 1910/11
The Joan Brinsmead Trust
A drawing made during a meeting of the London Sketch Club

Above: The Lark
From Queen Mary's Dolls' House, Windsor Castle
Pen and ink, 1920/21
37 × 25 mm
Reproduced by gracious permission of Her Majesty the Queen

Right: The King of Troy
Pencil and watercolour, 1912
From *Bill the Minder*
Private Collection

champion baby-sitter employed to look after a family of ten children. With the children (and the King of Troy whom they somehow pick up on the way) Bill wanders the world in search of adventure. They meet Good Aunt Galladia, who loved birds; Plain Jack, the ninth mate of the Swedish ship *Turnip* that sailed from Cherry Garden Pier for Margate in 1840 with a cargo of camels and was never seen again; and The Lost Grocer, who had been beguiled from his shop by a Druid, and who had disappeared for years. Finally, Bill and his troop reach Troy, and restore the King to his rightful throne. As in his comic illustrations, Will piles absurdity upon absurdity in a story that is packed so full of incident that its narrative thread nearly drowns. Though one critic in *The Athenaeum* called *Bill the Minder* 'richly imaginative and original,'[53] another pointed out that Will's habit of piling up incongruities goes far towards 'ruining his natural endowments. It is largely owing to this failing that we should speak of his most serious work rather as highly decorated than as highly decorative.'[54]

A curious, scrawny, featherless bird makes its appearance in Will's drawings at this time, and its regular presence can be seen as a sign that he felt he was now well enough known to have a trademark of his own. He had invented this bird in 1902, when it appeared as the offspring of the unscrupulous Bag-Bird, the tormentor of Uncle Lubin. It first appeared in *The Bystander* in the 1905 *Seven Ages of Man* series, and so familiar had it become by 1908 that the author of the *Strand* profile told of how a five-year-old girl, on seeing a plucked chicken for the first time, announced to her mother that 'one of Mr. Robinson's birds had flown in downstairs and gone to sleep'.[55] Another child was so taken with Will's drawings that he wrote to ask a special favour of the artist: 'I do so love your pictures that I want to call my hedgehog after you. May I please?'[56] Heath Robinson fever had even spread as far as Hong Kong. To celebrate their imminent return to England, the 25th and 40th Companies of the Royal Engineers had played 'Bouncing the Beecham', a game that Will had invented in his *Sketch*

Good Aunt Galladia Glowmutton, who loved birds
Pen and ink and wash, 1912
From *Bill the Minder*
The Joan Brinsmead Trust

Will was forever fascinated by formidable women who wore enormous hats.

series *Little Games for the Holidays* (August–September 1910). The 25th Company won by two catches to nil.[57]

Accolades such as these proved that Will's fame was fully established. So secure was he now, with the sureness of his talent and the weight of A. E. Johnson's agency behind him, that he was able to disregard two new approaches that Grant Richards made in 1911 and 1917, suggesting that the pair collaborate again.[58] If Will had convinced himself that his guiding spirit was that strange little genius Uncle Lubin, his audience already knew better – the strange little genius was William Heath Robinson.

Joan, aged about eight years old
Photograph, *c.* 1912
The Joan Brinsmead Trust

CHAPTER FOUR

MOONSHINE AND FANCY AND WAR 1914–1918

WILL'S FIRST INTIMATION OF WAR came when, with members of the Frothfinders, he was walking across the Chiltern Hills in South Buckinghamshire on August Bank Holiday 1914. 'The sun had long since set, and we were tired as we tramped along the country lanes.' The friends heard horses galloping towards them, and soon, in the failing light, they were passed by a uniformed orderly riding home with a second animal on a leading rein. The horses vanished into the darkness. 'The sound died down and the woods and fields resumed their sleep; but for us, this was the first evidence of the war that was immediately to break out.'[1]

By the time war had been declared, and soldiers were setting off cheerily to France, Will had completed the series of illustrations to *A Midsummer Night's Dream* which are the summit of his achievement as a book illustrator. The laboured theatricality of his illustrations to *Twelfth Night* had been overcome, being replaced with a frothy extravaganza of fairies, rustics and the petulant magic of Puck. Rackham's *A Midsummer Night's Dream* (1908) was stiff competition, but Will's version of the play had a different nature. It was essentially a black and white book, lightened with twelve colour plates, rather than a sumptuous colour plate production such as Rackham had created. In his *Dream*, Will took his black line technique to a peak of subtlety, and combined two graphic traditions that might otherwise have seemed utterly incompatible. Illustrations such as *'Help me, Lysander, help me!'* and the Act III heading of the Ass's Head on an obelisk, fuse the cool elegance of Aubrey Beardsley with the intricate surface textures that Will knew so well from the work of the wood-engravers of his father's generation. He used his knowledge of stage effects in these illustrations, many of which are lit from

Hermia: 'Help me, Lysander, help me'
Pencil, pen and ink, 1914
From *A midsummer Night's Dream*, Act II sc ii
Private Collection

Fairies and gnomes running to Theseus' palace
Pen and ink, 1914
From *A Midsummer Night's Dream*, Act V sc i
Private Collection

below with a kind of white, undiscriminating but appropriate theatrical limelight which throws the foreground into strong relief.

Freeing himself from the restraint of margins and borders, Will tosses cascades of fairies across the page with such exuberant flourishes that they seem to need all the magical powers they can muster to stay in place. Like his *Twelfth Night*, this *Dream* has a strongly architectural centre, with ruins, obelisks, temples and columns, giving a solid classical framework to the action. In illustrations such as *Exeunt Bottom, Quince, Flute, Snug, Starveling and Snout*, in which the six figures wander diagonally up the page, Will's sense of control of blank space is masterly. The colour plates in the *Dream* are tighter than those Will had painted for *Twelfth Night*, having outlines to their figures which echo his black line work, but which are irksome and dominant when used with colour.

When the newspapers were filled with stories of the war, mention of Will's *A Midsummer Night's Dream* squeezed its way into *The Times Literary Supplement*: '... full of moonshine and fancy,' the critic wrote, '... a riot of decoration ... Midsummer dreaminess permeating the whole book.... This book stands alone.'[2]

In Shakespeare's fantasy, Puck shook his wings and bragged to Oberon that he would 'put a girdle round about the earth in forty minutes'.[3] Even as Will was drawing Puck, the language of Parliament rose to wild heights of invention as politicians argued the need for the nation to increase expenditure on flying: 'It occurred to me,' the Secretary of State for War maintained in a statement that Puck might have welcomed, 'that we might make flying safer if we were to have spare wings.'[4] Colonel Seeley went on to point out that flying in Britain was more difficult and dangerous than flying on the Continent because 'we are subject to much stronger and more gusty winds, so that it is very difficult to carry on flying operations. We live in a very enclosed and very hilly country.... Before coming down [the aviator] must look for a suitable place, and having found [one] ... he may come down in a particular field and find that there is a wire fence at the end of it.' Another MP brought the attention of Members to the problems faced by pilots of observation aeroplanes: 'If you go too low, ... the position of the unfortunate aeroplanist sitting on a seat like a bicycle seat and with perhaps a battalion of marksmen below him, is a very disagreeable one.'[5]

Puck
Pen and ink, 1914
From *A Midsummer Night's Dream*, Act III sc ii
Private Collection

Bottom's head, as a classical herm
Pen and ink, 1914
From *A Midsummer Night's Dream*
Private Collection

If MPs nodded sagely at these points, such growing and gaudy talk both at home and in Germany of the inventions of war gave Will a new springboard for his imagination. Having completed *A Midsummer Night's Dream*, he faced the possibility of his opportunities for work diminishing as the pre-war publishing market altered its priorities. He realized that he, too, would have to adapt, and as the war developed he found new openings for his comic drawings: '... the much advertised frightfulness and efficiency of the German army, and its many terrifying inventions, gave me one of the best opportunities I ever enjoyed.'[6]

Will had been satirizing the threat of a German invasion since 1910, at the time when the articles of Robert Blatchford (1851–1943) were appearing in the *Daily Mail*. Blatchford, a highly perceptive and respected Socialist journalist, warned the nation in a series of ten articles published in December 1909 of the dangers presented by the growth in German militarism: '... Germany will attack Britain because she knows herself to be strong, and because she believes that Britain, her rich and influential rival, has grown fat and impotent and would fall an easy victim to a well-planned, resolute and powerful attack.'[7] Where Blatchford's warnings put a serious, well argued and measured case for the nation to beware the threat from Germany, Will's drawings, in the series *Am Tag* [*The Day*], firmly backed him up by making exactly the same point through a series of telling and incisive jokes. *Am Tag! Die Deutsche Kommen (Very)!* (April–June 1910) gave Will's view of what might happen in the event of a German invasion of Britain.

The first drawing in the series, *German Spies in Epping Forest*, had the caption:

So many authors have described in detail the invasion of England by Germany that Mr. Heath Robinson's patriotism has led him to make a thorough investigation of the subject, with some most remarkable results. He finds, for instance, German spies galore in Epping Forest, soldiers of the Kaiser ingeniously disguised in many ways and very much on the watch. His other revelations will be published week by week.[8]

This drawing and its caption were taken so seriously by the German authorities that it was reprinted in a German magazine to show how fearful of invasion the British were becoming.

Will's three collections of satirical wartime drawings contain some of his most biting and uncompromising

The Germans come! German Spies in English Woods
Die Deutschen kommen! (Deutsche Spione in englischen Wäldern)
· Karikatur auf die englische Invasionsfurcht von W. Heath Robinson

Above: The Curious Old Town Clock, Buntingford
Ian Jefferies Collection

H. G. Wells called Buntingford in Hertfordshire 'Heath Robinsonville', on account of its extraordinary architecture.

Will's cartoon 'German Spies in Epping Forest' (*The Sketch*, 1910) was taken literally by German propagandists, and widely circulated in Germany to show how well the Kaiser's spies were doing.
The Joan Brinsmead Trust

work. The collections, *Some 'Frightful' War Pictures* (1915), *Hunlikely* (1916) and *The Saintly Hun – A Book of German Virtues* (1917) are assemblies of full-page black and white drawings that had originally appeared predominantly in *The Sketch*, *Illustrated Sporting and Dramatic News* and *The Strand*. Of course, they are funny, mocking what Will (and the nation) saw to be German efficiency, formality and cunning, in comparison with the Tommy's good humour and cheerfulness against the odds. Although he was working during the course of a dreadful war, with the intention of keeping up spirits both amongst the soldiers at the Front and civilians at home, his characters seem to be indulging in highly inventive playground games.

One of Will's most ardent followers was H. G. Wells. 'It may amuse you to know,' Wells wrote in the early months of the war,

> ... that you are adored in this home. I have been ill all this Christmas-time and frightfully bored and the one thing I have wanted is a big album of your absurd beautiful drawings to turn over. Now my wife has just raided the Sketch office for back numbers with you in it and I am turning over lots of you. You give me a peculiar pleasure of the mind like nothing else in the world. I can feel myself getting better.[9]

Will's reply suggests that he remained anxious about his popularity being maintained: 'I shall certainly do my best to keep this work going and still further develop it as I think it capable of development – until everyone is tired of it – a dread I sometimes have. ...'[10]

A typical example of Will's wartime satire is *The Tommy Scalder*. This shows a cunning German device for the aerial bombardment of the British lines by pouring boiling water from kettles flown over No Man's Land by means of a squadron of kites. In Will's world of the absurd, the kettles boil immediately from cold when pla-

Huns injecting chilblain serum into British feet
Pen and ink and wash, *c.* 1915
Private Collection

ced over a candlestick, the kites stay aloft without the need for a line to any kite flyer, and they advance together in a menacing formation to the British trench. Despite the fact that each kettle can only hold two pints at the most, their supply of boiling water is constant, pouring out across No Man's Land as the kites make their journey. Although most of the British seem to dismiss the attack phlegmatically, equipped as they are with a supply of stout black brollies, some fainter hearts appear to wave the white flag. So within Will's patent absurdity, there is a vein of realism, grounded in the observation that perhaps this really *could* work, and if so the device would be so terrifying that it could break the resolve of the more highly strung of the Tommies.

The Tommy Scalder was one of a group of drawings under the title *Hague Convention Defied*, made in response to press reports of the 'frightfulness and efficiency' of the German army, with its many supposedly terrifying war machines which were in breach of the Hague Convention. Postcard pictures of some of the new weapons were circulated as propaganda by the German authorities to frighten the civilian population of Britain. By inventing weapons such as *The Tommy Scalder*, *Chilblain Serum* or *The Trench Presser*, weapons that even the Kaiser had not contemplated, Will played an important rôle in the British war effort by defusing the effect of the German terror through laughter.

'Frightfulness' was a recognized quality, tactic even, of the German army in the First World War, and Will's use of the word with inverted commas in the title of his first collection of war drawings indicates the immediacy with which it was understood by the general public. In *General von Sneak: A Little Study of the War*, published in 1918, Robert Blatchford summed up its meaning:

Right: A malevolent Santa Claus putting bombs into soldiers' stockings. Christmas card designed by Will for troops at the Western Front, 1915
Imperial War Museum, London

The Trench Presser
Pen and ink and wash, 1915
From *Some 'Frightful' War Pictures*

For fifty years the Gospel of Frightfulness has been preached in Germany; and the Germans, prone to violence, prone to hatred, rude in their language, coarse in their manners, have been apt pupils. ... Frightfulness is part of the German code of war and is looked upon by soldiers and civilians alike as a useful and proper part of the tactics – and business.[11]

When they reached the Front, Will's drawings gave fresh heart to the serving soldier, and led him to receive 'an immense correspondence' from all ranks of the army.[12] He quotes a letter sent in November 1916 which told him: 'Your "Some Frightful War Pictures" has just reached our mess within the last few days and you can have no idea how much the illustrations are appreciated out here. All the members of this mess have been "At it" since the very beginning and your sketches in the various magazines &c have always been a source of great amusement to us.'

By drawing a veil over the horrors of war and enabling the participants to laugh, Will's cartoons had a cathartic effect on their audiences in the trenches. In the view of the artist Percy Bradshaw, the comic drawings were Will's self-imposed contribution to the war effort, with the object of stopping it by reducing the combatants to hysterics.[13]

In their letters, officers and men suggested ideas to Will, some of which, in due time, he took up. *Training Wasps to Sting Highlanders in Flanders* was suggested by a Lieutenant-Colonel, and became a subject in the series *The Hague Convention Defied!* Later in the war, a suggestion that enemy troops could be sucked out of their trenches inspired Will's drawing of *The American Suction Tank for Drawing the Enemy from his Dugout*.

The long hours of waiting to go over the top, with hushed conversations in the dark and damp of the trenches, spawned the letters and ideas sent by soldiers to Heath Robinson. In his novel *Under Fire* (1916),[14] the Anglo-French novelist Henri Barbusse (1873–1935) described the army in which he served as 'a waiting machine', a poignant and double-edged description. The products turned out by the 'waiting machine' were

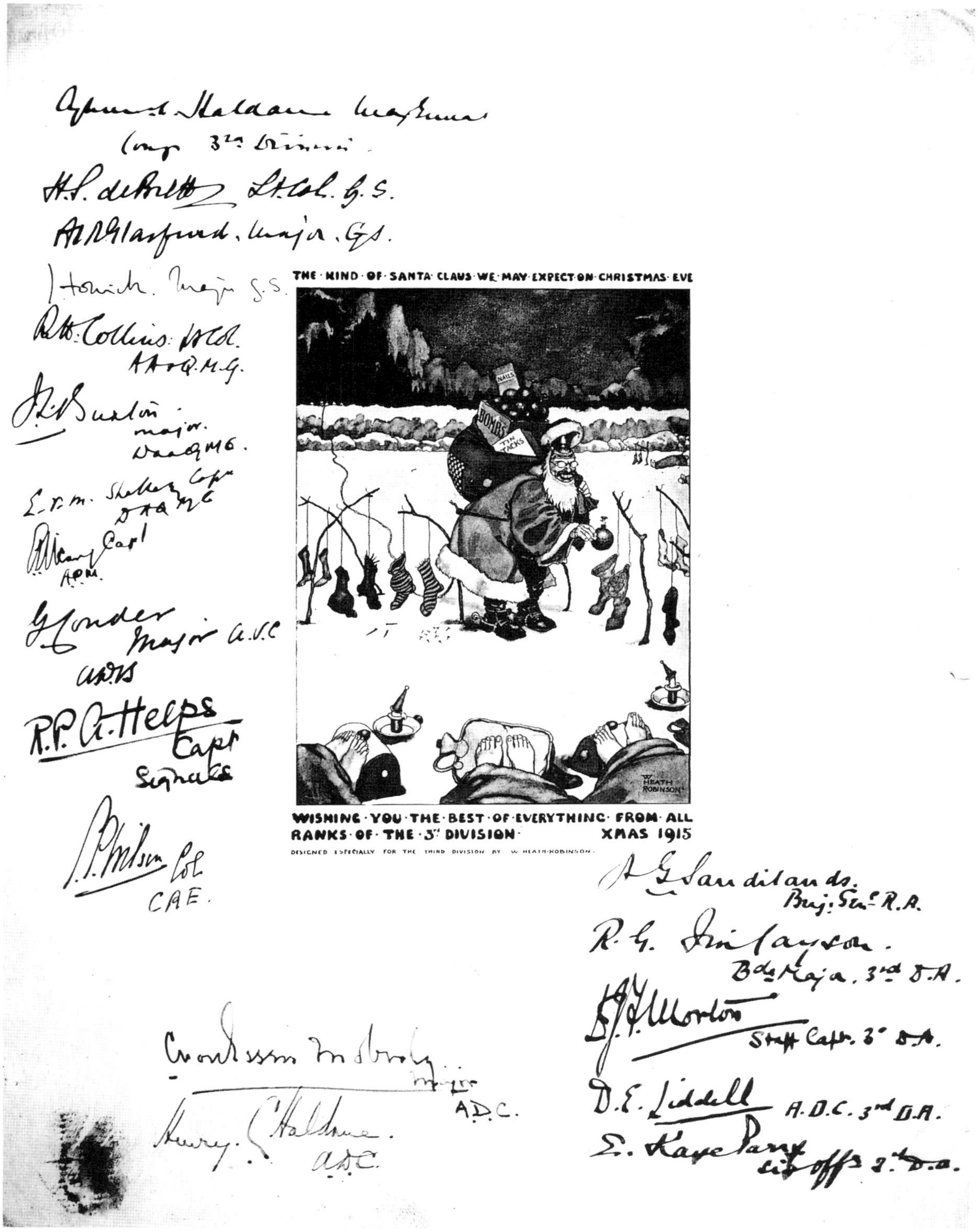
THE · KIND · OF · SANTA · CLAUS · WE · MAY · EXPECT · ON · CHRISTMAS · EVE
NAILS
BOMBS
TIN TACKS
HEATH ROBINSON
WISHING · YOU · THE · BEST · OF · EVERYTHING · FROM · ALL RANKS · OF · THE · 3RD DIVISION · XMAS 1915
DESIGNED ESPECIALLY FOR THE THIRD DIVISION BY W. HEATH-ROBINSON.

inventive and various – toys made from barbed wire, pencil cases from used rifle cartridges, poems and parodies sent to *The Wipers Times*. Many of the soldiers' proposals for 'Heath Robinson' machines were illustrated with drawings for Will to elaborate upon, and he recalled that without exception they were written in great good humour by men who were doing their best to make light of their hard life. 'No greater testimony could there be ... to the brave spirit that was abroad amongst our men in France, Salonica, Mesopotamia or wherever they were stationed.'[15]

The smile on the face of war soon faded, however. It seemed to fade, too, in Will's drawings, for there are some in which poison spills unbidden from his pen. In *The Hatcher*, the victim is, or will soon be, one of Heath Robinson's characteristic scrawny birds, which sits on a bomb with a fizzling fuse. 'Tis an unusual kind of egg, no doubt,' the bird observes, '... but thank Heaven it is still

Tommy (at a loss what to say when suddenly confronted by the enemy): 'Er, er, Third return to Ammersmith.'
Pen and ink and wash, *c.* 1915
Private Collection

Will's style here comes close to that of his contemporary Bruce Bairnsfather.

warm, and I feel the throb of young life within.'[16] An illustration in *The Saintly Hun*, too, shows inevitable destruction. A German soldier is taking delivery of a shell on his enormous chest, in an example of his nation's 'Tenderness of Heart'. The shell is sharp, the chest is soft, and though Will does not dwell upon it, he takes us to within the barest moment of an event such as Barbusse described: '... men squashed, cut in two, or divided from top to bottom, blown into showers by an ordinary shell, bellies turned inside out and scattered anyhow, skulls forced bodily into the chest as if by a blow with a club.'[17] In *The Trench Presser or Bosch Bayonetter* a platoon of German soldiers is about to be massacred from above. Will's inventions, slapstick and absurd though they may be, can turn very nasty.

Heath Robinson's satire does not have the same kind of political edge with which the drawings of George Grosz (1893–1959) or Otto Dix (1891–1969) savaged the morals and militarism of their German compatriots. It is different, reaching its target by mockery rather than by polemic or hatred. A comparable series of drawings to Will's are those by Edmund J. Sullivan, *The Kaiser's Garland*, published in the same year as *Some 'Frightful' War Pictures*.

Sullivan, born in England of Irish parents in 1869, was a highly respected and influential magazine and book illustrator, who taught illustration at Goldsmith's College in London. Like many illustrators of his generation, he contributed to *The Graphic*, *Punch*, and *The Pall Mall Budget*, and had come to prominence as an illustra-

Above: Nach Paris! First Lessons in Goosestep
Pen and ink and wash, 1915
From *Some 'Frightful' War Pictures*

Right: Preparing war films. The arrival of German prisoners at Margate jetty by the night boat to Boulogne
Pen and ink and wash, 1916
From *Hunlikely*
Private Collection

tor with editions of Carlyle's *Sartor Resartus* (1898) and Tennyson's *Dream of Fair Women* (1901). Rackham named him as one of his '33 Greatest Painters [*sic*] of the XIXth Century', and described him as being 'about as unconventional as possible'.[18]

Sullivan was moved to make his series of 44 powerfully satirical drawings in *The Kaiser's Garland* as a response to German imperialism at the beginning of the First World War. In a draft letter to the Rt. Hon. C. F. G. Masterman, Sullivan described them as 'a spontaneous expression of an Irish artist's opinion of German Kultur'.[19] Where Will's collections of First World War drawings are lowbrow and mockingly funny, Sullivan's have a tougher satire, being more potent in their savagery than the more widely published political cartoons of the day, such as those by Sir Bernard Partridge (1861–1945). The unerring venom of his ink made Sullivan the Gillray of his day, the British Grosz.

In his Foreword to *The Kaiser's Garland*, Sullivan describes how, during a pre-war State Visit by the Kaiser to London, he threw a bunch of roses into the Kaiser's carriage as he passed, driving in state to the Guildhall. 'The roses glanced down from the parasol of the Empress, caught his helmet, and grazed his cheek; and it is this little episode that suggested to me the title of my present bunch of drawings. If this garland that I have prepared should, on his last ride between the crowds, drop into the Imperial tumbril and graze his cheek, I shall not be sorry.'[20]

This passage marks the difference between the

The Return of the Conqueror by Edmund Sullivan (1869–1933)
Pen and ink, 1916

From The Kaiser's Garland, *Sullivan's angry satire on the futility of war. This intensely melancholic drawing parodies Dürer's engraving* Knight, Death and the Devil.

Right: Trading with the enemy on Yarmouth Sands
Pen and ink, *c.* 1915
Victoria and Albert Museum, London

outspoken, angry and controversial Sullivan and the reserved and popular Heath Robinson. Where Sullivan uses anger, horror and the iconography of their compatriot Dürer to attack German aggression, Will saw the war as one of the best opportunities he ever enjoyed, one with which to play on the resilience of the British sense of humour. 'I believe,' he wrote, 'that our sense of humour played a greater part than we were always aware of in saving us from despair during those days of trial.'[21] Sullivan pushed decorum about as far as it could go;[22] Heath Robinson played the clown.

There is, however, a toughness in Will's humour when he satirizes the enemy's pomposity. *Nach Paris! First Lessons in the Goose-Step*[23] shows a column of eighty or ninety German soldiers being controlled on puppet strings by a small gosling who steps bravely out in front of them. *Washing Day on Board a Zeppelin*[24] returns us to the calms of domesticity. A silhouetted battle-scarred Zeppelin floats gently above a roofscape of chimneys and church spires, while its crew busies itself with boiling, washing, mangling and ironing its clothes. The detail of the crew hanging up the washing on a line stretched from one end of the airship to the other is a magical evocation of the style of Arthur Rackham.

Although Will was unique as a comic draughtsman, his manner was ripe for pastiche. Two regular contribuors of cartoons to *The Bystander* during the war, Lieutenant-Colonel E. G. O. Beuttler and Bernard Hugh, produced regular Heath Robinson look-alikes. Their work, published when Will had temporarily left *The Bystander* for the rival *Sketch*, betrayed itself by having a wilder, more frantic humour than Will's.

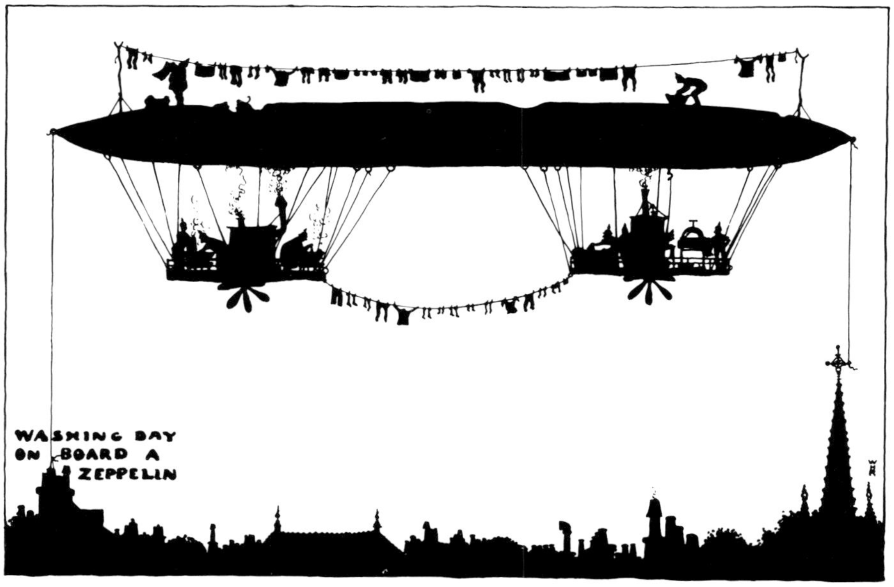

Washing day on board a Zeppelin
Pen and ink, 1917
From *The Saintly Hun*

A parallel to Will in popular literature was *The Book of Artemas*, an important and widely circulated parody of an Old Testament prophet by Arthur Telford Mason (Artemas). The book was published in 1917, and within a year it had reached its 99th edition. Its popularity mirrored Will's – where his inventions were drawn in the imagery of the playground or the amusement arcade, Artemas used Biblical language to satirize politicians and the war effort:

And the men of En[gland] did make them chariots of strange and wonderful design, and they *did* call them tanks. And there was no man throughout all the land that did say, I made not this chariot; but every man did draw his neighbour *unto the side*, and did speak unto him privily, saying 'Shush! Let it not be known. I tell thee that I, even I, did take *an hand* in this thing.

And the shape of the tanks was for a long time known only to the few. And some said they were *like unto* a lizard that is blown out mightily, that walketh as a man plagued with *the* corns.

And others said they were *like unto* an hippopotamus that doth wobble itself amazingly so that no man knoweth wither it intendeth; yet, *of a certainty*, doth it get there.

And others said they were like unto nothing on earth, being for the most part belly of a fashion *that is* given unto no living thing.[25]

When A. E. Johnson wrote his article about his friend and client's work for *The Studio* in 1916, he was at pains to play down Will's popularity as a humorous artist. *The Studio* was the leading art magazine devoted to the propagation and study of serious professional art. With its roots in the Arts and Crafts Movement, the magazine, which had since its inception in 1893 been edited by Charles Holme, carried topical reviews of current art exhibitions throughout Britain and abroad. It championed the cause of the young artist in its regular competition features, and brought artists of the highest quality to the fore in thoughtful illustrated articles. A feature in *The Studio* was, for any artist, a considerable accolade.

Johnson's article, 'The Line Drawings of William Heath Robinson',[26] was published only a few months after another, by Malcolm Salaman, on Charles Robinson.[27] It seems to have been an attempt by Johnson to remind readers of Will's reputation as a serious artist, and to present the Robinsons as an artistic dynasty. Both Salaman's and Johnson's articles speak of Grandfather Thomas Robinson as having been a wood-engraver con-

W. HEATH ROBINSON
PEACOCK PIE
A Book of Rhymes by
WALTER DE LA MARE
with illustrations by
W. HEATH ROBINSON
'He told me his dreams.....' ISAAC WATTS
CONSTABLE & CO LTD.
LONDON

Above: Jim Jay
Pen and ink, 1916
From *Peacock Pie*

Left: *Title page to* Peacock Pie, *a book of poems for children by Walter de la Mare, 1916.*

temporary and friend [*sic*] of Bewick, and Salaman writes of the art of Charles's father and uncle. With the coming of war, however, Will's public reputation had become resolutely linked with his inventions and his comic war drawings, and his earlier achievements as the illustrator of classics were at risk of being forgotten in clouds of laughter. Indeed, Percy Bradshaw, whose correspondence courses in sketching were heavily subscribed to during the First World War, was regularly asked by correspondents if Heath Robinson was mad.[28]

Johnson suggests in his article that Will's 'fancy' might be compared to Alice's observation on the Jabberwocky that 'somehow it seems to fill my head with ideas – but I don't exactly know what they are.' Defensively, Johnson goes on to say that 'by just so much as this constitutes, to the artist's legion of admirers, the chief imaginative charm of his work, one supposes that to others it must prove an exasperation.'

In his résumé of the artist's career to date, Johnson reminds the reader of Will's major books, and stresses that 'the history of his development so far has been one of continual experiment, and ... he has never fallen into the deadly trap of complacency.' As Johnson was Will's agent, the article smacks of special pleading in an attempt to recapture the admiration of those who might have thought that he had given up his place as one of the leading innovators in contemporary book illustration. Johnson reassures his readers that 'the artist is now engaged upon a new series of illustrations, which will doubtlessly be seen in the near future.' These were his illustrations to Walter de la Mare's *Peacock Pie* (1916).[29]

Johnson passes over Will's contribution to the war effort as a humorous artist in one sentence, as if it were at best an aberration, at worst an embarrassment.[30] By contrast, Malcolm Salaman emphasizes in his article how in wartime Charles had turned away 'from pictorial wonderland ... devoting himself as a zealous section-commander in his local Volunteer Training Corps, to the stern realities of drill, trench digging, and military map-making, in which last he is as expert and suggestive as he

'A very distinguished lobster . . .' (left) and 'Quick children, here is somethng . . .'
Pen and ink, 1915
From *The Water-Babies*

And clapped his little hands

is in illustrating a fairy tale.' The contrast in these two attitudes is a remarkable example of how narrow could be the perception of the rôle of the practising artist in the First World War. Although both Will and Charles were over the age for active service, Charles's image was expected to be enhanced by the news that he is digging trenches rather than drawing fairies, while Will's, it was feared, might be damaged among the sophisticated readership of *The Studio* if they were reminded that *his* contribution to the war effort was to produce funny drawings to amuse the troops and civilians. In retrospect, Will's contribution was by far the greater.

Although it occupied the largest part of his energies, Will's production was not limited during the war to comic drawings for the press. On the same day that he signed the contract with Constable & Co. to illustrate *A Midsummer Night's Dream*, he signed another with the same company to follow that with an illustrated edition of Charles Kingsley's *The Water-Babies*.[31] The contract for *The Water-Babies* cushioned to a small extent the blow of the wartime publishing changes, and with his full-page silhouettes, his page decorations and the colour plates he produced a book that harks back to *Bill the Minder*. He continued to work, too, for *The Strand Magazine* and *Pearson's Magazine*, making illustrations for stories that appealed mainly to children. This kind of decorative illustrated journalism, for stories such as 'The Competition at the Castlebar' by Morley Roberts[32] or 'Two Goats, a Garden and – ' by Elizabeth Allison,[33] represented a third strand in Will's work, and one which made an important contribution to his income until the late 1930s.

So he had no one to speak to or play with

As the balance of the war shifted, and after the arrival of the American Expeditionary Forces in France in 1917,

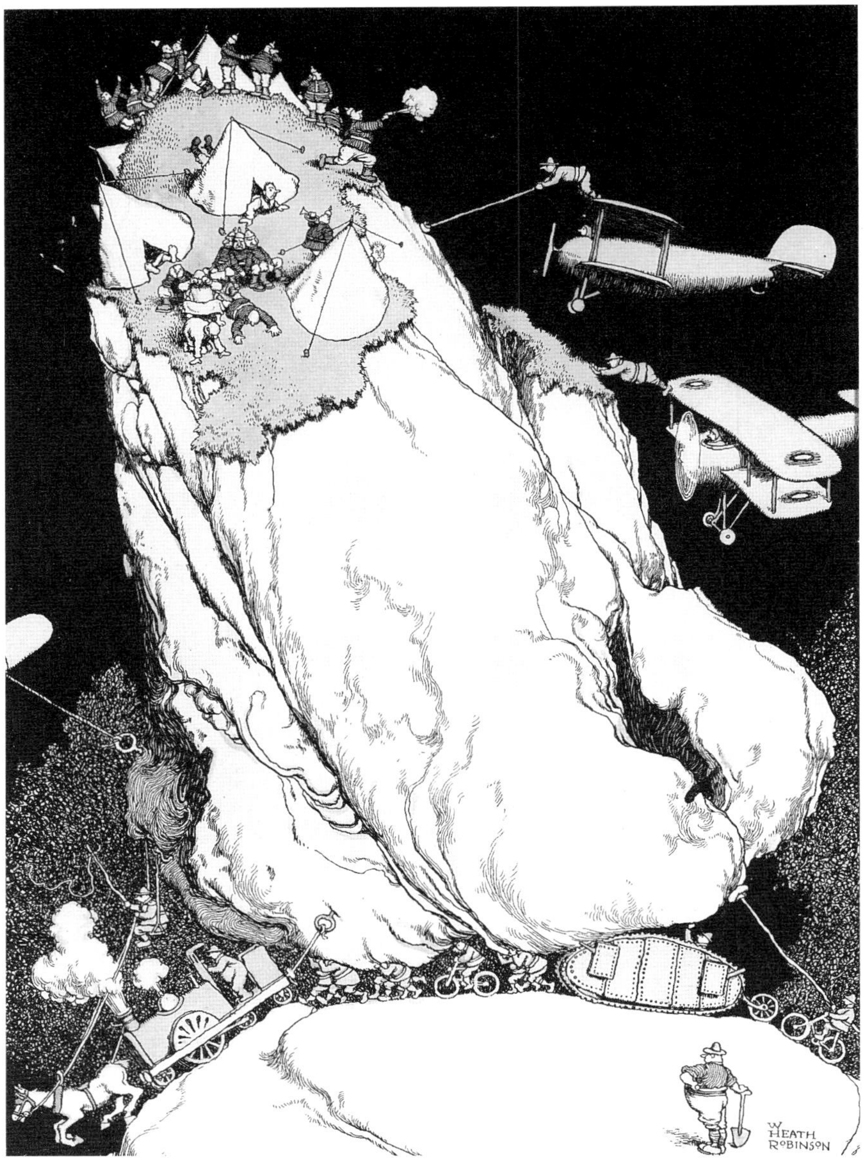

Amiability in Paris

Americans taking a peak in the Vosges
Pen and ink, 1918
Private Collection

Will did not actually see a mountain until he was 60. This drawing relies more on childlike imagination than on fact.

Will had his first opportunity to see the battlefields for himself. He was sent as a war correspondent attached to the International Feature Service to the American front in the Vosges in the spring and summer of 1918.[34] His selection by an American press syndicate reflects the widespread enjoyment of his drawings which, in America, had led to his winning a $250 prize from *Life* for an illustration to Benjamin Franklin's quotation 'God helps them who help themselves.'[35] During this trip, in which he visited the battlefields of Old Lorraine, Toul, Nancy and Luneville, Will saw the debris of war, rather than the heat of battle. The German army had been driven out:

... there were shattered houses in the villages, trenches cut across the fields, and other evidences of the enemy who had now been driven far away.... I remember a wide field marked here and there in seeming haphazard positions with clusters of white stones. Here were buried little groups of defenders where they had fallen resisting the advance of the enemy.[36]

If Will was particularly sensitive to the trace of melancholy that hung over the battlefields, this appeared in his writing only, and not in the drawings that he produced subsequently for the International Feature Service. *The Americans Taking a Peak in the Vosges* and *The American Suction Tank for Drawing the Enemy from his Dugout* show the same comic ingenuity as Will's drawings for the British press, only now the uniform of the soldiers is changed, and the platoons sport the Stars and Stripes.

At the end of the war, Will's contribution to the Allied victory was celebrated by the publication of thirty cartoons, which had previously appeared in magazines, in the collection *Flypapers*. Here is Will's expression of the ecstasy of peace after war, and, in his Introduction, his prose loops the loop in joy as his fairies in *A Midsummer Night's Dream* had done five years earlier: 'Friend, my small contribution to this good end lies before you – a souvenir of the triumph of planes over avoirdupois, of gas-bags over boilers, and a humble tribute to our deliverers.'[37]

CHAPTER FIVE

ART AND COMMERCE AND CRANLEIGH 1918–1929

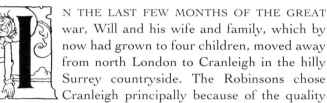

IN THE LAST FEW MONTHS OF THE GREAT war, Will and his wife and family, which by now had grown to four children, moved away from north London to Cranleigh in the hilly Surrey countryside. The Robinsons chose Cranleigh principally because of the quality of the schools in the area. Joan, now aged fourteen, started at St Catherine's, Bramley, while Oliver, followed by Alan and Quentin, went as day-boys to Cranleigh Prep School. When they left Pinner, Josie was pregnant with Tom, the couple's last child. The family's home, The Copse, about a mile outside Cranleigh on the Horsham Road, was a detached four-bedroom brick house built on the edge of The Vachery, a large estate with woods and a lake. It was as substantial a house as any successful businessman might acquire, and was a sign of Will's growing professional prosperity. The house was surrounded by the beginnings of a garden, which Will struggled to carve out of the difficult clay soil. The size of the garden, too, enabled him to indulge his passion for keeping chickens.

His income during the 1920s came almost exclusively from his magazine and advertising work. His output of illustrated books fell to a trickle after the publication of Perrault's *Old Time Stories* (1921), but included his own illustrated children's story *'Peter Quip in Search of a Friend'* (1922) and *Topsy Turvy Tales* by Elsie Smeaton Munro (1923).

Will feeding his chickens at Cranleigh
Photograph, 1920s
The Joan Brinsmead Trust

Joan, Oliver, Alan, Quentin and Tom Robinson at home in Cranleigh
Photograph, early 1920s
The Joan Brinsmead Trust

A warning that this might be a permanent change in the pattern of his production as an artist, came to Will in 1922, when his commission from Jonathan Cape for illustrations to a new edition of *The Complete Works of Shakespeare* was abruptly halted. The commission, for what must have been an eight or twelve volume edition, was an ambitious one for a young publisher. It had been placed in January 1921, and by December Will had completed well over four hundred subject drawings, character illustrations and colophons for twenty-one of the plays and poems. He submitted a second group of illustrations, some of which were most probably in colour, in February 1922. In March, however, the commission was called off, principally because Cape was unable to find an American co-publisher. Over 350 of Will's lost Shakespeare drawings were identified by the present writer in June 1991, having been discovered earlier that year by Kathy Arrington and Valerie Kettley of Cape.

The drawings that Will made for Jonathan Cape are remarkable for their strength of characterization and their bold design. The works he illustrates include plays as familiar as *The Merchant of Venice* and the rarely read, and still more rarely illustrated, poems such as *The Passionate Pilgrim*. Will's approach to this commission seems to have been cautious, however, and his illustrations do not in general have the zest of his work for his 1914 edition of *A Midsummer Night's Dream*. Exceptions include the silhouette headpiece for *The Taming of the*

Left: Will's passport photograph, 1918
Height 5′ 9″; Eyes hazel; Slim built
The Joan Brinsmead Trust

Will went abroad for the first time at the age of 44.

Character from *Henry VI pt 1*
Pen and ink, 1921/22

Shrew, strongly influenced by Rackham's silhouettes for *The Sleeping Beauty* (1920), showing a furious Petruchio throwing a ham at some despairing servants and a weeping Katharine. Other illustrations, such as the powerful head from *King Henry IV Part I* or the scene of the storming of Rouen from *King Henry VI Part I*, have a new sophistication. Their forebears seem to be the woodcuts of William Nicholson, or, in the light calligraphy of smoke and action, the etchings of James McBey and Seymour Hayden. Will's own, spare, black line technique is present too, and it is the drawings in this manner, with their stagey costume and exaggerated expressions and gestures, that make these Shakespeare illustrations so clearly Will's own.

There are, however, few jokes in this group, as if they represented Will's attempt to rebuild the career as a serious book illustrator that had been so obstructed, first by the collapse of his relations with Grant Richards in 1904, and then by the suffocation of pre-war publishing patterns in 1914. This new disappointment, and the effective loss of an important body of his serious work into the limbo of a publisher's filing cabinet for seventy years, was an unhappy echo of Will's troubles with *Rabelais*, and could not have been fully softened by the £200 payment he received from Cape in March 1922 for work to date.[1]

The intervention of the First World War had a profound effect on the career pattern of book illustrators. Those who, like Arthur Rackham, Edmund Dulac and William Heath Robinson, had achieved popularity in the pre-war years, found themselves forced to compromise as the market for the illustrated gift book collapsed. Rackham earned $24,000 from Colgate Soap over the years 1922–5 for a series of thirty coloured drawings of well-scrubbed young *belles* and *beaux* in eighteenth-century costume,[2] while Jessie M. King (1875–1949) boosted her income by decorating pottery.[3] The limited editions market provided a life-raft for some, particularly the wood-engravers of a younger generation, but this too was short-lived, being stifled by the Crash in 1929.

Character head from *Henry IV Pt 1*
Pen and ink, 1921/22

The blinded Earl of Gloucester from *King Lear*
Pen and ink, 1921/22

A Heath Robinson drawing of Heath Robinson drawing a Heath Robinson drawing
Pen and ink and wash, 1920
From *The Bystander*
British Library

In his *Studio* article of 1916, A. E. Johnson had made a case for Will as a serious book illustrator, but in retrospect it is clear that in doing so Johnson was documenting an artistic career that had already practically ceased to exist, and certainly did not survive for long after the war. Will had to make enough of a living to support and educate a growing family, and commercial pressures, reflected in his reputation as the public now perceived it, pushed him further and further towards the humorous and the lightweight. However much he might long to be a serious illustrator again, he was trapped by public demand. A wry self-portrait of the bind he was now in was his 1920 *Bystander* cartoon *A Heath Robinson Drawing of Heath Robinson Drawing a Heath Robinson Drawing*.[4]

Nine years after A. E. Johnson's article, *The Studio* published another piece on Will's work by the critic A. L. Baldry.[5] This time the writer took his subject at face value, refreshingly describing him as he was, rather than as the artist that he had been. Further, Baldry goes out of his way to show that it is because of Will's rare talent as a serious artist that his comic art is so authentic and satisying.

When an artist gains a wide popularity by dealing regularly with a particular type of subject matter which makes a considerable appeal to the public, there is always a danger that he may not be given the credit that is due to him for the quality of his achievement...[I]t is, perhaps, less widely realized that the secret of [Heath Robinson's] success as a humorist is to be sought in the soundness of his work as a serious artist, [and] that the point of his comic excursions is made plain by the artistic resource with which they are conducted. He never forgets that whatever his subject may be the presentation of it must be by means of a studied and logical design.... It is his consciousness of artistic responsibility that enables him to play the fool so persuasively.

If comedy had taken Will away from serious illustration, it was the seriousness of purpose in his comic art that led his career into its next stage. By 1920, this had already become deeply rooted, for shortly after the publication of *Uncle Lubin*, Will's text and illustrations had been noticed by Charles Edward Potter of Toronto, a representative of the Lamson Paragon Supply Company. Perhaps it was the ingenuity and resourcefulness of Lubin, the brevity of Will's narrative or the clarity of his drawings that attracted Mr Potter. Whatever it was, Potter, as mysterious and enigmatic a figure as Uncle Lubin himself, popped up and commissioned Will to make advertising drawings for his company.

The Annual Dance given to spirit mediums by the Psychological Society. Dancing with spiritual partners to spiritual music played by spiritual instruments
Pen and ink and gouache, exhibited 1924
Private Collection

Will, however, remained cautious in his negotiations with Potter, and in his account of their first meeting he plays a pantomime role:

I had so often heard of the nefarious dealings of unscrupulous tricksters from the other side of the Atlantic, that I felt this was a case for using caution. ... I was shown into his [hotel] room.... I cannot remember what I expected to see, but he was not at all of the gangster type; on the contrary he was the most amiable little man, who beamed at me in a friendly way through a pair of gold-rimmed glasses. I could easily imagine that Uncle Lubin and he got on very well together. Nevertheless I remained on my guard; for you never know what wiles may be practised to take advantage of an innocent artist.[6]

Potter, however, appeared to have none of the cunning that Will feared. He agreed to Will's terms of payment for the drawings one by one, cash on delivery.

In 1915 and 1916, the year A. E. Johnson attempted to shore up the Heath Robinson that was, his series of cartoons advertising the *Twelve Virtues of Chairman Tobacco* were published in *Punch* and other newspapers and magazines, and in 1919 his advertisement for Eno's Fruit Salt appeared on the flyleaf of *Flypapers*. Almost certainly on the strength of these and the 1915 Johnny Walker whisky advertisements, John Mackintosh commissioned Will to contribute the first in a series of cartoons by seven artists on the subject of *Toffee Town*, as advertisements for Mackintosh's Toffee. In his autobiography, Mackintosh writes of Will's drawing:

Every time you looked at it you could discover some new flight of exuberant fancy: the shaping of the toffee, as though from marble, with sculptor's hammer and chisel; boiling and cooling machines, all working with the precision of their own lunatic logic; and the testing apparatus, which drove along a patched conveyor belt an endless stream of small boys who, as they reached the vital spot, were fed with toffee from a gigantic tin and were finally decanted on the manager's desk, to be checked and recorded for happy smiles. The Marx Brothers and Billy Bunter combined couldn't have done it better.[7]

As a result of the Mackintosh advertisement, A. E. Johnson was approached on Will's behalf by a film company who wanted to dramatize his drawings with actors and three-dimensional working machinery in a film. This was one of a series of proposals made during his lifetime and since his death by third parties who wanted to translate his genius into an alien medium. Johnson strongly advised his client to have nothing to do with the proposal, and in doing so provided a shrewd insight into the essence of Heath Robinson humour:

A Half Hour in Toffee Town, 1921
Rowntree Mackintosh Archives, York

'Every time you looked at it you could discover some new flight of exuberant fancy.'

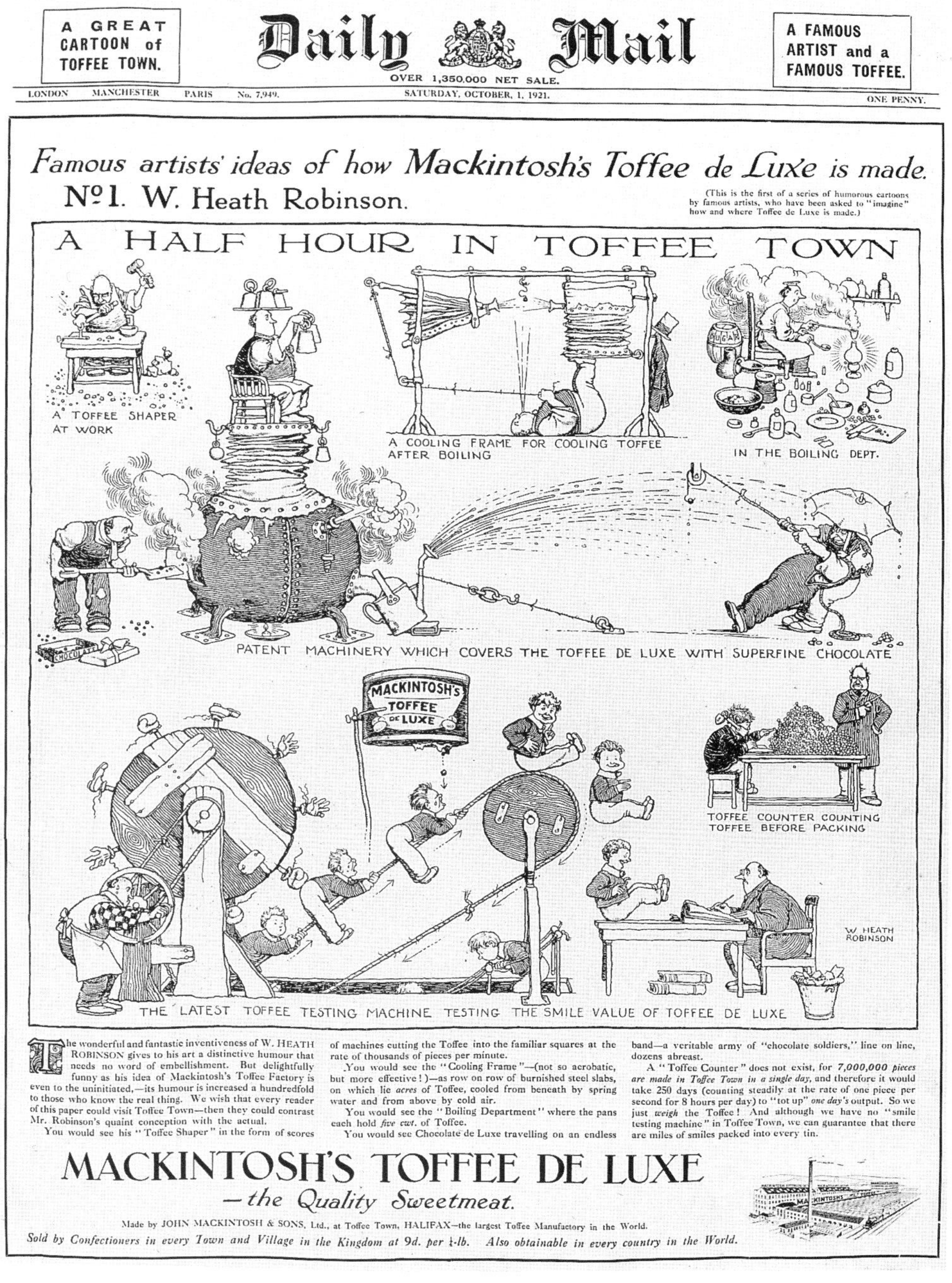

A GREAT CARTOON of TOFFEE TOWN.

Daily Mail

OVER 1,350,000 NET SALE.

A FAMOUS ARTIST and a FAMOUS TOFFEE.

LONDON MANCHESTER PARIS No. 7,949. SATURDAY, OCTOBER, 1, 1921. ONE PENNY.

Famous artists' ideas of how Mackintosh's Toffee de Luxe is made.
Nº1. W. Heath Robinson.

(This is the first of a series of humorous cartoons by famous artists, who have been asked to "imagine" how and where Toffee de Luxe is made.)

A HALF HOUR IN TOFFEE TOWN

A TOFFEE SHAPER AT WORK

A COOLING FRAME FOR COOLING TOFFEE AFTER BOILING

IN THE BOILING DEPT.

PATENT MACHINERY WHICH COVERS THE TOFFEE DE LUXE WITH SUPERFINE CHOCOLATE

MACKINTOSH'S TOFFEE DE LUXE

TOFFEE COUNTER COUNTING TOFFEE BEFORE PACKING

W. HEATH ROBINSON

THE LATEST TOFFEE TESTING MACHINE TESTING THE SMILE VALUE OF TOFFEE DE LUXE

The wonderful and fantastic inventiveness of W. HEATH ROBINSON gives to his art a distinctive humour that needs no word of embellishment. But delightfully funny as his idea of Mackintosh's Toffee Factory is even to the uninitiated,—its humour is increased a hundredfold to those who know the real thing. We wish that every reader of this paper could visit Toffee Town—then they could contrast Mr. Robinson's quaint conception with the actual.

You would see his "Toffee Shaper" in the form of scores of machines cutting the Toffee into the familiar squares at the rate of thousands of pieces per minute.

You would see the "Cooling Frame"—(not so acrobatic, but more effective!)—as row on row of burnished steel slabs, on which lie *acres* of Toffee, cooled from beneath by spring water and from above by cold air.

You would see the "Boiling Department" where the pans each hold *five cwt.* of Toffee.

You would see Chocolate de Luxe travelling on an endless band—a veritable army of "chocolate soldiers," line on line, dozens abreast.

A "Toffee Counter" does not exist, for *7,000,000 pieces are made in Toffee Town in a single day*, and therefore it would take 250 days (counting steadily at the rate of one piece per second for 8 hours per day) to "tot up" *one day's* output. So we just *weigh* the Toffee! And although we have no "smile testing machine" in Toffee Town, we can guarantee that there are miles of smiles packed into every tin.

MACKINTOSH'S TOFFEE DE LUXE
—*the Quality Sweetmeat.*

Made by JOHN MACKINTOSH & SONS, Ltd., at Toffee Town, HALIFAX—the largest Toffee Manufactory in the World.

Sold by Confectioners in every Town and Village in the Kingdom at 9d. per ¼-lb. Also obtainable in every country in the World.

Your ideas, and your vein of humour, as exhibited in the Mackintosh's series, can only be properly expressed through the medium of your own drawings. If one tries to analyse what makes your humour popular, I think the essential thing is that your inventions are sufficiently related to life and actuality to be plausible (once the basic absurdity is accepted), while nevertheless quite remote from it ... If one were to attempt ... to convert your preposterous old gentlemen into real flesh and blood, and your machinery into concrete facts, it seems to me that the fantasy is broken.... It is the very fact that nobody would dream of putting one of your machines into real operation that constitutes their charm, and I cannot help fearing that an attempt to reduce the whimsical imaginings of your fancy to concrete terms would be futile. I doubt whether the result would even be mildly amusing....[8]

From 1921 until the outbreak of the Second World War, Will was in constant demand from all types of manufacturing, process and service companies, to create single drawings or whole series to advertise their products. If the manufacture of Shuck McClean Printers Ink or of Crow, Catchpole Tarmacadam was not of immediate popular interest, Will's idiosyncratic interpretation of the processes involved brought him a new body of clients. These were the post-war generation of industrialists, advertising agents and readers of trade magazines, the very people, now demobilized, who less than ten years earlier had had their lives in the trenches brightened by Will's wartime fantasies. His approach to more everyday products brought him yet more admirers who were too young to have remembered his contributions to the First World War effort.

The new pussyfoot test for cat burglars
Pen and ink and wash, 1920
From *The Bystander*
Private Collection

Langston Day devotes an entire chapter of his book to quoting from an enormous file of letters written by A. E. Johnson to Will. The extracts he gives come from a mere nine-month span in 1921–2, the period in which Will was also working on his Shakespeare illustrations. The pressures on him were, therefore, intense, obliging him to switch from Shakespeare to commercial advertising requirements and, further, to illustrations and cartoons for the eleven different magazine titles to which he was also contributing over those two years. He reflected on this problem years later: 'The trouble about being versatile is that it is extremely difficult to switch from one subject to another. You have to be very careful to see that the humorous touch is not detected in your serious work and *vice versa*.'[9]

Will's commercial patrons were often pedantically specific about their requirements. One, for example, wanted the office cat to be shown sealing envelopes in his Accounts Department, while another specified that his advertisement should show a man on a ladder pouring sugar from a bag into a tub. Will usually obliged – he had no time available to argue the toss about such trivial matters.[10] Some of the advertising commissions were adapted for foreign-language magazines. The 1928 advertisement for Ransome's Lawn Mowers, for example, was translated into German and Dutch versions.[11]

Perhaps as an inevitable result of these pressures, Will tended to repeat himself. In one of the earliest of his post-war advertisements, *Then and Now*, the collection of drawings for the Port of Manchester Warehouses Ltd in 1921, he reused ideas that he originally devised for *The Strand Magazine* the year before. In 1920, his group of five cartoons under the title *Outside Line of History* were published in *The Strand* in a satire on H. G. Wells's recently published and controversial *Outline of History*.[12] Among a liberal scattering of Stonehenges on hilltops, these cartoons depict a cave-dwelling society which, in Will's imagination, invented the first umbrella, the first drama, the first lodger and so on. In *Then and Now* the same cave-dwellers appear, and demonstrate the supposed origin of the warehouse, in their efforts to preserve a filbert, or hazelnut, through the winter months.

Will was extremely diligent in paying visits to the companies that commissioned him, so that he could gain an idea of their manufacturing processes. Travel took up a great deal of his time. 'I find that I must saturate myself in the real thing first,' he told a feature writer for the *Statesman of Calcutta*,

> ... and then I am able to make fun of it more effectively. As regards the actual drawing, I try to retain the principle of the process and twist it to my own, humorous, point of view.... It really is a formidable task to treat some of these intricate processes humorously. They are so scientific that it is extremely difficult to reduce them to wood and bits of string.[13]

Only once is he recorded as being lost for inspiration by what he saw. On being shown round the factory of Connolly Brothers, Curriers, at Wandle Bank in Wimbledon, he looked at the Company's Turner Measuring Machine and commented: 'I can't improve on that, Mr. Connolly.'[14] For the Sheffield Mining and Manufacturing Company, Newton Chambers, Will made a series of nineteen drawings in 1932 for two book-

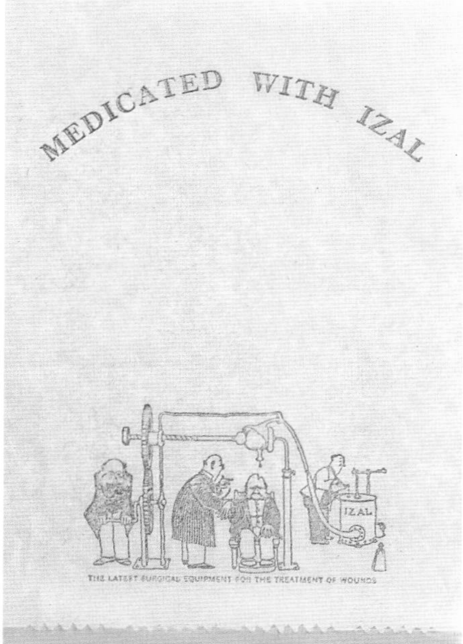

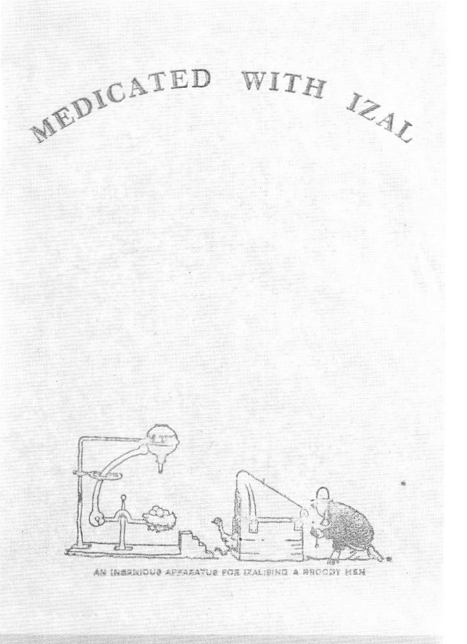

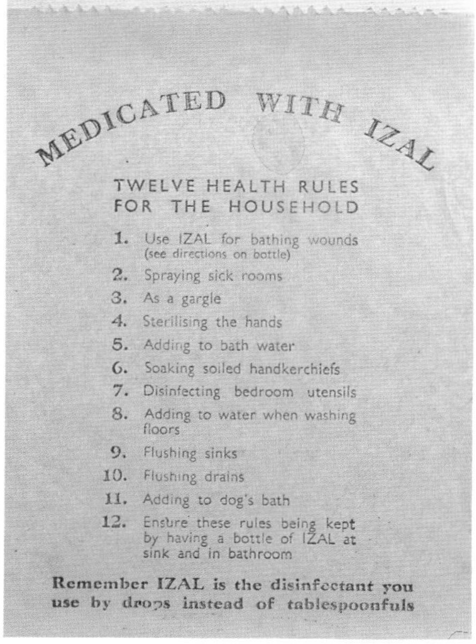
MEDICATED WITH IZAL

TWELVE HEALTH RULES FOR THE HOUSEHOLD

1. Use IZAL for bathing wounds (see directions on bottle)
2. Spraying sick rooms
3. As a gargle
4. Sterilising the hands
5. Adding to bath water
6. Soaking soiled handkerchiefs
7. Disinfecting bedroom utensils
8. Adding to water when washing floors
9. Flushing sinks
10. Flushing drains
11. Adding to dog's bath
12. Ensure these rules being kept by having a bottle of IZAL at sink and in bathroom

Remember IZAL is the disinfectant you use by drops instead of tablespoonfuls

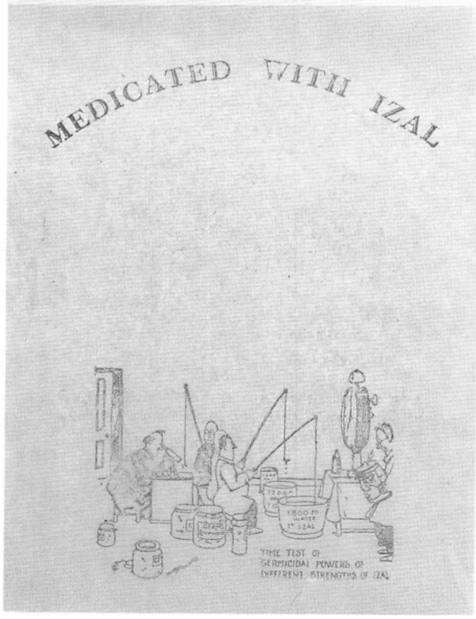

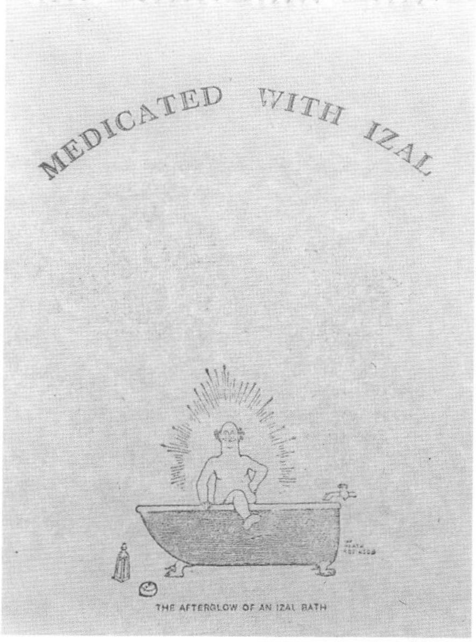

Left: The Turner Measuring Machine in use in Connolly's factory in Wimbledon in the 1960s. Will said that he was unable to improve upon it
Photograph: Connolly Brothers (Curriers) Ltd

Left: Sheets of Izal Medicated Toilet Paper decorated by Will for Newton Chambers Ltd, Sheffield, 1932.

Left: The Passing Cloud
Pen and ink and wash, 1930s
Sheffield City Art Galleries

Below: A Demonstration of the Tenacity of Duroid Tarmacadam
Pen and ink, 1932

Will makes his point by a charming exaggeration and by waiving the Law of Gravity.

lets, *Thorncliffe Visited* and *Heath Robinson Sees Izal Made*, to advertise the applications of coaltar to such widely ranging products as Duroid Tarmacadam, Izal Disinfectant and Medicated Toilet Paper. Newton Chambers went so far with one group of Will's drawings as to print them on their toilet paper.

Some companies, in acknowledgement of Will's reputation as a writer as well as an illustrator of his own books, employed him to engage his deadpan literary style on the introductions to their brochures. For Ruston-Bucyrus Excavators of Lincoln, for example, he not only contributed ten line drawings, but also a four-page essay to the booklet *The Gentle Art of Excavating*. Once again, H. G. Wells comes in for a gentle dig in the ribs, when Will writes:

> It is quite wrong, by the way, to conclude, as some writer whose name escapes me has permitted himself to do in a fit of unbridled imagination, that because machines grow more powerful and vaster year by year they will eventually overpower their masters. Take, for example, the Electric Shovel. Though with the strength of a giant, what could exceed in obedience its almost childlike response to the driver in the luxuriously appointed cab? It scoops up great masses of earth at the bidding of its master as easily as you or I spoon up our porridge at breakfast.[15]

Mixing, selecting and putting on the colours in the Connolly leather factory
Connolly Brothers (Curriers) Ltd

Will continues by writing lyrically about the Ruston-Bucyrus Grabbing Crane:

> I have only one fault to find with the Grabbing Crane, and that is its name. It somehow brings to mind those marauders who gain a precarious living by snatching and grabbing from shop windows. I never quite believed the story that one of these machines was used by an unscrupulous gang of this description. Far from deserving so evil a reputation, the Grabbing Crane may be described as a Machine with a Conscience. It is quite true that it has a habit of lifting things which rightly do not belong to it, but on the other hand it faithfully deposits those things where the rightful owner wishes them to be placed. Nothing is too large for its grasp. Had Mohammed possessed a Grabbing Crane he would have had no difficulty in bringing the mountain to him and thus have saved an unnecessary and tiresome walk.

In common with other examples of his advertising work, Will emphasizes the personal nature of his observations in the Ruston-Bucyrus booklet by writing in the first person, and including himself as a character both in the text and the margin drawings. He describes himself as a butterfly collector 'in search of data for a work I am compiling on the ravages of the lesser lepidoptera', who had been wandering in the neighbourhood of Lincoln and had been lured into the Ruston-Bucyrus works by a rare butterfly evading capture.

This disarmingly dotty image is characteristic, and is one he also cultivates elsewhere in, for example, some of the ten booklets he produced during his long association with Connolly Brothers. In a Foreword to *Connolly Chronicles* (1933), Will describes himself as usually spending his Saturday afternoons in the British Museum Library 'poring over that wonderful catalogue of works on leather'. Of course, he did no such thing, but nevertheless he assures us that on discovering the title *Connolly Chronicles* in the Library index, he filled in the necessary forms 'and presently the thirty-three volumes were brought to me by as many perspiring attendants, and two boys carrying the maps, graphs and charts appertaining to the work.' This procession of librarians and their assistants serving a waiting scholar is as 'Heath Robinson' an image as he ever drew, and shows him to be cultivating a public persona which fits perfectly into the image of the world that he created in his drawings.

Illustration from Leather Breeding on the Wandle, *1927, Will's vision of cattle husbandry as practised in the 1920s by Connolly Bros, of Wimbledon.*

A busy morning in the sumptuous studio of a fashionable hair artist
Pen and ink, 1925
From *Hutchinson's Magazine*
Private Collection

Although his drawings are peopled with a whole range of characters, workers concentrating intently on their task, pompous inspectors, naughty boys and haughty women, a stock character that recurs time and again, in his advertising and magazine drawings alike, is that of The Artist. This is only rarely Will himself, and is more usually a shock-headed, velvet-suited individual wearing a large floppy bow-tie and a deeply preoccupied, distant or aloof expression. In the Connolly drawings he appears with eight assistants overseeing the mixing and testing of colours in 'the new Connolly Studios'. The Johnnie Walker Whisky advertisement has him standing at one corner of the studio gallery carpet, plum-line dangling from his hand, checking that the angle of the label on the Johnnie Walker bottle is exactly right. With The Artist is a designer assistant carrying the label design on a drawing board, two junior artists brandishing palettes, brushes and a maul-stick, and two connoisseurs. One of these is a stylish aesthetic dandy in a long coat, carrying a top hat and stick and minutely examining a displayed Johnnie Walker bottle with his magnifying glass.

The regular repetition of The Artist and Connoisseur, the kind of characters that might have strayed out of a production of *Patience*, suggests the presence of a profound feeling of antagonism towards some quarters of the art world. These figures are usually treated with a harsher degree of mockery than any other of his 'types', and this mockery drifts into his writing. In *My Line of Life* he writes of being visited at Cranleigh by a Belgian refugee artist and writer, dressed in a broad-brimmed black hat and black

A true exquisite

An example of Will's decorative illustrations for magazine articles. What lingered of his practise of 'serious' illustration had shrunk by the mid 1920s to the pages of magazines.

velvet knee-breeches and stockings. He invents for this vision, who interrupted him and his son Alan as they were gardening, the music-hall name 'M. Renée de Boudoir'. The visitor may perhaps have been one of Will's Sketch Club pals playing a practical joke on him, but the vein of mockery, of laughing *at* 'M. de Boudoir' remains. 'A true exquisite', Will writes under his line drawing of this dainty individual.[16]

In his earliest student days, Will had cherished the ambition to become an artist of standing and distinction, an embryonic Old Master. This ambition, however, had been frustrated by bad luck and circumstance in 1897, 1904, 1914 and 1922, and each time he had been obliged to amend his plans. Although Will's comic drawings brought him eternal popular acclaim, they also led inexorably to his drift away from fine art, as represented by the velvet-jacketed artists and aesthetic connoisseurs, to decorative and popular illustration. It is little wonder, then, that such spikes as do recur in his humour should largely be directed towards the art world.

In the nine years from 1924 to 1932, Will's published output was devoted entirely to magazine and advertising work, with the exception of a book cover for *If I Were You* by P. G. Wodehouse (1931). Two books published

Opposite page: Cover design for Nash's Magazine Christmas Number
Pencil gouache, watercolour and gold
Private Collection

Nash's
& Pall Mall
Magazine
December
1/6
NETT
W. HEATH
ROBINSON
CHRISTMAS NUMBER

Farmyard and Barns, Norfolk
Watercolour, 1920s
273 × 357 mm
The Joan Brinsmead Trust

An example of the careful watercolour paintings Will made when he was relaxing at home.

during this period which were described as being illustrated by him, *Everyland Annual of Boys and Girls, III* (1926) and *Arabian Nights* (1932), both contained drawings which he had made thirty years earlier in 1899, and were undoubtedly being reissued now to cash in on his fame. What lingered of his practice of 'serious' illustration had shrunk to the pages of *Nash's Pall Mall Magazine*, from 1921, and *Good Housekeeping*, from 1925. His cartoons continued to appear primarily in *The Bystander*, until 1928, and in *London Opinion*, *Pearson's Magazine*, *The Sketch*, *The Strand Magazine* and *The Humorist*.

In his post-war *Bystander* cartoons Will continues occasionally to comment on current affairs, as he had in the pre-war *Sketch*. A recurring theme, the threat of strikes after the Great War, is illustrated for example by *The Man Who Didn't Care if North Bound Trains Went on Strike or Not*,[17] and *In Case They Strike: An Intelligent Suggestion in Anticipation of Cold Mornings and Coal Shortages*.[18] Will gives his views on world politics and sport in *The Soviet and the Serviette*[19] and *Why We Lost – Some of the Things that Made Cricket so Difficult for Englishmen in Australia*.[20]

Will's life in Cranleigh in the 1920s continued on its gregarious way, as it had in London and Pinner before the war. Old friends came to stay – the artists Alfred Leete (1882–1933), H. M. Bateman (1887–1970) and Bert Thomas (d. 1966) brought their children, while Will and Josie made other friends in Cranleigh. Lawson Wood (1878–1957), the cartoonist famous for his animal subjects, lived nearby, as did the artists Bertram Prance, John Eyre RI (d. 1927), Joseph Longhurst, E. H. Shepherd (1879–1976) and Edmund Dulac (1882–1953). Another close friend and neighbour was the writer Frank Swinnerton, whom Will had first met as a young man in the offices of J. M. Dent.

The rump of the Frothfinders Federation regrouped after the war, but they were never able to gather again with the same Arcadian passions that they had had in Pinner. They were more than ten years older now, had new responsibilities, and had all seen the war. The haunt of artists and drinkers in the Surrey hills was the White

Mother Courage
Watercolour, 1920s. 294 × 237 mm
Private Collection

Will (right) with Dickie Askew (centre) and perhaps the painter Bertram Prance (left) at Cranleigh
Photograph, 1920s
The Joan Brinsmead Trust

Horse Inn at Shere, a five-mile walk from Cranleigh. This deep, dark, smoke-stained inn, with oak beams, wattle-and-daub walls, fireside settles and Snugs, was run by Dickie Askew himself a painter, and a man who enjoyed the company of artists. Whenever Will walked to the White Horse – whenever he walked, indeed – he carried his sketchbook, pencils and watercolours with him. It was on and after these long walks, ending at the Crown Inn at Stanmore, and since 1918 at the White Horse Inn at Shere, that Will painted watercolours such as *Figures under Trees* or the pencil and wash *Farmyard Scene*. He was probably at his happiest and most relaxed on these occasions. Pressures of art for commerce and illustration were put aside for a while, and he was able to steep himself in the landscape of Surrey and to imagine himself as the wandering landscape painter that might have been.

A new friend in the area was a fiery, curry-eating Colonel, A. I. R. Glasford, and his wife Mabel. The Glasfords lived at The Old Court, Cranleigh, where they acted as guardians to two Cranleigh schoolboys, Vivian Cox and his brother Leonard, school friends of Quentin. Vivian Cox remembers the Colonel, who had fought in France, as 'a terrifying Anglo-Indian Army officer of Scottish descent',[21] but nevertheless also as a sensitive amateur pianist and watercolour painter, and as the author of such evocative works as *Rifle and Romance in the Indian Jungle* and *Musings of an Old Shikari*. Mabel Glasford, by contrast, seemed to Vivian Cox to have been 'a faded saint of a lady, tall and gentle and rather Pre-Raphaelite in appearance'.

Will's elder brothers, Tom and Charles, and their families, and his sisters Mary and Florence, were regular visitors at Cranleigh, as were Josie's nephews. Will and Josie were a popular couple, greatly loved among their extended family. Alison Greenwood, Tom's second daughter, remembered how her Uncle Will would sit on her bed and sing to her when she was homesick on a visit to Cranleigh. Alison spotted her uncle in the garden one afternoon wearing a colander on his head.

'It's my hat,' said Uncle Will.

'But it's got holes in it,' observed Alison.

'I've been in battle,' Will replied, witheringly.[22]

At mealtimes, Will told stories which put the children into fits of giggles. He kept a solemn tone in his voice as he spoke about his porridge sandwiches or his colander hat, so it was sometimes impossible for the children to tell if he was being serious. One of his stories concerned a man who got up in the morning and put his feet on back to front. Another, a long, rambling and much repeated tale that amused but exasperated his wife, concerned the invented Mrs McGraskin, the 'other' Mrs Robinson, who was violently unattractive, who wore tremendous hats, and by whom he had had many children.

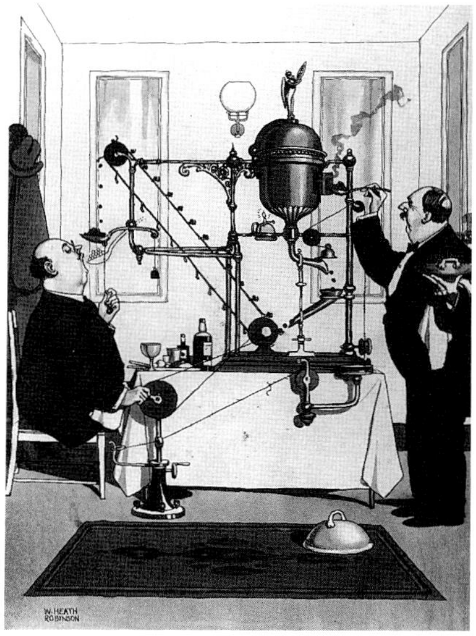

Above: An elegant and interesting apparatus designed to overcome once and for all the difficulties of conveying green peas to the mouth
Pen and ink, 1929
From *The Sunday Graphic*
Private Collection

Left: Carrying out the correspondence course for mountain climbing in the home
Pen and ink and colour wash, 1928
Private Collection

'You know, you are all love children,' he once announced to his assembled brood.[23]

'Don't be stupid, Will. Nonsense,' Josie protested. Josie took it in her stride; *her* mother, however, the children's Granny Latey, felt compelled to explain the joke away when she was staying at Cranleigh as 'just Will's fun', in case other guests got the wrong idea.

Alison's elder sister, Christine, remembered how the professional side to her uncle was never far from the surface. He spotted a group of workmen using a pneumatic drill beside the railway line at Cranleigh when he was taking Christine to the train.

'Hang on, Christine,' he said, rushing over to the men. 'I want to have a look at that.'[24]

Will called Christine, who had dark hair, Night, and Alison, a fair girl, Day. Each child had a story, invented and told by Will, that was entirely his or her own. Tom, his youngest child's, began: 'Henri de Trouville, who lived on the banks of the River Loire, went into the woods to pick strawberries....' Alan's told of a tall stack of rock in the Scilly Isles, on which a cow was tethered to a single tree. At the bottom of the rock was a cave, from which the children sallied forth each day to carry out great activities. All these stories carry echoes of the tales in *Bill the Minder*. Here, looking after and entertaining the countless children who flung themselves at him, was Will the Minder, William Heath Robinson, funny, eccentric, spry and unique. While Will told his stories, wild stories were told of him too: that he lived in a locked house surrounded by models of his machines; that reports of his eccentricities had robbed him of the offer of a very valuable appointment; that he growled at intruders.[25]

Right: Overtime at a Christmas Cracker Factory to cope with the demand of the approaching festive season
Pen and ink and watercolour, 1929
From *The Sunday Graphic*
Photograph: Christies

MOTTOES
CAPS
JEWELS
SWEETS
SCRAPS
W. HEATH
ROBINSON

Above: Lads v. Dads
A souvenir of the Annual Parents' Cricket Match at Preparatory House, Cranleigh School
Pen and ink and wash, 1922
745 × 545 mm
Presented by the Artist to Cranleigh Prep School

Left: The Right Spirit
Pen and ink and gouache, 1920s
Private Collection

The Robinsons' circle of friends encompassed artists and writers as well as romantic and original people such as the Glasfords. When Will and his family left Cranleigh for a holiday, it might be to spend Christmas in Crouch End with the Charles Robinsons, or with Tom and his family in Hatch End. One year they came up from Cranleigh in a hired bus, so many of them were there, and so loaded were they with presents and holly. 'I can't remember how Mother slept us all,' remarked Will's niece Bay. 'Probably in some drawers made into beds.'[26]

During summer holidays, Will and the family went to the Norfolk or North Kent coasts, or rented a house by the sea at Seaford or Bognor. All the nephews and nieces were invited, although no sooner had he arrived than Will himself longed to get home. He rarely, if ever, dressed for the beach, but sat on the sand in his town trilby, his suit and tie, quietly sketching. 'He didn't like going away for holidays. He didn't care for it at all,' Oliver remembered.[27] This made him nervously concerned about the children's safety, even on so safe a beach as Bognor's. 'You've gone too far,' he would call when the sea had reached to the children's knees. 'Come back! Come back!'

Occasionally, Will's humour betrayed a cutting edge. Christine recalled his referring to a neighbour's dog, which spurned the advances of other dogs, as 'the Bromide Bitch'. When he was brooding on a drawing in progress in his studio, Will would be a silent presence at meals as the chatter went on around him. Josie's nephew, Sir John Latey, recalled how 'every now and again, when people were having a drink, he would not participate as he usually did for a little while. He could be an abstracted figure, preoccupied.'[28]

Will's working day was as regular and as organized as the day of a nine-to-five businessman. Josie was up by seven, and brought him a cup of tea in bed. As he drank, he told his stories to the children who were still young enough to cuddle up beside him. This was followed by breakfast at eight and a solo sing-song in front of the

Beach Scene, Norfolk
Watercolour, 1920s
236 × 345 mm
The Joan Brinsmead Trust

An interesting movement to be inaugurated in our parks in spring to lightly turn young men's fancies to thoughts of intellectual development
Pen and ink and wash, exhibited 1924
Private Collection

A SOUVENIR OF THE
PERFORMANCE OF
"TREASURE ISLAND"
BY THE BOYS OF THE
PREPARATORY HOUSE
CRANLEIGH SCHOOL
DEC. 1924
RUM
W.
HEATH
ROBINSON

Treaure Island
Pen and ink and gouache, 1924
578 × 472 mm
Presented by the Artist to Cranleigh Prep School

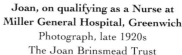

Joan, on qualifying as a Nurse at Miller General Hospital, Greenwich
Photograph, late 1920s
The Joan Brinsmead Trust

drawing-room fire, an early morning burst of 'Farmer's Boy' or 'The Man who Broke the Bank at Monte Carlo' to get the air into his lungs. Then with purposeful strides he would walk the mile into Cranleigh and back, to post a packet of drawings to a magazine and for the exercise which helped him start thinking things through for the day. He would settle down to work by about 9.30 and only emerge for lunch. He worked on until about seven in the evening, when he would join the family in the drawing-room and read or sketch as he sat.

Soon after the family moved to Cranleigh, Will had a pine plank studio built beside the house. From the outside it looked like any scout hut, but inside, with its wide windows and high pitched roof, tables, shelves and cupboards, it was a quiet and reserved working place. The studio had one, and only one, concession to the developing myth of its occupant. Between the hut and the house, fifteen feet away, Will rigged up a 'Heath Robinson' gadget, a speaking tube which ran down outside the studio wall, under the garden path, and up into the kitchen.[29] Through this he was summoned to lunch and supper, and could call for a cup of tea. The studio was Will's own domain. A sign on the door reading PRIVATE made that point perfectly clear. For friends and neighbours with problems, Will's studio became a kind of confessional, but nevertheless Alison recalled that her uncle did not talk about his work, and did not like children to watch him drawing.

Will's jollity and good humour was famous beyond the family boundaries. Vivian Cox remembered:

> Although we were dimly aware that he was a household name, he was so funny and friendly that we treated him more as an eccentric uncle than with the awe due to such a celebrity. He used to amuse us by drawing little caricatures of us, which to our shame we never valued any more than he did.[30]

He made caricatures of school events, too, commemorating one important annual event at Cranleigh Prep School, the 'Lads v. Dads' cricket match. His drawing of 1922 recalls the appalling indignities that can overtake adults when they allow themselves to play cricket with small boys. Will made a poster for a school performance of *Alice in Wonderland* (1922), in which Alan played the Mad Hatter, and did the same in later years for school performances of *Treasure Island* (1924) and *H.M.S. Mantelpiece* (1927).[31]

In 1929 the Robinsons left Cranleigh to move back to Highgate. Joan had by now qualified as a nurse at the Miller General Hospital in Greenwich. Oliver, too, had started his career as a printer with Hazell, Watson and Viney. Alan, aged 20, had been accepted as a student at the Royal College of Art, where he was taught in the Sculpture Department by Richard Garbe RA (1876–1957) and Henry Moore, having spent two years at the Central School of Art and Design. Now that the children had nearly all grown up, the family's centre of gravity had moved towards London, and this made Josie uneasy. She was anxious that the home influence over her sons in particular should not be weakened. The presence of Uncle Charles and Uncle Tom in north London was not enough to ease her anxieties, and she asked her brother, Jack Latey, a solicitor in London, to have a word with Oliver and Alan. In the only hint of sex education that Alan received throughout his youth, Uncle Jack invited the young men to lunch, and after much hesitation eventually said: 'My services will always be available to you if you get into difficulties.'[32]

Despite his wife's misgivings about their distance from home influences, Will gave the greatest encouragement to his children in their choice of careers. He had bought a small printing machine for Oliver, and set it up in his

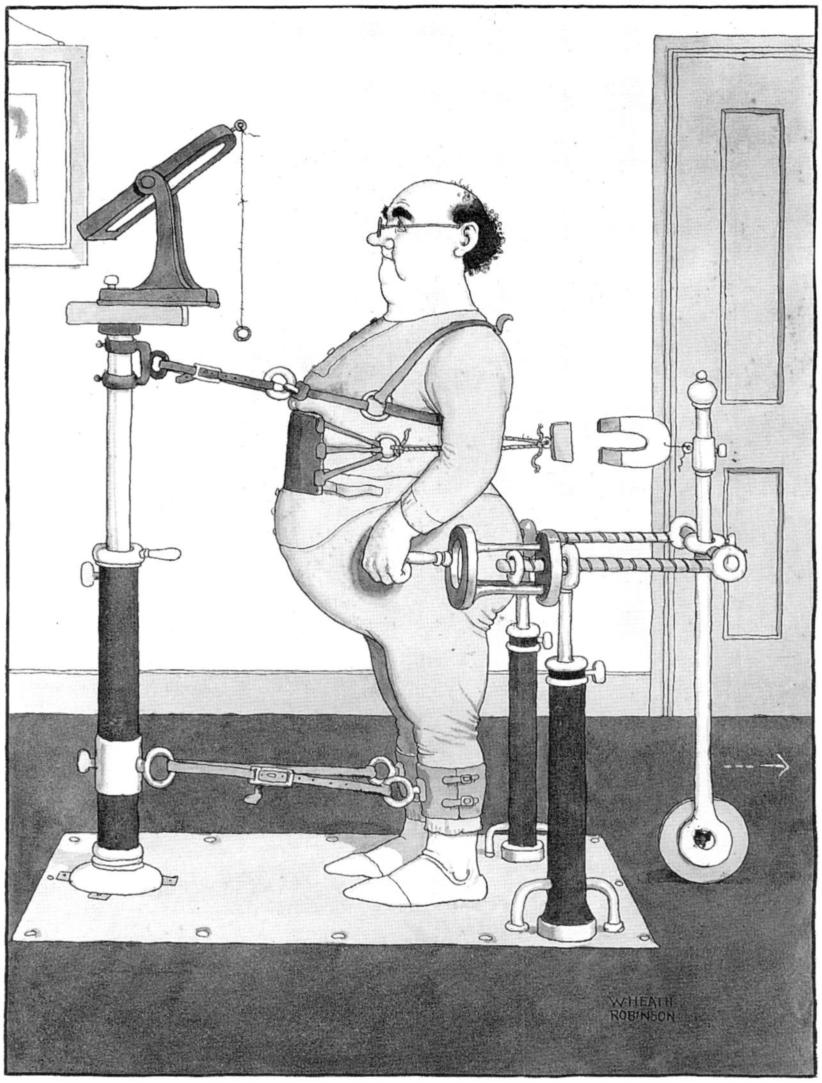

A convenient magnetic contraption (with mirror attachment) for reducing the figure. Recently placed on the market.
Pen and ink, 1926
From *The Bystander*
The Science Museum, London

studio where it was used to print the family magazine. He used his contacts to ensure that his children met the right people. Through Frank Swinnerton, for example, he arranged a meeting for Oliver with Harold Curwen, 'the kind of printer I would like my boy to be associated with'.[33] Both Oliver and Alan, in their different ways, were echoing the beginnings of Will's own career. Alan, however, becoming increasingly unsettled by growing religious feelings, failed his final examinations at the Royal College and, in 1932, became a novice monk attached to the Benedictine Order at Prinknash Abbey in Gloucestershire. This bewildered Alan's friends at the Royal College. Indeed, the Registrar, Hubert Wellington, bumped into him one evening on the Tube and roundly upbraided him for deciding to become a monk – though Alan later had the satisfaction of hearing that Wellington had himself become a Roman Catholic.

Will's reaction to Alan's conversion was one of puzzlement, even uncertainty, a feeling that he never fully resolved. In *My Line of Life* he writes of Alan's 'unlooked for conversion' to Roman Catholicism.[34] Will felt trespassed upon by a genial Irish bishop who told him at Alan's ordination: 'Oh, you'll be a Catholic any day.' Josie, on the other hand, was deeply affected by the change in her son, and she herself was received into the Catholic Church eighteen months later. Once Will was fully convinced that Alan had taken the right decision, he gave his son the fullest encouragement. As a gesture of faith and approval he presented the Abbey with a watercolour cartoon showing the monks putting the finishing touches to repairs to its roof in 1932. The figure leaning out of the central window is Alan, pointing at the bell calling the monks to lunch.

As the children grew up, Will's rôle as the 'funny uncle', moulded rather in the spirit of the character John Betjeman describes in *Indoor Games near Newbury*, gradually became redundant. What his children now needed was not a father who would make model theatres with them or tell them ludicrous stories, but a counsellor. Oliver, however, found him a little remote, his shyness interfering with any serious father-son relationship. Alan's bouts of irregular and irresponsible behaviour as a young student, left Will, as Alan recalled, saddened and disappointed. There were rarely, if ever, any rows in the Robinson household, no shows of fury or temper from their father at displays of youthful bad behaviour. Instead, Will bore his cross quietly, retreating to his studio when words seemed to fail.

One unlooked-for trial that Will had to endure concerned his youngest brother George, the only one of Will's generation of Robinson boys who had not taken the customary route of becoming an artist. George instead became a businessman in a variety of concerns that always seemed to collapse, although he rarely

Putting finishing touches to the roof at Prinknash Abbey

Pen and ink and watercolour, 1932. Presented by the Artist to Prinknash Abbey, Gloucestershire.

The central monk in black, calling his Brothers to lunch, is Will's son Alan, who later took the monastic title of Dom Basil.

Little Red Riding Hood
Pen and ink, 1921
From Perrault's *Old Time Stories*
Photograph: Bonhams

allowed this to affect his good spirits. He ran a poultry farm during the First World War, and then a publishing company, Robinson and Birch, for which Will contributed cartoons. After this firm failed, George became sales manager of Sizaire-Berwick, manufacturers of luxurious motor cars. Alan recalls how George once turned up at Cranleigh, grinning and dressed to kill in a chauffeur-driven Sizaire-Berwick. To Will's sons, Uncle George was a romantic character, who had privately admitted to Alan that Will had 'got him off the rocks' more than once. The discovery after George's death in 1935 that he had kept a mistress and two households came as a bitter blow to Will, but he took the news philosophically. Will's jokes about Mrs McGraskin, the 'other' Mrs Robinson, had come back to haunt him in the behaviour of his younger brother.

Illustration to Ben Travers' retelling of Little Red Riding Hood *in* The Passing Show, *1920s*

CHAPTER SIX

HOME TO HIGHGATE 1929–1944

20 Shepherds Hill, Highgate
Photograph, 1930s
The Joan Brinsmead Trust

Will named this house Hascombe after the hill on the North Downs, one of his favourite walking destinations in the 1920s.

WHEN THE ROBINSONS MOVED from Cranleigh to Highgate in 1929, Will was coming home. Their new house in Shepherds Hill was barely a mile from Will's childhood home in Benwell Road. Shepherds Hill itself joined Archway Road near the spot where, on his childhood walks with Tom and Charles along the Great North Road, he and his brothers would stop to eat their sandwiches.

20 Shepherds Hill is a large, dark, detached house like an overfed Swiss chalet. It had a bedroom for each of the Robinson children, and Will's studio was on the top floor at the front of the house, with a view of the quiet, tree-lined road. From this vantage-point he made a large ink and watercolour drawing looking down on the neighbouring drive and across into the road. A policeman walks past on the pavement, a car lumbers up the hill. The trees are in full, exuberant leaf. Nothing is out of place, and all seems well with the world. In its reflective, philosophical mood, its obsessive intensity of detail and its joy-in-suburbia, the picture echoes Charles Ginner's townscapes or Stanley Spencer's visions of Cookham, and speaks of Will's own desire for domestic security, contentment and order.

In 1935, when all the children except Tom had finally left home, Will and Josie moved a few hundred yards across Archway Road to 25 Southwood Avenue, a smaller hillside terrace with high bay windows and a pedimented door. This house, where Will spent his last years, was almost identical in type and size to his father's last house in Granville Road. In all the years he lived in London, each of Will's houses was within the same four square mile patch of north London in which he had been born, and in which his parents had also had their houses. This return to his roots, and the endless opportunities it

Above: William Heath Robinson by Guy Worsdell (1908–79)
Oil on board, 1943. 407 × 302 mm
National Portrait Gallery, London: bequeathed by Mrs Joan Brinsmead

Will proposed himself for the Cabinet post of Warden of Well-Being in the New World Order expected after the Second World War.

Right: The Knickerbocker Bar on board *The Empress of Britain*, 1930
Canadian Pacific Archive, Montreal

Left: View from the Studio Window at 20 Shepherds Hill
Charcoal and watercolour, 1920s. 767 × 542 mm
The Joan Brinsmead Trust

gave him to reflect upon them, contributed to the dominance of childhood stories in *My Line of Life*.

Thanks to A. E. Johnson's skill as an agent, Will's fame had hardly quavered since he had become a household name twenty years earlier. *Uncle Lubin* led the way, being described in 1912 as 'a rare good thing' by H. G. Wells in his novel *Marriage*,[1] and by the early 1930s Will's own name had sufficient momentum to enter popular literature on its own account. 'Not very lively,' mused Lord Peter Wimsey, dreaming of a machine designed to spot a murder weapon in Dorothy L. Sayers's novel *Five Red Herrings* (1931), 'better, I think, for a Heath Robinson picture.'

It is likely that Johnson had to push Will to overcome his shyness at taking part in activities that became more and more public in the years between the wars. Will had become a popular, if occasional, broadcaster when he lived in Cranleigh. In 1923 he spoke to the nation about his own home-made wireless set, which he had constructed out of the inevitable pieces of frayed string, egg cups, a bottle and a kettle.[2] Two years later, he asked his listeners to be ready with a pencil and a sheet of paper, ruled into numbered squares. With this in hand he took his audience step by step through the process of drawing what turned out to be Noah's Ark. Though the programme was billed as 'The Week's Feature', it was broadcast between 10.37 and the 11 p.m. 'Closedown' on 30 December 1925, and so its audience will have been limited to night watchmen and insomniac draughtsmen rehearsing for Hogmanay. A larger audience, however, would have attended to Will in conversation with the inventor K. M. Gleeson in 'In Town Tonight', a programme broadcast at the time that Will's full-scale working house was on show at Ideal Home Exhibition in 1934.[3]

In his years in Highgate, Will carried out some of the largest commissions of his career, in terms of physical scale. In 1930 he worked on his designs for the Knickerbocker Bar and the First Class Children's Room on the Canadian Pacific ship *The Empress of Britain*, then being

built on Clydebank.[4] The ship's architects, Staynes and Jones, made strenuous efforts to engage some of the leading Royal Academicians of the day to decorate one of the most important liners on the North Atlantic route. Artists whose work also adorned the ship's public rooms included Sir Charles Allom (1865–1947), Sir Frank Brangwyn RA (1867–1956), Edmund Dulac, Maurice Grieffenhagen RA (1862–1931) and Sir John Lavery RA (1856–1941). With Alan's help in his Highgate studio, Will painted a frieze about a hundred feet long depicting the Legend of the Cocktail, while he made nursery rhyme and fairy-tale panels and designed a special tea-set for the Children's Room. When his panels were due to be fitted into the ship, Will travelled to John Brown's Shipyard, where his presence was announced with a newspaper interview under the headline 'The Gadget King is Here.'

Architectural commissions of this kind were still new to Will. The largest scale his work had previously reached was in the backdrop for the sketch 'Epsom Ups

Will decorating an aeroplane to be used in a Hospitals' Pageant, 1933.

Mr & Mrs Churchill looking at 'The Gadget Family' at The Ideal Home Exhibition, 1934
British Library, Colindale

You must call at "THE GADGETS"!
Heath Robinson's "Ideal Home" is having its house warming at Olympia from now on until April 28, and thousands of visitors are rocking with laughter at the quaint conceits of Britain's favourite humorous artist.
In "The Gadgets" at Olympia all the merry jests of Heath Robinson's funniest creations have been given form and life and movement.
"The Gadgets" is the joke of the year, and the laughter it raises will soon be echoing all over London.
Come to Olympia to-day and enjoy your share of the fun Heath Robinson has provided for you.
Other Special Features of the Exhibition include :—
STAYBRITE CITY—"THE VILLAGE OF TO-MORROW"—GARDENS OF HISTORY AND ROMANCE—THE PAGEANT OF FASHION—NEW ROOMS FOR OLD—BATHROOMS WITH IDEAS—The HISTORY of WRITING—THE B.T.H. HALL of MAGIC—TELEPHONE TERRACE—THE EMPIRE TEA LOUNGE—THE STREET OF CARPETS—DAVY JONES' LOCKER—TEDDY TAIL'S CASTLE—ADVENTURES IN COLOUR, ETC., ETC.
600 DISPLAYS AND DEMONSTRATIONS OF ALL THAT IS NEWEST AND BEST IN EVERY SPHERE OF HOME-MAKING.
Daily Mail
IDEAL HOME EXHIBITION
NOW OPEN
OLYMPIA London, W.
10 a.m. to 10 p.m. ADMISSION 2/4 (Including Tax)
1/2 AFTER 6 p.m.

Advertisement for The Ideal Home Exhibition, Olympia, 1934
British Library, Colindale

and Downs', performed at the Alhambra Theatre in 1913. His work was, however, essentially one of a small scale, the intricate machinery being at its best when reduced to the size of a magazine page to be pored over as if it were a blueprint of a more than usually animated kind. The intricacy, and the corresponding spider's web delicacy of Will's inventions, do not translate happily to a large scale, and when this is attempted the joke tends to become laboured.

Nonetheless, public demand urged Will on to larger things. *The Empress of Britain* commission was followed by an invitation to him to create a full-scale working house for 'The Gadget Family', at the 1934 Daily Mail Ideal Home Exhibition at Olympia. The Gadgets' house was deliberately commissioned to act as an archaic foil to the major feature of the exhibition, the stainless steel Staybrite City. 'At the heart of the exhibition,' the *Daily Mail* reported, 'set where it can poke a bad-dream kind of fun at all the exhibitions of inventions the world has ever seen, the Heath Robinson House turns the creaking wheels of its wood-and-string machinery. ... Yet, like everything else in Olympia, this grotesque satire on an ideal home works perfectly.'[5]

The early morning activities of the Gadget Family's ideal home was demonstrated to the public in consecutive Acts. The house had an alarm clock which delivered a morning drink, a bucket shower bath activated by the bather, and a breakfast gong that operated two bosun's chairs. These carried Mr and Mrs Gadget through the bedroom floor down to their breakfast. The chairs, on landing, turned on the radiogram, squirted milk towards the cat and lifted the lids of the bacon and eggs by means of springs. The baby was washed by a revolving wheel of sponges, and eggs were beaten by a rotary machine worked by the cook on a bicycle.

The Lord Mayor of London was wary of the Heath Robinson house, ironically voicing fears of a Brave New World born of the union of Aldous Huxley and William Heath Robinson: 'I do not know whether I am to be fed through a tube in the future,' he said on his official visit.[6] Winston Churchill, on the other hand, wanted to see the house more than anything else when he and his wife visited Olympia. 'Mrs Churchill's amusement was a noticeable contrast to Mr Churchill's absorption and

The man who tried to make a Heath Robinson wireless set
Pen and ink, 1920s

amazement. Laughter to him was secondary to admiration for the artist's ingenuity.'[7]

If the Gadgets' house was a sign of Will's prescience in conjuring up archaic versions of the Teasmade, the in-bath shower, the invalid's domestic chair-lift, the Jacuzzi and the Magimix, it also suggests that pressure of work was once again forcing him to repeat himself with such large-scale re-creations of his graphic work. He was paying the price of his fame, and probably also paying the price of coming back to London from the country, for in moving back into the orbit of the London commercial world he was making himself available for catch-penny projects that may have widened his fame but also weakened the authority of his name. 'Have a good laugh with Heath Robinson,' the *Daily Mail* urged, stressing that the watchword of the Ideal Home Exhibition of 1934 was Simplicity, 'for this excellent joke of a house is made at the expense of the bad old days when "labour saving" gadgets were more trouble than they were worth.'[8]

Langston Day reports how, at the opening of the Ideal Home Exhibition, people rushed to see 'the Great Man, lifting up their children to catch a glimpse of him. And curiously enough they gazed at the Gadgets in embarrassment, fearing to laugh lest it might hurt the inventor's feelings.'[9] By allowing his own myth to get out of hand, and by contributing to its distortion and misunderstanding, Will was tying himself down as a kind of ageing one-turn pantomime clown. The laugh was on him. This trend continued when, in 1938, he appeared on BBC Television with a three-dimensional recreation of a Sonata Chair, in which a musician could play sonatas while sitting at his ease, a Heath Robinson Car with television early-warning device, and the Pea Splitting Machine. Will's performance with the Pea Splitting Machine was announced with the ironic assertion that the concept was 'so vital to our digestion and general well-being that we have persuaded the inventor to bring it to the studio and tell us something of the way in which it is intended to work, and of the mechanical ideas which lie behind its construction.'[10] The make-believe with which Will enchanted his early life was interfering with its end.

Will did, nevertheless, see that there were limits to his popularization, beyond which he was not prepared to be pushed. Approached by a Blackpool fun-fair designer, he was asked to paint a hoarding outside the building, showing what Langston Day described as 'not very respectable ladies and gentlemen careering round outside the building to suggest the joys within'.[11] He declined the invitation. He also declined an invitation that his image in wax be included in the display at Madame Tussaud's, a refusal that suggests that he considered waxworks to be *infra dig*.

More than a quarter of a century after making his first machine, Will at last found in literature the man who has been credited as being an inventor after his own heart. This was Professor Branestawm, the character created by Norman Hunter in stories first published in the 1920s. Will was invited to illustrate them when they were published in a collected edition by Bodley Head in 1933. If Professor Branestawm was conceived in response to the publication of Will's early inventions, Hunter's popular mad professor was very far from being the kind of man who could possibly have created Will's inventions. The Professor, a great man with simple tastes and a multitude of spectacles scattered about his shiny bald head, invented machines such as a Burglar Catcher, a Spring-Cleaning Machine and a Pancake Making Machine. Indicating the latter, the Professor explains:

'Here are the flour bin, the egg receptacle, the milk churn, and the sugar canister and the lemon squisher.... This is the pancake pan, and this is the thickening regulator, by means of which you can have pancakes any thickness you like. Here is the centrifugal tossing gear with adjustable self-changing height regulator, and my own patent device for calculating the number of tosses required for pancakes of different thicknesses.'

'Will it go wrong?'

'Certainly not.'[12]

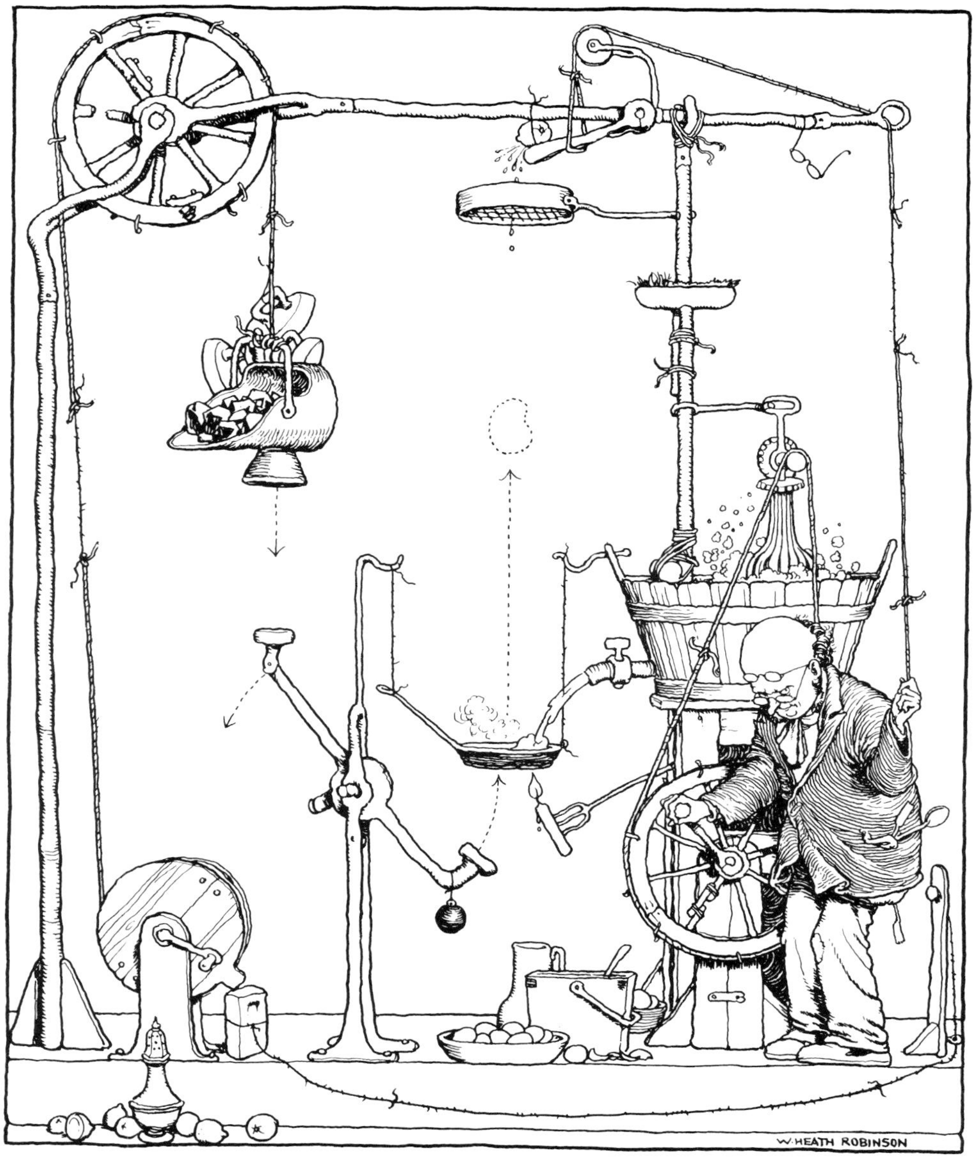

The certainty of his ideas, and the torrent of talk to which Branestawm subjects his audience, differentiates him from the true inventor of Heath Robinson's machines. Where Branestawm's inventions are made in a trice, for the coherence of Norman Hunter's story-line, Will's have all the air of having taken a very long time to manufacture, or to evolve through trial and error and repair. It is the operators of Will's machines who have built them, or who at the very least have adapted them to their own requirements. Branestawm has intellect and ambition, whereas Heath Robinson's workmen are slow, practical men with long memories but few prospects. The inventions, therefore, that Will devised to illustrate Norman Hunter's stories have none of the frenzy in their activity that Hunter's writing suggests, and it is significant that Will's drawing of the Pancake Making Machine lacks many of the features that Branestawm so proudly shows off: there is no centrifugal tossing gear, no adjustable self-changing height regulator, no toss calculator. Will's illustration is, in fact, a different machine, and ignoring the brainstorming of Branestawm, Heath Robinson remains his own man.

Despite the pressures upon him from commerce and entertainment to become a madcap showman, a personality of the new television age, Will continued in Highgate to retreat when he could into his own private work, making the plywood and plaster teapot stand showing an ageing Adam and Eve with the serpent, and ruminative watercolour paintings such as the imaginative landscape of *c.*1934. At the same time he produced advertising material and an inventive series of books which gave readers tips and encouragement on how to survive the modern world. His most enduring advertising commission came from the directors of the Great Western Railway Company which, in 1935, was celebrating its centenary. His series of 93 drawings for the railway, made at express speed in two months, if Langston Day is to be believed,[13] represent one of his finest comic achievements. They have also remained his best-known advertising campaign, remembered long after its time through their gentle, earnest invention, their unhurried humour and their sheer archaism. More to the point, we all know and have all used the railways, and feel that Will's drawings may not be that far from the truth.

Adam and Eve teapot stand, 1920s
The Joan Brinsmead Trust

Left: Hascombe Hill, Surrey
Watercolour, 1930s
Private Collection

'The Company is not without a sense of humour,' the Foreword to *Railway Ribaldry* states. Among its pages we learn how the first locomotive was built; we see what happens when the communication cord is pulled; we witness an episode during Night Duty at one of the first railway signals; and we see what can happen when a train travels at 102mph. Within the myriad details of the pictures, we see, for example, a short apprentice, standing on a book to gain height, enquiring of an older colleague if he is screwing the tap on the side of the locomotive in the right place. Another workman polishes the locomotive's dome, as if he were a hatter and it were the finest solar topee. Elsewhere, an elderly couple trundles a sleeping baby in its soap-box pram across the rails, while two night-gowned signalmen solicitously stop an oncoming passenger train to let the family pass. The passengers all lean out to watch. These drawings, teeming with detail, are so full of 'asides' that Will runs the risk, as he did in *Bill the Minder*, of losing the narrative thread in the overwhelming exuberance of his ideas.

Left: Professor Branestawm's Pancake Making Machine
Pen and ink, 1933

A Speed of 102 mph
Pen and ink, 1935
From *Railway Ribaldry*

An artistic way of hiding an unsightly view
Pen and ink, 1936
From *How to Live in a Flat*

Railway Ribaldry has, however, a gentleness and a gentility that are unique. The inventiveness of the drawings is of so poetic a strain that if Puck, Bottom, Flute or Snug from Will's own edition of *A Midsummer Night's Dream* were to appear bewildered beside the rails, they would hardly look out of place. It is perhaps no coincidence that the Heath Robinson element that looked so much at home in Sue Blane's sets for the 1989 Royal Shakespeare Company production of *A Midsummer Night's Dream* was not the Heath Robinson of the Shakespeare illustrations, but the Heath Robinson of the comic drawings.

The Sinking Body

How to Live in a Flat, the first of Will's extended series of *How to...* books, was launched in 1936 as a comic response to the 1930s housing boom in which blocks of flats were constructed for people of all grades of income in London and the provinces. The developments ranged in social and physical scale from the Quarry Hill Flats, designed for the City Council in Leeds in 1935, to the exclusive Dolphin Square in London (1937). The common factor in all these developments was their shrunken internal space, a necessity made tolerable by virtue of

The "Home From Home" Caravan

good internal planning, and by gadgets of the kind promoted at the annual Ideal Home Exhibitions. In one ambitious gadget illustrated in *How to Live in a Flat*, 'An artistic way of hiding an unsightly view', the trees and architecture of *A Midsummer Night's Dream* meet the smoking chimneys and gas-holders of an industrial city.

This and four other titles were illustrated by Will to texts by K. R. G. Browne, the grandson of Dickens's illustrator, 'Phiz'. If some of Will's ideas are now surely dated, others have become prophetic. Which would-be husband in the 1990s would take the advice given in *How to be a Perfect Husband* (1937) and test his fiancée's nerves by dropping coal on to a tin bath hidden behind a screen? None, of course; he would take her to see *The Silence of the Lambs* instead. Drawings in *How to be a Motorist* (1939), however, show a remarkable prescience: *The Sinking Body* of a saloon car (lowered to enable the driver and friend to play table tennis on its roof) has long been standard in some Citroën cars. The *Home from Home Caravan* is a regular feature of modern roads, and an improvement on the *New Rear Wheel Gear for Turning the Car in One Movement* can be found on the Honda Accord.

Will talked about the nature of his humour, as he perceived it, in 1938. 'My humour is, I suppose, a gentle satire on the fussiness of people, the people who take

Testing a Fiancée

Right: Sensible collaboration between a short story writer and an illustrator to make both ends meet
Pen and ink, 1930s
Private Collection

themselves very seriously and have no sense of humour ... a satire not on a type, but on a real human trait. There is nothing cynical in it.'[14] This was certainly true in 1938, though as a recollection of some of Will's abrasive cartoons of the 1906–18 period it was misleading. The famous, contented and secure Heath Robinson seemed by 1938 to have forgotten the frustrations that had toughened his cartoons thirty years earlier. *My Line of Life*, published in 1938, has a mood of gentle reminiscence that charms the reader but does not bite.

After K. R. G. Browne's death in 1940, Will continued the *How to ...* series in collaboration with Cecil Hunt, the publisher and writer. Hunt wrote in his autobiography of treasuring the happy evenings in Will's studio hatching ideas with him, and watching him at work. Hunt, who persuaded him to write *My Line of Life*, also remembered the public appearances Will made to mark the book's publication:

[He was] one of the least seen of all public personalities with a comparative following. ... When I took the chair for him at a great meeting at a *Sunday Times* Book Exhibition he was deeply moved by the insistence of crowds who surrounded him, not for the superficial autograph, but to thank him for his refreshing humour and the unforgettableness of many of his finest absurdities.[15]

For Will, the 1914–18 war had been a 'good war'. The opportunities that it presented enabled him to become part of the propaganda campaign against the Kaiser's Germany. The coming of the Second World War caused Will once again to reach for his tin hat and lead pencil and to make himself available in his own special way for service. It was as if he, with the support of his audience, saw himself as a one-man Home Guard, the Graphic Division of Dad's Army. Perhaps it was just a fit of pre-war nerves that caused him to suppress in *My Line of Life* the fact that Uncle Lubin's origins lay in the culture of two Fascist countries. Whatever the case, Heath Robinson in the 1939–45 war put his talents to the country's service, and made a series of magazine drawings that ridiculed the Nazi war machine and Hitler's invasion plans, and proposed the existence of a Sixth Column in Britain which outwitted the treacherous deeds of the Fifth.

Will's Second World War drawings were as important a part of the British war effort as *ITMA* and J. B. Priestley's fireside chats broadcast by the BBC. Unlike the First World War drawings, however, Will now brought personalities into his titles – so we have *A Contemptible Plot to Inject Flu Germs into Field Marshall Goering* and others which ran under the title of *The Ubiquitous Winston* in *The Sketch*. Hitler was directly satirized in Will's illustrations to *Mein Rant* (1940), a series of verses by R. F. Patterson

Endpaper from Mein Rant, *1940.*

Contemptible plot by the First Lord and his gang to inject flu germs into Field Marshall Goering
Pen and ink and wash, *c.* 1942
Private Collection

lampooning *Mein Kampf*. Whereas the First World War drawings had an edge to their humour that discomforted as well as amused, the Second World War drawings had none of this. Instead they tended to be militarized versions of Will's inter-war inventions, as if Branestawm's Pancake Making Machine had been commandeered by the Civil Defence. Nobody ever seems to have got hurt. Will's sting had been drawn.

He was part of a national movement now, following with others rather than leading as he had done in the First World War. The stage designer Oliver Messel, a camouflage officer in the Second World War, disguised pillboxes in Somerset with a bravura that rivalled even Will's outlandish proposals. Describing Messel's work, the painter Julian Trevelyan, a camouflage officer with Messel, wrote:

> ... we were given full rein to our wildest fancies. Oliver was here in his element, and he turned many of them into gothic lodges, and he even got special thatchers all the way from Norfolk to finish one of them. Others he ingeniously disguised as caravans, haystacks, ruins and wayside cafés, ... Some of his designs looked a bit theatrical, as might be expected, but he built them at a lucky moment when labour was unlimited and the urgency of the situation worked miracles.[16]

It seems that the Nazi party took Will as seriously in 1940 as had the Kaiser's propagandists in 1910. Will claimed during the war that Lord Haw-Haw had included him on a list of people who would be arrested when the Führer came to power in England. 'Now I really am famous,' Will retorted. The notoriously inaccurate Gestapo Arrest List, drawn up in May 1940, included a W. A. Robinson among the names of its intended targets. If this was indeed a misprint for W.

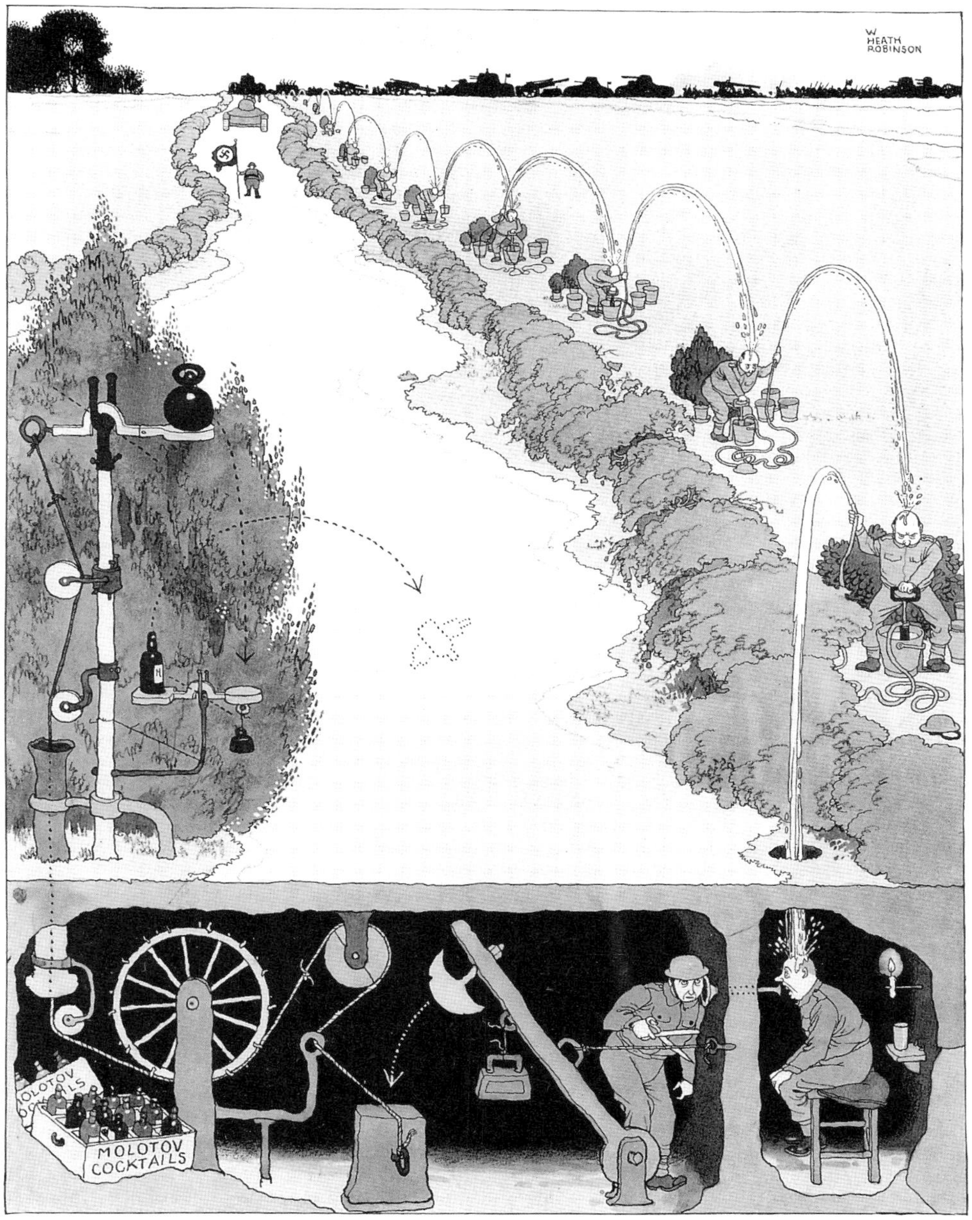

The stirrup pump relay system of signalling for giving warning of an invasion
Pen and ink and wash, 1940
From *The Sketch*
Victoria and Albert Museum, London

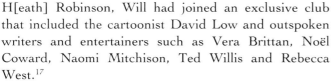

'And each of us you'll freely own is a regular out-and-out Adonis'
Pen and ink, 1940
from *Mein Rant*

H[eath] Robinson, Will had joined an exclusive club that included the cartoonist David Low and outspoken writers and entertainers such as Vera Brittan, Noël Coward, Naomi Mitchison, Ted Willis and Rebecca West.[17]

Before and during the war, Will and Josie made regular visits to Prinknash to see Alan, who had now taken the monastic name of Dom Basil Robinson. In *My Line of Life*, Will wrote lyrically of the monastery:

Dwarfed by the distance, a procession of white-hooded monks can be seen moving along the terrace and disappearing among trees. A faint smell of incense is drifted on the air. Soon a peal of bells sounds insistently and triumphantly. It reverberates all over the hills and countryside. It pauses, and a few last sad notes sing out a requiem to the passing day.[18]

The lyricism is, however, tinged with melancholy as Will stands looking over the landscape and the community that had enclosed his son. It is as if he is looking at a way of life that he was drawn to, but could not quite bring himself to join. When the monks took the decision to build a new Abbey in 1938, Will presented them with two more watercolour cartoons to use as they wished for fund-raising purposes. Cecil Hunt identified this latent desire, seeing a spiritual quality about Will which suggested that he frequently withdrew himself from the world.[19]

Will's religious feelings, though strong and deeply personal, were left unexpressed. He would, however, take himself off on the top deck of a bus (because he enjoyed the view) to visit a church, ostensibly to look at its architecture. Among his favourite destinations were St Saviour's, Aberdeen Park, and St Joseph's, Highgate

Bath night during an air raid on the Siegfried Line
Pen and ink and wash, *c.* 1942
Private Collection

Dying rose petals in a delftware bowl
Watercolour, 1930s
204 × 276 mm
The Joan Brinsmead Trust

Painted by Will as a present for his wife.

Hill. Will would slip in and sit quietly at the back, preferring his churches to be empty, in between services. Will had other reasons to feel uncomfortable in a church. He had a weak bladder, exacerbated by prostate trouble, and dreaded being caught in the middle of a crowded pew. Nonetheless, he felt a magnetic attraction to religion, a longing that he could still not bring himself to allow any established church to satisfy. Alan, however, remembered the great Catholic preacher Father Vincent McNab saying, 'I can understand why your father did not follow you into the Church. A lot of people lead others towards it, but do not go in themselves. Moses didn't go into the Promised Land.' The last communication with Alan that Will had before his death was to send his son a small, folded, secret drawing of an elderly William Heath Robinson floating up towards heavenly rays of light on tiny butterfly wings. His pipe and slippers have fallen away in his amazement. The light to which he flies, however, is a cobweb.

Will's health was weakened in the last fifteen years of his life by a heart condition, and as a consequence no insurance company would cover him. The weakness of

Dom Basil Robinson at work on a sculpture of The Sacred Heart, *1930s*

Left: Will and Josie Heath Robinson at home in Highgate, 1930s. On the wall is a print of Dürer's *Trinity*, and some of Will's collection of Japanese prints
The Joan Brinsmead Trust

A funeral procession
Watercolour, 1930s
410 × 370 mm
Private Collection

his heart prevented him from gardening, and he was now forced to leave this to others. In his old age he spent his evenings at Highgate reading Dickens, Trollope, Hardy and Scott, Frazer's *The Golden Bough*, Prescott's *History of the Conquest of Mexico* or the great Russian novelists. Over the drawing-room fireplace hung a print of Dürer's *Trinity*, a painting that Will's eyes returned to time and again. Surrounding him was his collection of Japanese prints, whose sense of space and dramatic diagonals had so firmly influenced his own work.

William Heath Robinson died at 25 Southwood Avenue on 13 September 1944, a few days before he was due to return to hospital to undergo a prostate operation. He had been sent home after exploratory surgery, but was still strung about with tubes and drips and catheters. He loathed the prospect of hospital, loathed looking like part of one of his own inventions, and loathed the thought of another operation. Left alone for five minutes, he wrenched the alien tubes from around his body, and shortly afterwards he died.

Will's vision of himself going up to heaven
Pen and ink, 1944
164 × 120 mm
Private Collection

The last drawing Will sent to his son, Dom Basil Robinson.

CHAPTER SEVEN

HOW TO BUILD A NEW WORLD

The Rescue
Pen and ink and wash, 1920s
Private Collection

UNSTABLE AND COMPLICATED though it may be, Will's machinery reflects his desire for order. The one area of his life over which his control was total was that contained within the eight square feet of his drawing-board. The technology that he developed there was for use, not ornament, and for the general improvement of everyday life in the civilized and ordered society of his imagination.

It is significant that even his many cartoons that have no mechanical associations, such as *A Public Demonstration for the Benefit of Professional Rugby Players* or *The Rescue*, follow seamlessly in this tradition. They celebrate behaviour in the kind of society that civilization aspires to, but will never reach outside art and literature, and one in which the Law of Gravity does not always apply.

The common and humanizing thread that runs through Will's machinery is that it all has to be operated by people, and carefully supervised. There would be no room for the microchip in his industrial pantheon. Will's sympathy with Aldous Huxley's melancholy reflections on invention were instinctive:

> Creative work [Huxley wrote in 1929], of however humble a kind, is the source of man's most solid, least transitory happiness. Leisure has now been almost as completely mechanized as labour. Men ... sit and are passively amused by mechanical devices. Machinery condemns one of the most vital needs of humanity to frustration which the progress of invention can only render more and more complete.[1]

Where Huxley grasped one of the central problems of scientific progress, Will, in his straightforward, unintellectual way, tried to present solutions through his own creative work. And his solutions were anti-inventions. He did not want to stop the clock, or run it backwards, but he tried instead to make it work in a different way in his desire to help to build a better world.

GENTLY
DOES IT
W. HEATH
ROBINSON

Right: Two rogues calling themselves weavers made their appearance
Pen and ink, 1913
From *Hans Andersen's Fairy Tales*
Sheffield City Art Galleries

Left: A public demonstration for the benefit of professional rugby players by those interested in the inculcation of gentler methods in the game
Pen and ink and gouache, 1923
From *Royal Magazine*
Private Collection

His obsession with order led naturally to an obsession with subject, which, in turn, led to his evolving a graphic style that was clear and intelligible. The lively penwork of his illustrations to the 1902 edition of *Don Quixote*, though ideally suited to convey the character and actions of this deluded Spanish grandee, was of no use in describing the intricacies of a Match Tipping Machine. The cartoons of his peers Phil May, George du Maurier, Harry Furniss or Lewis Baumer were drawn with highly energized, spontaneous lines. Will's later work, by comparison, is studied, even plodding, but nonetheless perfectly suited to its purpose.

The roots of this style lie in the work of Aubrey Beardsley and the Japanese printmakers, and in the technical drawings of engineering draughtsmen. There were passing influences from artists such as Daniel Vièrge (1851–1904), Caran D'Ache [Emmanuel Poiré (1858–1909)] and other English and Continental artists discussed elsewhere, but the influence of Beardsley and the Japanese endured. Like engineering blueprints, Will's machines are presented in frontal elevation with very little background detail, but with the assistance here and there of arrows or dotted lines to show the direction of movement. Will's open line has the clarity of Beardsley's, and his sense of design, particularly in non-mechanical subjects, is dependent on the high viewpoints and exaggerated perspectives of Japanese art. This is particularly apparent in Will's illustrations to *A Midsummer Night's Dream* and *The Water-Babies*, and from these and earlier examples of his serious work, the manner spread directly to his comic drawings.

Behind the bland screen of a computer monitor we know that a logically enacted sequence of events takes place, because that is what we are told. With a Heath Robinson machine, however, we can *see* that it is the case. The machines have a peculiarly Anglo-Saxon sense of amateurism, of make-do-and-mend, of triumphal solution in the face of an intractable problem. The operators of the machines show no surprise that they work, because they, or people very like them, put the machines together. They are not amused, because they are getting on with the job.

When A. E. Johnson was approached in the 1920s by a film company eager to translate Will's drawings into 'reality', he perceptively recognized that the attempt would fail. 'If one were to attempt to convert ... your machinery into concrete facts, it seems to me that the fantasy is broken.... I doubt whether the result would even be mildly amusing.' Johnson was right. It would be as tedious as trying to explain a joke to a person with no sense of humour. A further problem that would always haunt such attempts is that the machinery would be prone to breakdown. The machinery in Will's drawings never breaks down.

This quality may point to the reason why Will's work was so popular among industrialists, a breed which is no

Right: A Christmas deed of kindness
Pen and ink and gouache, 1925
From *Hutchinson's Magazine*
Private Collection

Right: Some occasions when a gentleman is not expected to give up his seat to a lady
Pen and ink and wash, 1920s
Private Collection

stranger to coping with mechanical breakdown. Will, however, did not see it that way, finding a different but equally rational explanation:

> ... of course, for most of my mechanical drawings it is essential for people to have some knowledge of the processes caricatured. They appeal chiefly, therefore, to men with specialized technical ability. That is why the most successful of them are used for brochures and prospectuses which are read almost exclusively by experts.... These experts seem to appreciate my humour immensely: it tickles them to death and enhances their pride in their great machines.[2]

Heath Robinson appeared at a perfect historical moment, which suggests that his existence was inevitable. If he had not done the job of mechanizing the funny-bone of the nation, somebody else most certainly would have, and at precisely the same time. In the nineteenth century the machine itself was the oppressor. Wood-engravers, for example, were not permitted to keep the printing machine waiting 'a single hour' in the 1860s and 1870s.[3] A Lancashire cotton manufacturer wrote in 1832: 'Whilst the engine runs the people must work – men, women and children are yoked together with iron and steam. The animal machine – breakable in the best case, subject to a thousand sources of suffering – is chained fast to the iron machine, which knows no suffering and no weariness.'[4] No serious artist could make fun of that beast. By the 1920s, after countless Factory Acts and a devastating war, the beast had been tamed in production lines throughout the world, and harnessed to do what each was designed for and no more.

W HEATH ROBINSON

COLLECTING THE NEW PROPERTY TAX

Collecting the New Property Tax by Michael Heath
Published in *The Independent*, 1991

At that point the machine could safely be caricatured until its next escape with the splitting of the atom and the birth of the Nuclear Age. At a future time in which humanity completely loses its fear of nuclear power and feels it is fully in control of this knowledge, then a new Heath Robinson will emerge to caricature and cosset this pet. That is not prophetic, it is inevitable.

In the meantime, the spirit that inspired William Heath Robinson has inspired others. The American sculptor Alexander Calder (1898–1976) rigged up a household of gadgets, as Julian Trevelyan recalled: 'Over his bed were a series of strings that put on the light, turned on the bath, lit the gas under the kettle and so forth; often they failed to function and he would have to hop out of bed to fix them. When I saw him last he told me he was making a machine for tickling his wife Louisa in the next room.'[5]

The inventions of the American artist Rube Goldberg are in the Heath Robinson mould, as are the proposals of the many contestants in the annual competition for inventors in France, the Concours Lépine. In 1989 Walt Disney Studios released *Honey I Shrunk the Kids*, a story of a Middle American inventor who is forced to search for his miniaturized children with the aid of a series of 'Heath Robinson' machines.

The mechanical fantasies of the Englishman Rowland Emett (1907–1990) are heirs to the Heath Robinson tradition. Many of Emett's machines have been built to operate, but their success owes more to the wizardry of their electronics than to the logic of their mechanics. Nearer to the Heath Robinson tendency, however, are Tim Hunkin's explanations in drawings and sculpture of the workings of domestic machinery, and Glen Baxter's ironic series of drawings such as his *Great Failures of Our Time*.

Will's style is extraordinarily integrated, the change between his serious and his comic work being one of subject and mood, not of style. A work which straddles his comic and serious moods is his watercolour *The Christening Party*, one of a series of ruminative figure compositions, painted in the late 1920s and 1930s. This Will considered to be his best work, and Langston Day tells that he vowed he would rather sell his clothes than part with it.[6] In the crowded but brilliantly orchestrated composition, reminiscent of the populous paintings of Breughel or Frith, an enormous extended family, their friends, servants and a brass band, enjoy a christening feast in a luxuriant garden where the chestnuts, rhododendron, broom and laburnum are in full flower. One old man talks to another; a mother blows her child's nose; a maid puts down a great pile of cups and saucers; the detail is intense and deeply felt.

There is, however, a hint of reflective melancholy amid the merriment: somewhere in the crowd is the baby with its mother standing quiet and distracted in the midst of the hubbub. Directly below her is a child with a skipping rope, staring directly out at the viewer with a perspicacious gaze, the only witness that this party is being watched. This may not have been Will's own garden, but it was the garden of his imagination, the setting for this reverie in late Victorian dress. And whose christening was it? Perhaps it was his own.

'In summer the gardens were full of bloom,' he recalled of Hatch End in *My Line of Life*, though he might have been writing about any golden memory of his past. 'There were many horse-chestnut trees. In the spring they set ablaze their glorious candle clusters of white and pink. In the autumn the roads and paths were ankle-deep in their crimson, brown and yellow litter. The sun shone brightly for us in those days.'[7]

The Christening Party
Pen and ink and gouache, 1930s
Harry Ransom Humanities Research Center, University of Texas at Austin

The penultimate title in Will's *How To...* series was *How to Build a New World* (1941), written and illustrated with Cecil Hunt in the gloomiest days of the Second World War. At a time of darkness, Will's proposals made happy, skittish nonsense, and helped to keep hope alive in the free world. Long after his death, Will's son, Dom Basil Robinson, offered copies of this book and *How to Make the Best of Things* (1940) through the Benedictine Order to Pope John Paul II. His Holiness graciously accepted the gift for the Vatican Library. Will Heath Robinson, in his life wary of religion, was received into the Roman Catholic church at last.

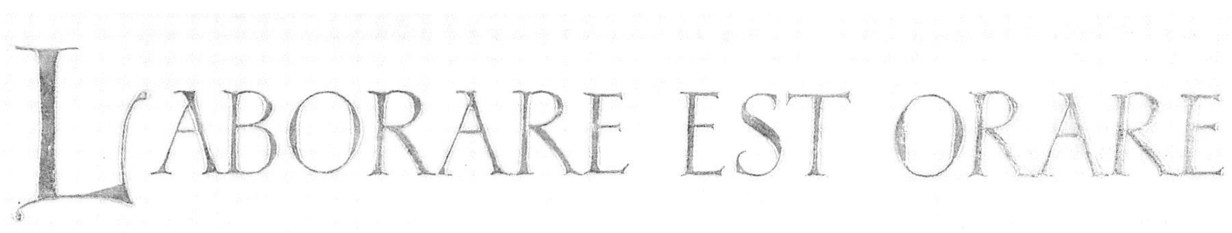

Laborare est Orare [To work is to pray] by Will's sister, the calligrapher Mary Robinson (1874–1974)
Gold on vellum, 1920s
85 × 563 mm
The Joan Brinsmead Trust

Titania: Full often hath she gossip'd by my side
And sat with me on Neptune's yellow sands
Pen and ink, 1914. From *A Midsummer Night's Dream*, Act II sc i
Sheffield City Art Galleries

NOTES

ABBREVIATIONS IN NOTES

BA: Bell Archive, University of Reading Library

BEARE: Geoffrey Beare: *The Illustrations of W. Heath Robinson*; Werner Shaw, 1983

CHM: Chadwyck-Healey Microfilm

DAY: Langston Day: *The Life and Art of W. Heath Robinson*; Herbert Joseph, 1947

GRA, ILLINOIS: Grant Richards Archive, University of Illinois Library at Urbana-Champaign, USA

MLOL: William Heath Robinson: *My Line of Life*; Blackie, 1938

RHC: Rider Haggard Collection, Butler Library, University of Columbia, New York

RP: Robinson Papers, University of Reading Library

ROGERSON: Ian Rogerson: *The Robinson Brothers – An Exhibition of Book Illustration by Thomas Heath, Charles and William Heath Robinson*; Manchester Polytechnic Library, 1987

WHR: William Heath Robinson

Abbreviations for dates are given in the UK format throughout: e.g., 1.2.03 signifies 1 February 1903.

INTRODUCTION

1 DAY, p. 136. I have failed to find any reference to the remark in *Hansard*'s records of House of Commons debates. Day's observation may be apocryphal. JH.

2 *Oxford English Dictionary*; 1989, Vol. VII, p. 77.

3 OED; Vol. III, p. 842.

4 A note on the back of an envelope containing the love letters of Tom Robinson and Lizzie Heath (1867) suggests that the Robinsons felt that they were a cut above the Heaths, who dropped their aitches. R.P.

5 Nick Nuttall: 'Engineer plans to snuff out oilfield fires like candles'; *The Times*, 15.3.1991.

CHAPTER ONE

1 WHR's birth certificate, Office of Population and Census Services.

2 Letter Charles Lamb to Bernard Barton, 1823. Quoted David Cecil: *A Portrait of Charles Lamb*; Constable, 1983, p. 164.

3 *A History of Middlesex*, Vol. VIII; Victoria History of England, OUP, 1985, pp. 13, 83.

4 *Islington Gazette*, 7.6.72.

5 *Islington Directory*, 1877.

6 George and Weedon Grossmith: *The Diary of a Nobody*; J. Arrowsmith, Bristol, 1892, pp. 21–2. The *Diary* first appeared serially in *Punch* in 1888.

7 MLOL, p. 3.

8 *Ibid.*, p. 8.

9 The 1871 Census return for 19 Benwell Road, Islington, records his birthplace as Gateshead, Co. Durham, but the 1881 return for 37 Benwell Road has it as Durham, Co. Durham.

10 *A Memoir of Thomas Bewick Written by Himself* (1822); ed. Montague Weekley, London, Cresset Press, 1961, p. 189.

11 *Ibid.*, pp. 203–4.

12 A long ballad, sent to Thomas Robinson the elder at Cold Bath Street, Cold Bath Fields, is dated Feb. 1834. RP.

13 1881 Census return for 37 Benwell Road.

14 Address given on Thomas Robinson the younger's birth certificate, 1838. RP. Further addresses recorded among the Robinson Papers for Thomas Robinson the elder are: 63 Margaret Street, Spa Fields (on an undated letter from William Cobbett); 23 Pulteney Street, Islington (1851); 34 Westbourne Road, Barnsbury (letter dated 8.8.67). See also Rodney K. Engen: *Dictionary of Victorian Wood Engravers*; London, Chadwyck Healey, 1985, p. 222.

15 Eric A. Willatts: *Streets with a Story – The Book of Islington*; Islington Local History Education Trust, 2nd edn, 1988, p. 26.

16 The Brothers Dalziel: *A Record of Fifty Years Work, 1840–1890*; Methuen, 1901, p. 160.

17 Thomas Robinson's birth certificate, 28.9.1838. RP.

18 Thomas Robinson the younger wrote to Eliza's father requesting her hand in marriage on 8.5.67. The couple were married at Holy Trinity Church, Islington on 26.8.68. RP.

19 1871 Census return for 29 Benwell Road.

20 Thomas Robinson rented the house for £30 p.a. Letter, undated [1872]. RP.

21 MLOL, p. 5. Thomas Robinson the younger, WHR's father, worked at 9 Essex Street, Strand (from *c.*1864), at 8 Dane's Inn (from 1871), and at 1 Dane's Inn from 1889 until his death in 1902. RP.

22 Thomas Robinson's invoice for work completed in August and September 1883 lists subjects drawn for *Penny Illustrated Paper* and *Illustrated London News*, and lists fees for visiting Holloway, Wimbledon, Scotland Yard, Woolwich and Bow Street to make sketches. RP.

23 Six-year indenture between Richard Henry Mather and Thomas Robinson, 5.3.79. RP.

24 Ref. letter of contract, Henry Sell to Thomas Robinson, 2.4.90. RP.

25 This was the fourth address the family had had since 1869. After leaving 25 Ennis Road, they moved to 33 Bryantwood Road, Islington, and are first listed at 51 Benwell Road in the 1878 *Islington Directory*, and in *Kelly's Directory*.

26 A third sister, Mabel Heath, had been born in 1876, but died the following year.

27 Lizzie Heath is listed in the 1871 Census, aged eleven, at 29 Benwell Road.

28 MLOL, pp. 7–8.

29 *Ibid.*, p. 134.

30 1881 Census: 49 Benwell Road: Margaret Horne, Wife of Mariner, and four children; 53 Benwell Road: Annie Wright, Wife of Master Mariner, and four children.

31 MLOL, pp. 14ff.

32 Ann Thwaite: *A. A. Milne – His Life*; Faber, 1990, p. 57.

33 MLOL, p. 18.

34 *Ibid.*, p. 25. Ref. letter Tom to his parents, n.d. [1880]. RP.

35 Photographic Interviews, V: A Favourite *Sketch* Artist – Mr W. Heath Robinson'; *The Sketch*, 4.1.11, pp. 398–9.

36 W. Heath Robinson: 'In the Days of My Youth'; *T.P.'s & Cassell's Weekly*, 18.4.25, p. 956ff.

37 Letter Tom Robinson to his parents, n.d. [25.12.82]. RP. Quoted by kind permission of Mrs Alison Greenwood.

38 Peter Ackroyd: *Dickens*, Sinclair-Stevenson, 1990, pp. 111–12.

39 R. L. Stevenson: 'A Penny Plain and Twopence Coloured'; collected in *Memories and Portraits*; Chatto and Windus, 1887, pp. 213ff.

40 George R. Sims: 'Trips About Town, VI: In the Heart of Hoxton's; *The Strand Magazine*, Vol. 30, Sep. 1905, pp. 325ff.

41 MLOL, pp. 25–6.

42 Letter WHR to his parents, n.d. [*c.*1880]. RP.

43 A production of *Sinbad the Sailor* opened at the Drury Lane Theatre on 26.12.82.

44 MLOL, pp. 54ff.

45 Letter WHR to his mother, dated 1.4.[?]80. RP.

46 Letter Tom Robinson to his parents, n.d. [1883]. RP. Quoted by kind permission of Mrs Alison Greenwood.

47 MLOL, p. 56.

48 MLOL, p. 22.

49 *Ibid.*, pp. 41–2. I am grateful to Ms V. R. Hart, the Local History Librarian at Islington Library, for identifying the school for me. See *Islington Daily Gazette*, 24.8.23 and 30.8.23 for an account of Roston Bourke's life and funeral.

50 Roger Berthoud: *The Life of Henry Moore*; London, Faber, 1987, pp. 27ff.

CHAPTER TWO

1 MLOL, p. 71.

2 *Loc. cit.*

3 *Ibid.*, p. 82.

4 This is likely to be the same H. T. Bosdet, of 81 Charlotte Street, Fitzroy Square, who exhibited *A Portrait* at the Royal Academy in 1885.

5 MLOL, p. 48. Royal Academy Student Register.

6 W. Heath Robinson: 'In the Days of My Youth'; *T.P.'s and Cassell's Weekly*, *loc. cit.*

7 Royal Academy Student Register; admitted 26.1.92. WHR was student no. 4350, recommended by R. A. Warren. Ref. also J. E. Hodgson and F. A. Eaton: *The Royal Academy and Its Members*; John Murray, 1905, Appendix VII.

8 Five paintings by Hodgson are held in Wolverhampton Art Gallery. They include *A Philharmonic Rehearsal in a Farmhouse* (1860), *Holbein's Studio* (1861) and *Queen Elizabeth Reviewing the Fleet* (1864).

9 MLOL, p. 20. The Robinson family moved in 1886 to 313 Camden Road, Holloway (*Islington Directory*, 1886) and in 1888 to Hillside, 49 Ferne Park Road, Stroud Green (Insurance Policy. RP.)

10 MLOL, p. 86. See also *T.P.'s and Cassell's Weekly*, *cit.*

11 *Ibid.*, p. 72.

12 Frank Swinnerton, quoted BEARE p. 9. see also Frank Swinnerton: *Swinnerton – An Autobiography*; Doubleday, Doran & Co., N.Y., 1936, p. 77.

13 Billinghurst's published titles include: R. L'Estrange (trans.): *A Hundred Fables of Aesop*; J. Lane, 1899; *A Hundred Fables of La Fontaine*; J. Lane, 1900; *A Hundred Anecdotes of Animals* (written and illustrated by PJB; J. Lane, 1901) and L. Dalkeith: *Beasts Shown to the Children*; T.C. & E.C. Jack, 1906.

14 MLOL, p. 96.

15 *The Radio Times*, 31.12.37.

16 The first 59 pages of Will's illustrations do not carry his signature, but that of the blockmaker, Lemercier Gravure.

17 DAY, pp. 117ff. Speaking in 1991, Dom Basil Robinson felt that Day's observations, drawn from conversations with Will's friends, may have been exaggerated. 'My father wasn't *so* untidy. He could always find things to within a layer or two.' Tidiness, or lack of it, seems to be relative. Tom Robinson, too, defended his father. 'The untidiness must mainly have been confined to the earlier days. Under my mother's influence I am sure things were different later.'

18 Recalled by Dom Basil Robinson, 1991.

19 Ref. John Latey's obituary, *The Athenaeum*, 4.10.02, pp. 451–2.

20 Will's passport records that his eyes were hazel coloured, 30.4.18.

21 MLOL, p. 135.

22 *Aunty Bay's Autobiography*; typescript. RP. Quoted by kind permission of Mrs Joyce Cooper.

23 DAY, p. 118.

24 MLOL, p. 133.

25 WHR to E. Bell, 25.2.98 and 10.3.98. BA, 323/178 and 179.

26 WHR to E. Bell, 17.11.99. BA, 348/171.

27 Pencilled note by E. Bell, dated 2.1.00 at foot of letter from WHR to E. Bell, 29.12.99. BA, 348/172.

28 Ref. letter WHR to E. Bell, 29.3.00. BA, 313/218.

29 WHR to E. Bell, 7.1.01. BA, 315/188.

30 Number 3, 1899–1902; number 2, 1902–9.

31 MLOL, 137.

32 WHR to Grant Richards, 18.3.02. RHC, NY. WHR gives two spellings for the name of his hero: Schnitzel and Schnitzell. For simplicity, I have kept to the former.

33 WHR to Grant Ricahrds, 5.4.02. RHC, NY. The contract is dated 4.4.02. CHM, H.

34 WHR to Grant Richards, 13.10.02. RHC, NY.

35 *Aunty Bay's Autobiography*; typescript. RP. According to a note in RP, the epitaph on Thomas Robinson's grave in Highgate Cemetery reads: 'Contributor to the Illustrated London News for 20 Years.'

36 *Ibid.*.

37 MLOL, p. 136.

38 *The Studio*, Vol 21 (1901), p. 209.

39 *The Athenaeum*, 15.11.02, p. 650.

40 R. E. D. Sketchley: *English Book Illustration of Today: Appreciation of the Work of Living English Illustrators with Lists of their Books*; Kegan Paul, Trench, Tuibner & Co., 1903, p. 114.

CHAPTER THREE

1 GRA, ILLINOIS. CHM E2/3.

2 MLOL, p. 98.

3 Grant Richards: *Author Hunting*; London, Unicorn Press, 1934. New edn 1960, p. 41.

4 *Ibid.*, pp. 65ff.

5 *Ibid.*, p. 33.

6 Richards is described thus by Arthur Waugh. *Ibid.*, introduction by Alec Waugh, p. xiii and *passim*.

7 He paid Gordon Browne £150 for illustrations to Anstey's *Paleface and Redskins* (1878), and Bernard Shaw a 20% royalty for *Plays Pleasant and Unpleasant* (1898). *Ibid.*, p. 95.

8 2,677 copies sold (includes 1,280 to America) by 31 Dec. 1902. 3,897 copies sold by 17.11.04. WHR took a 10% royalty on a cover price of 6s, and 2d per copy on the American edition. GRA, ILLINOIS, *loc. cit.*

9 Letter WHR to Grant Richards, 11.1.03. RHC, NY. *The Child's Arabian Nights* by WHR was published 23.9.03. 5,000 copies were printed. Richards purchased the copyright outright from WHR for £35. See GRA, ILLINOIS, *loc. cit.*

10 'I shall not undertake this book unless I can get an American publisher to take one half of the edition.' Grant Richards to J. P. Lippincott, 22.9.03. GRA, ILLINOIS CHM A4/291–2.

11 The largest number of illustrations Heath Robinson made for a single book was more than 400 for a planned edition of Shakespeare's *Complete Works* for Jonathan Cape, Jan. 1921 to Mar. 1922. The edition was not published. See Chapter 5.

12 Figure given by BEARE, p. 118.

13 *The Works of Mr Francis Rabelais*, Vol. I, pp. 26, 27.

14 *Ibid.*, p. 179.

15 *Ibid.*, p. 309.

16 *Ibid.*, pp. 429ff.

17 *Ibid.*, pp. 11ff.

18 A. E. Johnson: *W. Heath Robinson*; A. & C. Black, 1913.

19 Letter Grant Richards to J. P. Lippincott, *cit.*

20 See Linda Gertner Zatlin: *Aubrey Beardsley and Victorian Sexual Politics*; Clarendon Press, Oxford, 1990.

21 Malcolm C. Salaman: 'Charles Robinson – Book Illustrator', *The Studio*, Vol. 66, 1916, p. 179.

22 Letter WHR to James E. Lyons, 28.4.02. RHC, NY.

23 Letter WHR to Grant Richards, 4.9.02. RHC, NY.

24 Letters WHR to Grant Richards, 13.10.02 and 29.10.02. RHC, NY.

25 Letter WHR to Grant Richards, 11.1.03. RHC, NY.

26 Letter WHR to Grant Richards, 20.4.04. RHC, NY.

27 Letter Grant Richards to WHR, 5.5.04. GRA, ILLINOIS. CHM A5/246; WHR to Grant Richards, 10.5.04. RHC, NY.

28 The hearing into Grant Richards's bankruptcy took place in Feb. 1905. *The Times*, 8.2.05, p. 12.

29 Grant Richards's recorded expenditure on the production of *Rabelais* was £434.11s.2d. This includes three cash payments of £37.10s.0d, possibly intended for WHR, and one of which was certainly received by him. GRA, ILLINOIS. CHM E2/733. [*Vide* receipt 20.4.04. RHC, NY.]

30 Letter Grant Richards to WHR, 3.11.05. GRA, ILLINOIS. CHM A7/202.

31 Letters Grant Richards to Alexander Moring, 19.10.05 and 13.11.05. GRA, ILLINOIS. CHM A7/137 and A7/228.

32 Grant Richards: *op. cit.*, p. 95.

33 Other editions were illustrated by Emile Boilvin, 1876–7, L. Chalon, 1892, J. Garnier, 1897–9, and Anon., 1897.

34 *The Athenaeum*, 7.12.12, p. 710.

35 *Times Literary Supplement*, 28.11.12.

36 MLOL, p. 99. See also n. 29.

37 *The Bookman*, Dec. 1909, p. 138. Others asked to write about their Christmases included Arthur Rackham, John Hassall, Tom Browne, Jerome K. Jerome and John Galsworthy.

38 MLOL, pp. 108, 110.

39 *Ibid.*.

40 *The Sketch*, 11.4.06, p. 409.

41 *Ibid.*, 1.8.06, p. 87.

42 *Ibid.*, 20.4.10–22.6.10. See also Chapter 4.

43 James Hamilton: *Arthur Rackham*; Pavilion Books, 1990, pp. 68–77 and *passim*.

44 *Times Literary Supplement*, 17.12.08.

45 Anon.: 'Mr. W. Heath Robinson and His Work'; *The Strand Magazine*, Vol. 36, Jul. 1908, pp. 41ff.

46 W. Heath Robinson: *The Adventures of Uncle Lubin*, 1902, p. 62.

47 *The Sketch*, 27.3.07–22.5.07; nine cartoons.

48 Peter Ackroyd: *op. cit.*, pp. 275–6.

49 *The Bystander*, 7.12.10, p. 475.

50 The original charter, dated 8.4.11, is among RP.

51 MLOL, p. 196.

52 For an account of the London Sketch Club see David Cuppleditch: *The London Sketch Club*; Dilke Press, 1978. Also Walter Churcher: 'The London Sketch Club'; *The Studio*, Vol. 63, 1915, pp. 243–55. For the Savage Club, see Percy V. Bradshaw: *Drawn from Memory*; Chapman and Hall, pp. 101ff.

53 *The Athenaeum*, 26.10.12, p. 498.

54 *Ibid.*, 7.6.13, p. 629.

55 *The Strand Magazine*, *loc. cit.*.

56 MLOL, p. 104.

57 'Bouncing the Beecham'; *The Sketch*, 10.8.10, p. 145; 'Beecham Bouncing in Hong Kong', photographic feature; *The Sketch*, 12.10.10, Suppl. p. 8.

58 Ten letters Grant Richards to WHR, A. E. Johnson and E. R. Dracott, 1911–12 and 1915–17. GRA, ILLINOIS. CHM A19, 20, 23–5 and *passim*.

CHAPTER FOUR

1 MLOL, p. 145.

2 *Times Literary Supplement*, 10.12.14, p. 549.

3 *A Midsummer Night's Dream*, Act II, sc. i.

4 *Hansard*, Vol. 53, 5.6.13, col. 1111.

5 *Loc. cit.*, col. 1566.

6 MLOL, p. 146.

7 *Daily Mail*, 13.12.09. Reprinted in Robert Blatchford: *The War that was Foretold – Germany and England*; Daily Mail, 1914.

8 *The Sketch*, 20.4.10, p. 49.

9 Letter H. G. Wells to WHR, 31.12.14, quoted MLOL, p. 106.

10 Letter WHR to H. G. Wells, 4.1.15; Wells Collection Correspondence, R–187. University of Illinois Library at Urbana-Champaign.

11 Robert Blatchford: *General von Sneak: A Little Study of the War*; London, Hodder and Stoughton, 1918. Chap. IV: 'The Cult of Frightfulness', p. 53.

12 MLOL, p. 147.

13 Percy V. Bradshaw: *The Art of the Illustrator: W. Heath Robinson and His Work*; London, The Press Art School, n.d. [1918], p. 4.

14 Henri Barbusse (trans. Fitzwater Wray): *Under Fire: The Story of a Squad*; Dent, 1917.

15 MLOL, p. 150.

16 *Hunlikely*, 1916.

17 Henri Barbusse: *op. cit.* Quoted in Alistair Horne: *The Price of Glory: Verdun 1916*; Macmillan, 1962, p. 74. (Penguin edition, 1964.)

18 James Hamilton: *op. cit.*, pp. 45, 58.

19 Draft letter E. J. Sullivan to Rt. Hon. C. F. G. Masterman, 12.4.16. Sullivan Notebooks, Pierpont Morgan Library, New York.

20 Edmund J. Sullivan: *The Kaiser's Garland*; London, William Heinemann, 1915.

21 MLOL, pp. 146, 150.

22 A letter inserted into JH's copy of *The Kaiser's Garland* reads: 'Xmas 1915. I hope you will like it, it is very gruesome but Ella and I though it so clever and well drawn that we chose it, hoping you will agree. C.S.F.'

23 *Some 'Frightful' War Pictures*, 1915, p. 2.

24 *The Saintly Hun*, 1917.

25 *The Book of Artemas. Concerning men and the things that men did do, at the time when there was a war*; W. Westall and Co., n.d. [1917], Chap. XIV, v. 25–8.

26 *The Studio*, Vol. 67, 1916, pp. 223ff.

27 Malcolm C. Salaman: *op. cit.*

28 Percy V. Bradshaw: *Drawn from Memory*; London, Chapman and Hall, 1943, p. 74.

29 See MLOL, p. 130.

30 'After the publication of *Rabelais* there came a pause in Mr. Heath Robinson's activities as an illustrator. He had begun to exploit, in *The Sketch* and elsewhere, that curious vein of absurdity which has earned for him so great a vogue as a humorist, and to this he devoted himself almost exclusively for some time. When presently he resumed illustration, it was to undertake *Twelfth Night....*' A. E. Johnson: 'The Line Drawings of W. Heath Robinson'; *The Studio*, Vol. 67, 1916, p. 228.

31 BEARE, pp. 43, 47.

32 *The Strand Magazine*, Dec. 1915, Vol. 50, pp. 603–12.

33 *The Strand Magazine*, Sep. 1916, Vol. 52, pp. 311–13.

34 US National Archives, Washington. Records of the American Expeditionary Force, 1917–23.

35 DAY, p. 108.

36 MLOL, p. 155.

37 W. Heath Robinson: *Flypapers*; Duckworth, 1919, p. 3.

CHAPTER FIVE

1 Ref. BEARE, pp. 66–7. The present writer is particularly grateful to Valerie Kettley of Jonathan Cape for showing him as many of WHR's original Shakespeare illustrations as she herself could trace. Some of the correspondence relating to the commission is held in the Cape Archive at the University of Reading Library.

2 Ref. James Hamilton: *op. cit., p. 126.*

3 Colin White: *The Enchanted World of Jessie M. King*; Edinburgh, Canongate, 1989, pp. 105ff. See also Michael Felmingham: *The Illustrated Gift Book 1880–1930*; Aldershot, Scolar Press, 1988, p. 28.

4 *The Bystander*, 20.10.20, p. 187.

5 A. L. Baldry: 'The Art of Mr. W. Heath Robinson'; *The Studio*, Vol. 89, no. 386 (May 1925), pp. 243ff.

6 MLOL, p. 103. For a good account of WHR's business relationship with Potter, see Geoffrey Beare: *Heath Robinson Advertising*, Bellew, 1992, p. 10ff.

7 Lord Mackintosh: *By Faith and Work*; Hutchinson, 1966, pp. 59–60. The Mackintosh *Toffee Town* advertising campaign ran for six months from Oct. 1921 to Mar. 1922, with one page a month taken in the *Daily Mail, Daily Express, Daily News*, Daily Mirror, *Daily Sketch* and 'several of the leading provincial newspapers'. The other artists commissioned were: Charles Harrison, Mabel Lucie Attwell, Fougasse, Bruce Bairnsfather, George Morrow and H. M. Bateman.

8 Letter A. E. Johnson to WHR, 18.5.22, quoted in Geoffrey Beare: 'Heath Robinson: The Illustrator'; *W. Heath Robinson The Inventive Comic Genius of Our Age*; Chris Beetles Ltd, 1987, pp. 29–30.

9 Maurice Sly: 'How They Make You Laugh'; *The Sunday Statesman Magazine Section*, Calcutta, 11.8.38, p. 18.

10 DAY, Chap. XVIII, pp. 187ff.

11 Ransome Archives, Institute of Agricultural History, University of Reading.

12 *The Strand Magazine*, Vol. 59, May 1920, pp. 493–6.

13 Maurice Sly: *op. cit.*

14 Anon.: 'Connolly Leather and William Heath Robinson'; *Connolly Leather 1991 Calendar*, Introductory Notes.

15 William Heath Robinson: *The Gentle Art of Excavating*; Lincoln, Ruston-Bucyrus Ltd, n.d. [*c.*1938]. Reprinted: William Heath Robinson: *The Gentle Art of Advertising*; London, Duckworth, 1979, pp. 9–19.

16 MLOL, p. 166.

17 *The Bystander*, 13.8.19, p. 441.

18 *Ibid.*, 8.9.20, p. 620.

19 *Ibid.*, 31.3.20, p. 913.

20 *Ibid.*, 16.3.21, p. 581.

21 Letter Vivian Cox to JH, 8.7.91.

22 Conversation with Mrs Alison Greenwood, Jun. 1990.

23 DAY, p. 184.

24 Conversation with Miss Christine Robinson, Aug. 1990.

25 Recounted in *Cookham Family Robinson*; exhibition catalogue, Cookham Festival, 1971, p. 4.

26 *Aunty Bay's Autobiography*; RP.

27 Conversation with Oliver Robinson, February 1991.

28 Conversation with Sir John Latey, July 1991.

29 I am grateful to the owners of The Copse, Dr and Mrs Cameron, for letting me see their house and studio, and for showing me what remains of Heath Robinson's speaking tube.

30 Letter Vivian Cox to JH, *cit.*

31 Ref. *The Cranleighan*, Dec. 1927, pp. 369, 371–2.

32 Conversation with Dom Basil Robinson, 1991.

33 Letter WHR to Frank Swinnerton, 9.2.27; Swinnerton Papers, University of Arkansas Libraries, Fayetteville.

34 MLOL, p. 195.

CHAPTER SIX

1 H. G. Wells: *Marriage*; Macmillan, 1912, p. 269.

2 19.4.23, 8 p.m.

3 21.4.34, 7.30 p.m.

4 For the fullest account of the decoration of *The Empress of Britain* see *The Shipbuilder and Marine-Engine Builder*, May 1931.

5 *Daily Mail*, 4.4.34, p. 12.

6 *Ibid.*, 10.4.34, p. 9.

7 *Ibid.*, 20.4.34, p. 11.

8 *Ibid.*, 10.4.34, p. 23.

9 DAY, p. 205.

10 *Ibid.*, p. 202.

11 *Loc. cit.*

12 From Norman Hunter: 'Pancake Day at Great Pagwell'; *The Incredible Adventures of Professor Branestawm*, Bodley Head 1933, pp. 173ff.

13 DAY, p. 208.

14 Maurice Sly: *op. cit.*

15 Cecil Hunt: *Ink in My Veins: Literary Reminiscences*; Robert Hale, 1948, pp. 113–15.

16 Julian Trevelyan: *Indigo Days*; MacGibbon and Kee, 1957, p. 122.

17 *Sonderfahndungsliste G. B.*; Imperial War Museum, London.

18 MLOL, p. 195.

19 Cecil Hunt: *Author-Biography*; Hutchinson, 1935, p. 232.

CHAPTER SEVEN

1 Aldous Huxley: *Do What You Will*; Chatto and Windus, 1929. Quoted Sybille Bedford: *Aldous Huxley – A Biography*; Chatto and Windus, 1973, Vol. 1, p. 220.

2 Maurice Sly: *op. cit.*

3 The Brothers Dalziel: *op. cit.* See Chapter 1.

4 James Phillips Kay: *The Moral and Physical Conditions of the Working Classes Employed in the Cotton Manufacture in Manchester*. Quoted in Humphrey Jennings: *Pandaemonium: 1660–1886. The Coming of the Machine Age as Seen by Contemporary Observers*; Picador, 1987, p. 185.

5 Julian Trevelyan: *op. cit.*, p. 30.

6 DAY, p. 233.

7 MLOL, p. 138.

CHRONOLOGY OF WILLIAM HEATH ROBINSON'S LIFE

1872 31 May. Born at 25 Ennis Road, Stroud Green, London, third child of Thomas Robinson and Eliza Heath. Two older brothers, Tom (b. 1869) and Charles (b. 1870).

1874 Family moved to 33 Bryantwood Road, Islington. Will attended Miss Mole's Dame School. Mary, his sister, born.

1876 Mabel, his sister, born, February.

1877 Mabel, his sister, died, March.

1878 Family moved to 51 Benwell Road, Islington. Robinson grandparents moved from 19 to 37 Benwell Road. Childhood summer holidays usually spent at Ramsgate.

1880 Attended Holloway College.

1881 Charles Robinson, his uncle, died.

1882 Attended St Mary Magdelene's Church, Holloway Road. Holiday in Brighton, March. Florence, his sister, born.

1883 Holiday in Brighton, June.

1884 Attended Islington Probationary School.

1885 Thomas Robinson, his grandfather, died, September.

1886 Harriet Robinson, his grandmother, died, May. Family moved to 313 Camden Road, Holloway, October.

1887 Left school to attend Islington School of Art.

1888 Family moved to 49 Ferne Park Road, Stroud Green.

1892 Enrolled at Royal Academy Schools, January.

1895 Family moved to 1 Granville Road, Stroud Green.

1896 Sold first drawings for publication in *Little Folks* and *The Sunday Magazine*.

1897 Left the Royal Academy Schools, January. Spent the summer painting on and near Hampstead Heath. Disappointment in the Balls Pond Road, followed by a holiday at Lelant, Cornwall. Met the painter Alfred East. Took first studio at Howland Street, Tottenham Court Road, shared with Percy Billinghurst. Charles, his brother, married to Edith Favett. *Danish Fairy Tales and Legends* and three other books illustrated by WHR published.

1898 Edith ('Bay'), his first niece, born, August. Corresponded with Edward Bell, publisher. Moved studio to 115 Gower Street with Percy Billinghurst.

1899 Became engaged to Josephine Latey. *Arabian Nights* published. Moved studio to 3 New Court, Carey Street, shared with E. Cockburn Reynolds, then to 2 New Court.

1900 *The Poems of Edgar Allan Poe* published.

1902 Harriet Robinson, his aunt, died, February. His father died, May. Josephine's father, John Latey, died, September. *Adventures of Uncle Lubin* published by Grant Richards, October. Proposed to Grant Richards that he illustrate an edition of *Rabelais*.

1903 Met Charles Edward Potter of Lamson Paragon Supply Co. Will and Josephine married. Lived in furnished flat in Holloway Road, then moved to Cathcart Hill, Tufnell Park. *Child's Arabian Nights* published. First press advertisements published by Lawson Paragon Supply Co.

1904 His first child, Joan, born, June. Exhibition of *Rabelais* illustrations, Dickenson & Foster, London. Grant Richards declared bankrupt, November.

1905 His first cartoon in *The Bystander* published, February. Cartoons published in *The Tatler* and *Pall Mall Magazine*. Exhibited at the Royal Academy. *Stories from Chaucer* published in England and USA.

1906 His first cartoons in *The Sketch* published, March. Appearance of first recognizable 'Heath Robinson' machine. *Fairy Tales from Hans Andersen*, illustrated by Tom, Charles and William Heath Robinson.

1908 Oliver born, April. Appoints A. E. Johnson as his agent. Work first published in *The Strand Magazine*, June, followed by a profile, July. Moved with family to Hatch End, Pinner. Relinquished his New Court studio. Exhibition of illustrations to *Twelfth Night* at Brook Street Art Gallery, London, October. *Twelfth Night* published.

1909 Alan born, October. *A Song of the English* published. Exhibition of *Song of the English* illustrations, Baillie Gallery, October.

1910 First cartoons satirizing the threat of a German invasion of England published in *The Sketch*, April. 'Bouncing the Beecham' played in Hong Kong. *Collected Verse of Rudyard Kipling* published in USA. Joined London Sketch Club. Moved to Moy Lodge, Moss Lane, Pinner.

1911 Profiled in *The Sketch*, January. Federation of Frothfinders founded at The Crown Inn, Stanmore, April.

1912 Quentin born, March. *Rabelais* published by Alexander Moring Ltd in London and by Lippincott in USA. *Song of the English* and *Bill the Minder* published in England and USA. *Uncle Lubin* praised in H. G. Wells' novel *Marriage*. Exhibition of *Bill the Minder* illustrations at Brook Street Gallery.

1913 Profile of WHR by A. E. Johnson published. *Hans Andersen's Fairy Tales* published. Designed stage set for 'Epsom Ups and Downs' in revue at Alhambra Theatre.

1914 *A Midsummer Night's Dream* published.

1915 *Some 'Frightful' War Pictures* published, November. *Bill the Minder* reissued. *The Water-Babies* published. *Twelve Virtues of Chairman Tobacco* advertisements appeared in *Punch*.

1916 *The Saintly Hun* and *Peacock Pie* published. Article on WHR's line drawings by A. E. Johnson published in *The Studio*.

1917 *Book of Artemas* published. *The Saintly Hun* published.

1918 Travelled to Northern France to draw US troops at Front. Met Louis Raemakers. Moved to The Copse, Cranleigh, Surrey. Contributed to *The Art of the Illustrator* by Percy Bradshaw.

1919 *Flypapers* published. Tom born, January.

1920 Elected President of London Sketch Club for the year.

1921 Commissioned by Jonathan Cape to illustrate *The Complete Works of Shakespeare*, January. Perrault's *Old Time Stories* published. Series of advertisements for Connolly Bros begun.

1922 Cape's *Shakespeare* commission curtailed, March. *Peter Quip in Search of a Friend* published.

1923 Made first radio broadcast, April. *The Humours of Golf* published in England and USA. *Mr. Spodnoodle* strip cartoon series published in *The Daily News*.

1924 Elected a member of the Savage Club. Exhibition at the Fine Art Society, London, December.

1925 'The Art of W. Heath Robinson' by A. L. Baldry published in *The Studio*. Made second radio broadcast, December.

1925 *Uncle Lubin* published in USA. Cover designs and illustrations began to be published in *Good Housekeeping*, and continued in *Nash's Magazine*. Wrote article on his early life in *T.P.'s and Cassell's Weekly*.

1928 Exhibited at Sunderland Art Gallery.

1929 Moved to 20 Shepherds Hill, Highgate.

1930 Designed and painted decorations for the liner *Empress of Britain*.

1933 *Professor Branestawm* stories published. Decorated aeroplane for British Hospitals Air Pageant.

1934 'The Gadget Family' featured in Daily Mail Ideal Home Exhibition, Olympia, London. Interviewed on 'In Town Tonight' radio programme. *Absurdities* published.

1935 *Railway Ribaldry* published. Designed 140ft backdrop for the Chelsea Arts Ball. Moved to 25 Southwood Avenue, Highgate.

1936 *How to Live in a Flat* published.

1937 *How to Be a Perfect Husband* published.

1938 *How to Make a Garden Grow* and *My Line of Life* published. Introduced working models of his machines on television. Guest speaker at Foyles Literary Lunch. Lectured at *The Sunday Times* National Book Fair. Interviewed in *The Statesman of Calcutta*, August.

1939 *How to Be a Motorist* and *Let's Laugh* published.

1940 *Mein Rant* and *How to Make the Best of Things* published. Wartime cartoons began to appear in *The Sketch*.

1941 *How to Build a New World* published.

1942 *Heath Robinson at War* published.

1943 *How to Run a Communal Home* published.

1944 Died at home, 13 September. Buried at St Marylebone Cemetery, Finchley.

1945 Memorial exhibition, Fine Art Society, London, February.

1947 *The Life and Art of William Heath Robinson* by Langston Day published. This book contained WHR's final unfinished story, *Uncle Lubin's Holiday*.

WILLIAM HEATH ROBINSON'S FAMILY TREE

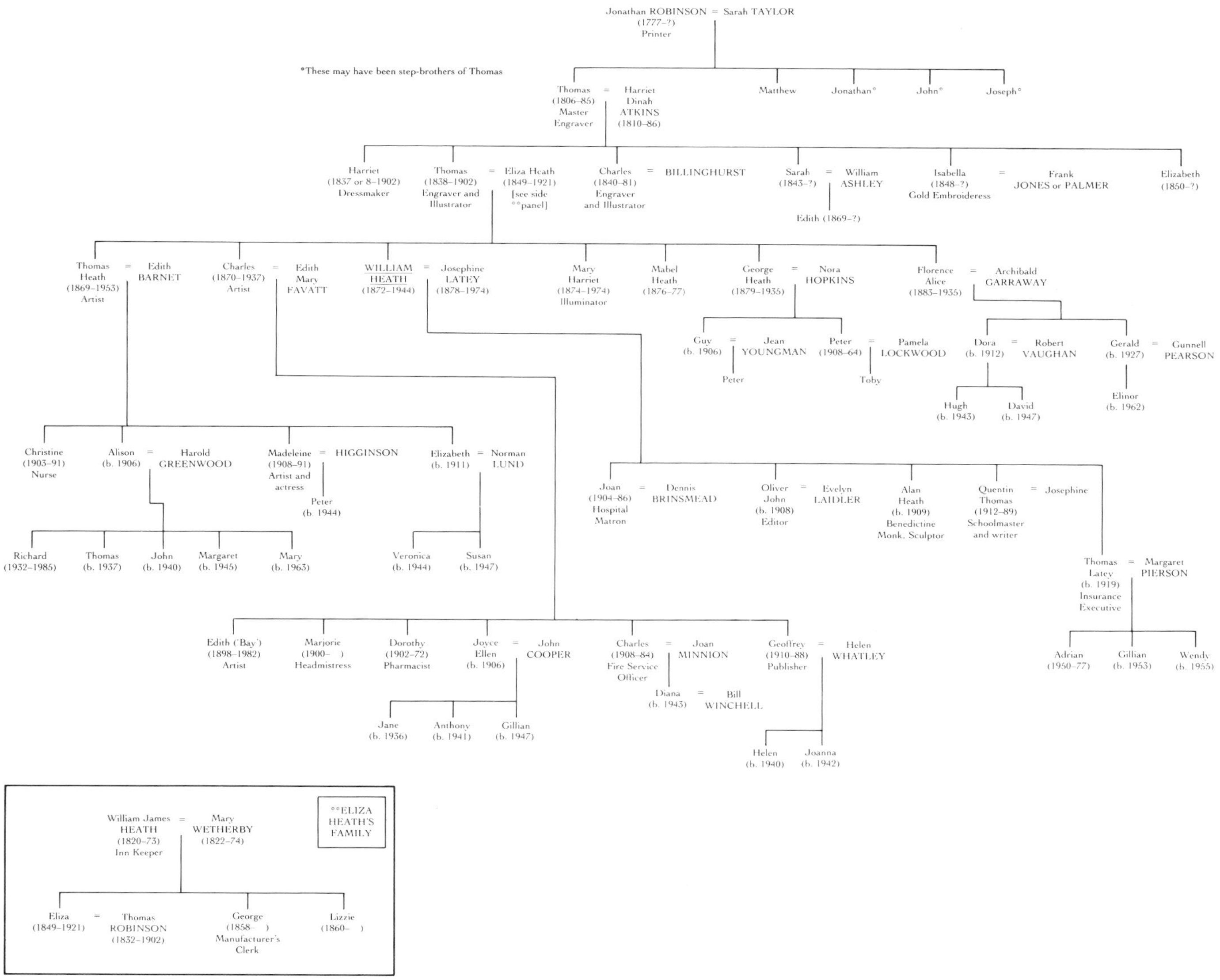

Jonathan ROBINSON = Sarah TAYLOR
(1777–?)
Printer
*These may have been step-brothers of Thomas
Thomas (1806–85) Master Engraver = Harriet Dinah ATKINS (1810–86)
Matthew
Jonathan*
John*
Joseph*
Harriet (1837 or 8–1902) Dressmaker
Thomas (1838–1902) Engraver and Illustrator = Eliza Heath (1849–1921) [see side **panel]
Charles (1840–81) Engraver and Illustrator = BILLINGHURST
Sarah (1843–?) = William ASHLEY
Edith (1869–?)
Isabella (1848–?) Gold Embroideress = Frank JONES or PALMER
Elizabeth (1850–?)
Thomas Heath (1869–1953) Artist = Edith BARNET
Charles (1870–1937) Artist = Edith Mary FAVATT
WILLIAM HEATH (1872–1944) = Josephine LATEY (1878–1974)
Mary Harriet (1874–1974) Illuminator
Mabel Heath (1876–77)
George Heath (1879–1935) = Nora HOPKINS
Florence Alice (1883–1935) = Archibald GARRAWAY
Guy (b. 1906) = Jean YOUNGMAN
Peter
Peter (1908–64) = Pamela LOCKWOOD
Toby
Dora (b. 1912) = Robert VAUGHAN
Hugh (b. 1943)
David (b. 1947)
Gerald (b. 1927) = Gunnell PEARSON
Elinor (b. 1962)
Christine (1903–91) Nurse
Alison (b. 1906) = Harold GREENWOOD
Madeleine (1908–91) Artist and actress = HIGGINSON
Peter (b. 1944)
Elizabeth (b. 1911) = Norman LUND
Richard (1932–1985)
Thomas (b. 1937)
John (b. 1940)
Margaret (b. 1945)
Mary (b. 1963)
Veronica (b. 1944)
Susan (b. 1947)
Joan (1904–86) Hospital Matron = Dennis BRINSMEAD
Oliver John (b. 1908) Editor = Evelyn LAIDLER
Alan Heath (b. 1909) Benedictine Monk, Sculptor
Quentin Thomas (1912–89) Schoolmaster and writer = Josephine
Thomas Latey (b. 1919) Insurance Executive = Margaret PIERSON
Adrian (1950–77)
Gillian (b. 1953)
Wendy (b. 1955)
Edith ('Bay') (1898–1982) Artist
Marjorie (1900–) Headmistress
Dorothy (1902–72) Pharmacist
Joyce Ellen (b. 1906) = John COOPER
Jane (b. 1936)
Anthony (b. 1941)
Gillian (b. 1947)
Charles (1908–84) Fire Service Officer = Joan MINNION
Diana (b. 1943) = Bill WINCHELL
Geoffrey (1910–88) Publisher = Helen WHATLEY
Helen (b. 1940)
Joanna (b. 1942)
**ELIZA HEATH'S FAMILY
William James HEATH (1820–73) Inn Keeper = Mary WETHERBY (1822–74)
Eliza (1849–1921) = Thomas ROBINSON (1832–1902)
George (1858–) Manufacturer's Clerk
Lizzie (1860–)

Based on information supplied by Geoffrey, Guy, Toby and Tom Robinson, 1992

BOOKS ILLUSTRATED BY WILLIAM HEATH ROBINSON

In compiling these lists, which aspire to completeness but may not achieve it, the author acknowledges his debt to the bibliographies compiled by Geoffrey Beare, John Lewis and Ian Rogerson, and to the British Library catalogue. Beare's and Rogerson's reference numbers are given. The numbers in bold after each entry indicate the quantity of black and white / colour illustrations by Heath Robinson in each book. The place of publication is London unless otherwise stated. The asterisk* indicates that the illustrations first appeared in earlier publications. The edition given is trade, except where stated.

1897 1 Hans Christian Andersen: *Danish Fairy Tales and Legends*; Bliss, Sands & Co. Beare 5a. Rogerson 2a. **16/0**. Later variant edition.

2 Miguel de Cervantes Saavedra (trans. Charles Jarvis): *The Life and Exploits of the Ingenious Gentleman Don Quixote de la Mancha*; Bliss, Sands & Co. Beare 6a–e. Rogerson 3a–b. **16/0**. Later variant editions.

3 John Bunyan (ed. George Offor): *The Pilgrim's Progress from This World to That Which is to Come Delivered Under the Similitude of a Dream*; Bliss, Sands & Co. Beare 7a–f. Rogerson 4a–c. **24/0**. Later variant editions.

4 W. H. D. Rouse: *The Giant Crab and Other Tales of Old India*; David Nutt. Beare 8a–c. Rogerson 9a–b. **52/0**. Later variant editions.

1898 5 Laurence Gomme (ed.): *The Queen's Story Book*; Archibald Constable & Co. Beare 9a–d. Rogerson 5a–c. **20/0**. Later variant editions.

6 Florence Marryat: *A Soul on Fire*; Sands & Co. Reprinted 1902. Beare 10. Cover design by WHR. **0/0**

1899 7 Anon.: *The Arabian Night's Entertainment*; George Newnes by arrangement with Archibald Constable & Co. Beare 14a–b, 58a–c. Rogerson 6, 23, 24a–c. **208/0** [Other illustrations are by A. L. Davis, Arthur McCormick, Edwin Norbury and Helen Stratton.] Later variant editions. Six WHR illustrations from this title were included in *The Children's Wonder Book*; Odham's Press Ltd, 1933. Beare 198. Rogerson 45.

8 Mrs E. Lucas (trans.): *Fairy Tales by Hans Christian Andersen*; J. M. Dent & Co. Beare 15, 20, 45. Rogerson 7a–b, 10, 21. **35/0**. [Other illustrations are by Charles and Tom Robinson.] Later variant editions.

9 W. H. D. Rouse with W. Crooke: *The Talking Thrush – Stories of Birds and Beasts*. J. M. Dent & Co. New edition 1938. Beare 16a–b. **29/0**

1900 10 *The Poems of Edgar Allan Poe*; George Bell & Sons. Beare 17a–d. [Also limited edition on Japanese vellum, 75 copies.] **103/0**. Reissued 1970.

11 Ascot R. Hope: *Tales for Toby*; J. M. Dent & Co. Beare 18. Rogerson 8. **11/0**. Additional illustrations by S. Jacobs.

1902 12 Miguel de Cervantes: *The Adventures of Don Quixote of la Mancha*; J. M. Dent & Co. Beare 23. Rogerson 11a–c. **45/0**. US edition 1925. A further edition was published posthumously in 1953 with 8 new colour plates and 26 line drawings, of which 10 were new. Beare 252.

13 W. Heath Robinson: *The Adventures of Uncle Lubin*; Grant Richards. Beare 24a–e. Rogerson 15a–c. **112/0**. US edition 1925. Later editions.

14 Walter Rippmann (ed.): *Dent's Andersen in German*; J. M. Dent & Co. Beare 25a–b. Rogerson 16. **12/0**. Additional illustrations by Charles Robinson.

15 W. A. Morgan (compiler): *The House Annual, 1902*; Gale & Polden. Beare 26. Rogerson 66. **6/0**

16 Prof. H. Shück (trans. W. F. Harvey): *Mediaeval Stories*; Sands & Co. Beare 27a–b. Rogerson 14. **10/0**

17 R. E. Raspe: *The Surprising Travels and Adventures of Baron Munchausen*; Grant Richards. Beare 28. Rogerson 13. **0/4**

18 Charles and Mary Lamb: *Tales from Shakespeare*; Sands & Co. Beare 29a–b. Rogerson 12. **16/0**. Later variant edition.

1903 19 W. Heath Robinson: *The Child's Arabian Nights*. Grant Richards. Beare 30. **25/12**

20 Geraldine Hodgson: *Rama and the Monkeys*; J. M. Dent & Co. Beare 31. Rogerson 251. **6/1**

21 Anon.: *Boys' and Girls' Fairy Stories*; J. M. Dent & Co. Beare 32. **3/3**

22 T. W. H. Crosland: *Grant Richards' Children's Annual for 1904*; Grant Richards. Beare 33. **1/4**

1904 23 Richard Johnson with Thomas O'Cluny: *The Merry Multifleet and the Mounting Multicorps*; J. M. Dent & Co. Beare 34. **16/0**

24 *The Works of Mr. Francis Rabelais, Doctor in Physic Containing Five Books of the Lives, Heroick Deeds & Sayings of Gargantua and His Sonne Pantagruel*; Grant Richard. Two volumes. Beare 35a. **254/0**. Rogerson 17a. Edition de luxe of 25 copies. Beare 35b. Published by Alexander Moring Ltd, 1912 (**238/0**); The Navarre Society, 1921 (**238/0**) (Rogerson 17b); and 1931, 1948 and 1954 (bound as one volume, **236/0**). Beare 35c–g. US editions 1912 and 1932.

25 T. W. H. Crosland and W. Collinge: *Grant Richards' Children's Annual for 1905*; Grant Richards. Beare 36. **0/2**

1904 26 C. Bearne: *Sanota: A Red Indian Story*; Wells Gardner Darton. Not in Beare. **7/0**

1905 27 Myra Hamilton: *Kingdoms Curious*; William Heinemann Ltd. Beare 38. **2/0**

28 Janet Harvey Kelman: *Stories from Chaucer Told to the Children*; T. C. & E. C. Jack. Beare 39a–c. Rogerson 18a–b. **0/8**. US edition 1905. Later variant editions.

29 *The Children's Christmas Treasury of Things New and Old*; J. M. Dent & Co. Beare 40. **4/3**

1906 30 W. M. Thackeray: *The Memoirs of Barry Lyndon* and *Men's Wives*; Caxton Publishing Co. Beare 42. Rogerson 22. **3/3**

31 Jeanie Lang: *Stories from the Iliad or the Siege of Troy*; T. C. & E. C. Jack. Beare 43a–c. Rogerson 20. **0/8**. US edition [?]1907. Later variant editions.

32 Jeanie Lang: *Stories from the Odyssey*; T. C. & E. C. Jack. Beare 44a–c. Rogerson 19a–c. **0/8**. US edition [?]1907. Later variant editions.

1907 33 Roland Carse: *The Monarchs of Merry England (William I to Richard II)*; Alf Cooke, Leeds and London. Beare 51a. Rogerson 29a–b. **73/20**

34 Eden Phillpotts; *The Secret Woman*; Collins Clear Type Press. Beare 52. **0/1**

1908 35 Roland Carse: *The Monarchs of Merry England (Henry VII to Edward VII)*; T. Fisher Unwin. Beare 51a. Rogerson 29a–b. **73/20**

36 O. M. Hueffer: *The Book of Witches*; Eveleigh Nash. Beare 56. **0/1**

37 William Shakespeare: *Twelfth Night or What You Will*; Hodder & Stoughton. Beare 57a–c. Rogerson 25a–b. [Also signed limited edition on hand-made paper, bound in vellum, 350 copies] **0/40**. Later variant editions.

1909 38 Rudyard Kipling: *A Song of the English*; Hodder & Stoughton. Beare 61a–b. Rogerson 26a–c. [Also signed limited edition on hand-made paper, bound in vellum, 500 copies.] **59/30**. Later variant editions.

39 Thomas Catling (ed.): *The Press Album*; John Murray. Not in Beare. Rogerson 27. **1/0**

1910 40 *The Collected Verse of Rudyard Kipling*; Doubleday, Page & Co., New York. Beare 63. **15/9**. Not published in England.

41 Rudyard Kipling: *The Dead King*; Hodder & Stoughton. Beare 64. Rogerson 28. **14/0**

1911 42 F. T. Palgrave: *The Golden Treasury of Songs and Lyrics*; Hodder & Stoughton. Beare 66. **0/1***

43 John G. Wilson (ed.): *The Odd Volume*; Simkin, Marshall, Hamilton, Kent & Co. Ltd. Beare 67. **1/1**

1912 44 W. Heath Robinson: *Bill the Minder*; Constable & Co. Ltd. Beare 69a–b. Rogerson 30a–c. [Also signed limited edition on hand-made paper, bound in vellum, 380 copies.] **126/16**. US editions 1912 and 1924. Later variant editions.

45 Harry Golding (ed.): *Happy Hearts. A Picture Book for Boys and Girls*; Ward, Lock & Co. Ltd. Beare 70. **0/2**

1913 46 *Hans Andersen's Fairy Tales*; Constable & Co. Ltd. Beare 74a–b. [Also signed limited edition on hand-made paper, bound in vellum, 100 copies.] **96/16**. Rogerson 31a–c. US edition 1924. Later variant editions.

47 Walter Carroll: *The Countryside – First Piano Lessons*; Forsyth Brothers Ltd. Beare 75. **1/0**

1914 48 *Shakespeare's Comedy of A Midsummer Night's Dream*; Constable & Co. Ltd. Beare 77a–b & e. Rogerson 32a–b. [Also signed limited edition on hand-made paper, bound in vellum, 250 copies. 100 issued in 1914, 150 in 1919.] **63/12**. Later variant editions.

49 Charles and Mary Lamb: *Tales from Shakespeare*; Hodder & Stoughton. Beare 78. **0/2***

1915 50 Charles Kingsley: *The Water-Babies. A Fairy Tale for a Land-Baby*; Constable & Co. Ltd. Beare 80a. Rogerson 34a–b. **104/8**. Later variant editions.

51 W. Heath Robinson: *Some 'Frightful' War Pictures*; Duckworth & Co. Beare A1. Rogerson 59. **25/0***

52 George Goodchild (ed.): *The Blinded Soldiers and Sailors Gift Book*; Jarrold & Sons. Not in Beare. Rogerson 33. **1/0**

1916 53 Walter de la Mare: *Peacock Pie*; Constable & Co. Ltd. Beare 89. Rogerson 38. **95/0**. Reprinted 1920. US edition 1920.

54 *The Queen's Gift Book*; Hodder & Stoughton. Beare 90. Rogerson 36. **3/1**

55 *Princess Marie-Jose's Children's Book*; Cassell & Co. Beare 91. Rogerson 37. **0/1***

56 Sir William Bull and 'Orion' [William Warren]: *The Book of Limericks*; Daily Express. Beare 92. **1/0**

57 Walter Carroll: *Forest Fantasies – Nine Miniatures for Pianoforte*; Forsyth Bros. Beare 93. **2/0**

58 *Playbox Annual for 1917*; Amalgamated Press. Beare 94. **6/0***

59 W. Heath Robinson: *Hunlikely!*; Duckworth & Co. Beare A2. Rogerson 35. **24/0***

1917 60 *Playbox Annual for 1918*; Amalgamated Press. Beare 104. Rogerson 71a. **9/0***

61 W. Heath Robinson: *The Saintly Hun: A Book of German Virtues*; Duckworth & Co. Beare A3. **24/0***

1918 62 *Playbox Annual for 1919*; Amalgamated Press. Beare 111. Rogerson 71b. **6/0***

1919 63 *Playbox Annual for 1920*; Amalgamated Press. Beare 114. **5/0***

64 W. Heath Robinson: *Flypapers*; Duckworth & Co. Beare A4. **30/0***

1920 65 R. L. Hine: *The Cream of Curiosity*; G. Routledge & Sons. Beare 117. **2/0***

66 *The Playbox Annual for 1921*; Amalgamated Press. Beare 118. Rogerson 71c. **6/0***

67 Max Pemberton (ed.): *Pelman Pie*; Hodder & Stoughton. Beare 119. **1/0**

68 W. Heath Robinson: *Get on With It*; G. H. Robinson & J. Birch. Beare A5. Rogerson 39. **30/0**

69 W. Heath Robinson: *A Jamboree of Laughter from a Boy Scout's Diary*; A. V. N. Jones. Beare A6.

1921 70 Charles Perrault (trans. A. E. Johnson): *Old Time Stories*; Constable & Co. Ltd. Beare 122a. Rogerson 40. **50/6**. Later variant edition.

71 *Playbox Annual for 1922*; Amalgamated Press. Beare 123. Rogerson 71d. **3/0***

72 W. Heath Robinson: *The Home Made Car*; Duckworth & Co. Beare A7.

73 W. Heath Robinson: *Motor Mania*; 'The Motor Owner'. Beare A8.

74 G. Heath Robinson (ed.): *The Toby Annual 1921–22*; G. Heath Robinson & J. Birch. Not in Beare. Rogerson 73. **3/0**

1922 75 W. Heath Robinson: *Peter Quip in Search of a Friend*; S. W. Partridge & Co. Ltd. Beare 129. Rogerson 41. **20/8**

1922 76 *The Complete Works of William Shakespeare*; Jonathan Cape. Commissioned and partly executed, but not published. Discussed in Beare, but not listed. [See Chapter 5]

77 *Ward, Lock Story Books*; Ward, Lock & Co. a) *The 'After You' Story Book*; b) *The Fairy Queen Story Book*; c) *The Rainy Day Story Book*; d) *The Sunny Day Story Book*; e) *The Buttercups and Daisies Story Book*; f) *The Summer Days Story Book*. Beare 130a–f. Each **2/0**

78 W. Heath Robinson: *Quaint and Selected Pictures*; G. H. Robinson & J. Birch. Beare A9.

1923 79 Elsie Smeaton Munro: *Topsy Turvy Tales*; John Lane The Bodley Head Ltd. Beare 135. **36/6**

80 *Ward, Lock Story Books*; Ward, Lock & Co. a) *The Bedtime Story Book*; b) *The Make-Believe Story Book*. Beare 130g–h. Each **2/0**

81 W. Heath Robinson: *Humours of Golf*; Methuen. Beare A10. Rogerson 42a–b. **50/0***. US edition 1923. Reissued by Duckworth 1975.

1924 82 *The British Legion Album*; Cassell & Co. Not in Beare. Rogerson 43. **1/0**

1926 83 W. E. Cule (ed.): *Everyland Annual for Boys and Girls III*; The Carey Press. Beare 149. **7/0***

1928 84 Harry Golding (ed.): *The Wonder Book of Aircraft*; Ward, Lock. Not in Beare. Rogerson 44. **2/0**

85 *BBC Handbook*, 1929. Not in Beare. **1/0**

1931 86 P. G. Wodehouse: *If I Were You*; Herbert Jenkins. Beare 188. **1/0**

1933 87 Norman Hunter: *The Incredible Adventures of Professor Branestawm*; John Lane The Bodley Head. Beare 197a. Rogerson 46a–b. **72/1**. Later variant editions.

88 John R. Crosland and J. M. Parrish: *The Children's Wonder Book*; Odham's Press Ltd. Beare 198. Rogerson 45. **6/0***

1934 89 George Maxwell Lyne: *Balbus. A Latin reading book for junior forms*; E. Arnold & Co. Beare 206. Rogerson 259. **10/0**

90 *Heath Robinson's Book of Goblins* (from Vernaleken's *In the Land of Marvels*); Hutchinson & Co. Ltd. Beare 207. Rogerson 47. **53/7**. Illustrations from this book were reused in *Goblins: Verses by Spike Milligan*; Hutchinson, 1978.

91 W. Heath Robinson: *Absurdities*; Hutchinson & Co. Ltd. Beare A11. Rogerson 48a–b. **96/0***. Reissued by Duckworth 1981.

1935 92 W. Heath Robinson: *Railway Ribaldry*; Great Western Railway. Beare A12. Rogerson 49a–b. **93/0**. Reissued by Duckworth 1974.

1936 93 Heath Robinson and K. R. G. Browne: *How to Live in a Flat*; Hutchinson & Co. Ltd. Beare 223a. Rogerson 50. **119/0**. Later editions.

1937 94 W. Heath Robinson and K. R. G. Browne: *How to be a Perfect Husband*; Hutchinson & Co. Ltd. Beare 229a. Rogerson 53. **117/0**. Later editions.

1938 95 Heath Robinson and K. R. G. Browne: *How to Make a Garden Grow*; Hutchinson & Co. Ltd. Beare 231a. Rogerson 52. **115/0**. Later editions.

96 A. M. Low: *The Wonder Book of Inventions*; Ward, Lock. Not in Beare. Rogerson 51. **2/0**

97 W. Heath Robinson: *My Line of Life*; Blackie & Sons Ltd. Beare 232a. **124/0**. Reissued 1974.

98 John B. Gledhill and Frank Preston: *Success with Stocks and Shares*; Sir Isaac Pitman & Sons Ltd. Beare 233. **4/0**

1939 99 Heath Robinson and K. R. G. Browne: *How to be a Motorist*; Hutchinson & Co. Ltd. Beare 237a. Rogerson 54. **109/0**. Later editions.

100 W. Heath Robinson: *Let's Laugh*; Hutchinson & Co. Ltd. Beare A13. Rogerson 55a–b. [Reissued as *Devices* in 1977.] **111/0***

1940 101 R. F. Patterson: *Mein Rant*; Blackie & Son Ltd. Beare 240. Rogerson 56. **12/0**

102 W. Heath Robinson and Cecil Hunt: *How to Make the Best of Things*; Hutchinson & Co. Ltd. Beare 241a. Rogerson 57. **124/0**. Later editions.

1941 103 W. Heath Robinson and Cecil Hunt: *How to Build a New World*; Hutchinson & Co. Ltd. Beare 243a. Rogerson 58. **135/0**. Later editions.

104 W. Heath Robinson: *Heath Robinson at War*; Methuen. Beare A14. Rogerson 63. **81/0***. Reissued by Duckworth 1982.

1943 105 W. Heath Robinson and Cecil Hunt: *How to Run a Communal Home*; Hutchinson & Co. Ltd. Beare 247a. **126/0**. Reissued 1980.

1944 106 Liliane M. C. Clopet: *Once upon a Time*; Frederick Muller Ltd. Beare 249. **43/0**

1945 107 Walter Carroll: *The Enchanted Isle – Music for Violin and Piano*; Forsyth Bros. Beare 251. **2/0**

1947 108 W. Heath Robinson: *Uncle Lubin's Holiday*. Unfinished story published in Langston Day: *The Life and Art of W. Heath Robinson*; Herbert Jenkins, pp. 249–60. Not in Beare. **8/0**

1953 109 Miguel de Cervantes: *The Adventures of Don Quixote de la Mancha*; Methuen. Beare 252. **26/8**. 16 of the black and white illustrations were first published in the 1902 edition. The other illustrations were made shortly before WHR's death.

New collections of WHR's cartoons have been published by Gerald Duckworth & Co. Ltd, as follows:

110 W. Heath Robinson: *Inventions*; 1973. **129/0**

111 W. Heath Robinson: *The Gentle Art of Advertising*; 1979. **75/0**

112 W. Heath Robinson: *Great British Industries and Other Cartoons from The Sketch 1906–14*; 1985. Intro. Geoffrey Beare.

ILLUSTRATIONS TO SHAKESPEARE COMMISSIONED BY JONATHAN CAPE

William Heath Robinson was commissioned by the publisher Jonathan Cape in January 1921 to illustrate a new edition of *The Complete Works of Shakespeare* for publication in eight or twelve volumes. The commission was cancelled in March 1922 after Heath Robinson had produced well over four hundred pen and ink drawings, with most probably some in colour, and the edition was never published. The works were lost for seventy years until more than 350 of them were discovered by Kathy Arrington and Valerie Kettley of Jonathan Cape in 1991. They were identified by the present writer in June 1991.

This list shows which of the plays WHR illustrated, and analyses the approximate number of character studies, colophons, illustrations to speeches and decorative headpieces WHR drew. The plays and poems are identified by an initial letter written in WHR's hand at the edge of each drawing, with a key number.

NB: For further contractual details the reader is referred to Geoffrey Beare: *The Illustrations of W. Heath Robinson*; Werner Shaw, 1983, pp. 66–7.

Play or Poem	Characters	Colophons	Speech illus.	Headpieces
The Tempest	6	13	5	2
The Two Gentlemen of Verona	6	11	5	–
The Merry Wives of Windsor	1	–	–	–
Measure for Measure	2	12	9	–
The Comedy of Errors	–	–	–	–
Much Ado about Nothing	–	4	1	–
Love's Labour's Lost	8	7	3	–
A Midsummer Night's Dream	7	5	4	2
The Merchant of Venice	14	5	–	1
As You Like It	–	–	–	–
The Taming of the Shrew	8	1	8	1
All's Well That Ends Well	–	1	–	–
Twelfth Night	9	1	15	–
The Winter's Tale	9	2	3	–
King John	–*	–	–	–
Richard II	–	–	–	–
Henry IV part 1	15	4	1	1
Henry IV part 2	–	–	–	–
Henry V	–	–	–	–
Henry VI part 1	12	4	7	1
Henry VI part 2	–	–	–	–

Play or Poem	Characters	Colophons	Speech illus.	Headpieces
Henry VI part 3	–	–	–	–
Richard III	–	–	–	–
Henry VIII	–	–	–	–
Troilus and Cressida	–	–	–	–
Coriolanus	–	–	–	–
Titus Andronicus	3	–	6	1
Romeo and Juliet	–	–	–	–
Timon of Athens	–	–	–	–
Julius Caesar	–	–	–	–
Macbeth	2	2	2	–
Hamlet	10	5	6	–
King Lear	5	–	–	–
Othello	9	–	7	–
Antony and Cleopatra	4	9	–	–
Cymbeline	11	3	6	–
Pericles	9	3	6	–
Venus and Adonis	–	1	–	–
The Rape of Lucrece	–	2	8	–
The Passionate Pilgrim	1	1	2	1
The Phoenix & the Turtle	–	–	–	1

* Inscription (Pandulph, *King John*) deleted; renamed for *Henry VI part 1*.

The drawings are all unsigned except one, a full-page illustration to *The Tempest*, Act II, sc. ii, of Trinculo with Caliban: 'What have we here?'. This is signed bottom left W. HEATH ROBINSON.

ADVERTISING BROCHURES, BOOKLETS AND EPHEMERA BY WILLIAM HEATH ROBINSON

Heath Robinson's prolific output as an artist for advertising has been extensively chronicled by Geoffrey Beare in his *Heath Robinson Advertising* (Bellew, 1992). For further details the reader is referred to Beare's bibliography, which, though acknowledged by the author to be incomplete, is extremely thorough. In drawing up the following list, which is also inevitably incomplete, the author is endebted both to Beare's published research and to *The Gentle Art of Advertising*, the collection of Heath Robinson's drawings compiled by Quentin Robinson and published by Duckworth in 1979. For their help in tracing Heath Robinson's advertising work, the author would also like to thank Barbara Arnold, Jonathan Brown, D. D. Dunkley, J. F. Earle, Sally Goldsmith, Anthony Hussey, E. Longbottom, Monty Moss, Nicholas Morgan and Peter Wright.

Heath Robinson designed advertisements for the following companies and their products:

1903 City Dairy Co. Ltd, Toronto, Canada. **0/1**

Lamson Paragon Supply Company, London, 1903–09

1915 *Chairman Tobacco*; R. J. Lea Ltd, Manchester. **13/0**

Johnnie Walker Whisky, Kilmarnock. **6/0**

1919 *Eno's Fruit Salts*; J. C. Eno, Ltd, London. **1/0**

1920 The longest and most fruitful association Heath Robinson had with a single company was that with Connolly Bros (Curriers), Ltd, Wimbledon. This lasted from 1920 to 1936, and 12 advertising booklets resulted: *Nothing Like Leather* (1920) **9/0**; *Light on Leather* (1922) **23/0**; *Tough Testimonials* (1924) **4/0** [9 other artists contributed to this publication]; *Nothing Takes the Place of Leather* (1925) **23/0**; *Leather Breeding on the Wandle* (1927) **20/0**; *Cattle Culture at Connolly's Leather College on the Wandle* (1930) **20/0**; *Leather for Ever* (1931) **20/0**; *Heath Robinson on Leather* (1932) **110/0**; *Connolly Chronicles* (1933) **23/0**; *Connolly-Land* (1934) **14/1**; *The Business Man's Encyclopedia Connollyca* (1935) **36/0**; *Connolly Customers* (1936) **20/0**

Meccano Ltd. **4/0**

Pear's Solid Brilliantine; A. & F. Pears Ltd. **1/0**

1921 Christmas card for Bassetts Birmingham Asphalt Ltd. **1/2**

Horrockses' Crewdson & Co. Ltd, Cotton Manufacturers, Manchester. **3/0**

Limmer & Trinidad Lake Asphalt Co. Ltd. **0/1**

Mackintosh's Toffee; J. Mackintosh & Sons Ltd, Nottingham. **3/0**

Mazda Light Bulbs. **1/0**

Port of Manchester Warehouses Ltd, Manchester. **22/0**

1922 Burroughs Adding Machines Ltd, London. **1/0**

Robert Cort & Sons Ltd, Coke Manufacturers, Reading. **1/0**

Fletcher Burrows & Co. Ltd, Colliers, Atherton, Lancs. **5/0**

MacDonald, Greenlees & Williams (Distillers) Ltd. **0/1**

Stiff & Co., Starch Manufacturers. [Published in Belgium.] **1/0**

Thomas & Green Ltd, Papermakers. Calendar for 1922. **0/9**

1923 Cuthbert C. Smith, Pig Farmer, Nottinghamshire. **1/0**

1924 *Comfort Soap*. Lever Bros Ltd, Port Sunlight. **1/0**

Wireless Valves. Philips Glowlamp Works Ltd. **12/0**

1925 Inecto Hair Restorer. **1/0**

1926 Barclay's Lager. **1/0**

Hovis Bread. Hovis Ltd, Macclesfield. **10/0**

1927 *Safety Matches*; Bryant & May Ltd. **1/0**

Rogers Peet Company, Gentleman's Outfitters, New York. **6/0**

1928 Clarkhills Automatic Water Heaters Ltd. **1/0**

G. & T. Earle, Ltd, Cement Manufacturers, Hull. **5/0**

Ransomes' Motor Mowers; Ransomes, Sims & Jefferies Ltd, Ipswich. **3/0**

1929 The Gre-Solvent Company, Leeds. **11/0**

1931 Practical Etching Service Ltd, London. **11/1**

1932 *Izal Medicated Toilet Paper*, *Izal Disinfectant* and *Duroid Tarmacadam*. Newton Chambers, Ltd, Thorncliffe, Sheffield. **19/0**

1933 William Crawford & Sons Ltd, Biscuit Manufacturers. **0/1**

1934 The Nithsdale Silver Fox Ranch, Thornhill, Dumfries. **2/0**

[The following eight advertisements were also exhortations for the New Year, and were published on Jan. 1st.]

Co-operative – Permanent Building Society, London. **1/0**

Luvisca Shirts. Courtaulds Ltd. **1/0**

The Direct Supply Aerated Water Co. Ltd. **1/0**

Ever-Ready Razor Products Ltd. **1/0**

Nugget Boots Polish. **1/0**. [Also 1937, 1939 and 1940.]

Prudential Assurance Co. Ltd. **1/0**

Smith's Sectric Clocks. **1/0**. [Also 1937, 1939 and 1940.]

Wright's Coal Tar Soap. Wright, Layman & Umney Ltd. **1/0**. [Also 1937, 1939 and 1940.]

1935	Great Western Railway Company, London. **93/0**
	Hercules Cycle Co. **0/1**
1936	Cylindo Tea. **1/0**
	International Stores. **1/0**
	Moss Bros & Co. Ltd, Gentlemen's Outfitters, Covent Garden. **16/0**
	Douglas Stuart, Bookmaker, London. **8/0**. [Also 1937.]
1937	Rhodian Cigarettes. **1/0**
1938	Ruston-Bucyrus Ltd, Crane Manufacturers, Lincoln. **16/0**
1940	Burberry's Ltd. **1/0**
	Shredded Wheat; Nabisco. **1/0**
1941 and 1942	High Duty Alloys Ltd. **8/0**

Undated advertising ephemera for the following companies:

Asbestos Cement Building Products, London.

Barford & Perkins Ltd, Garden Machinery Manufacturers.

Bayliss, Jones & Bayliss Ltd, Fencing Manufacturers.

John Booth & Sons, Structural Engineers (*c*.1930)

Continental Tyre Company, Germany (*c*.1927)

William Cook & Co. Ltd, Wire Rope Makers, Sheffield.

The Daimler Co. Ltd, Motor Car Manufacturers (*c*.1926/27).

A. Duckham & Co. Ltd.

Thomas Foreman & Son, Printers, Nottingham.

General Electric Co. Ltd (*c*.1934)

Goodall, Backhouse & Co.

Luis Gordon & Sons Ltd, Sherry Makers.

W. P. Hartley, Jam Makers (*c*.1925)

Hazelbourne Laundry, Balham, London.

T. Kerfoot & Co., Bardsley, Lancs. (?1922)

Allen Lane, Publisher, London (*c*.1933)

Hector Powe, Tailors, London (*c*.1924)

Shuck Maclean & Co. Ltd, Printers' Ink Manufacturers (*c*.1926)

Thomas Tapling Ltd, Bedding Manufacturers.

Vickery's Ltd, Paper Mill Specialities, London.

Wagon Repair Company.

Wellington & Ward Ltd, Photographic Film Manufacturers (*c*.1925)

Youngman Ladders.

Zerkall Butten, Paper Makers, Germany.

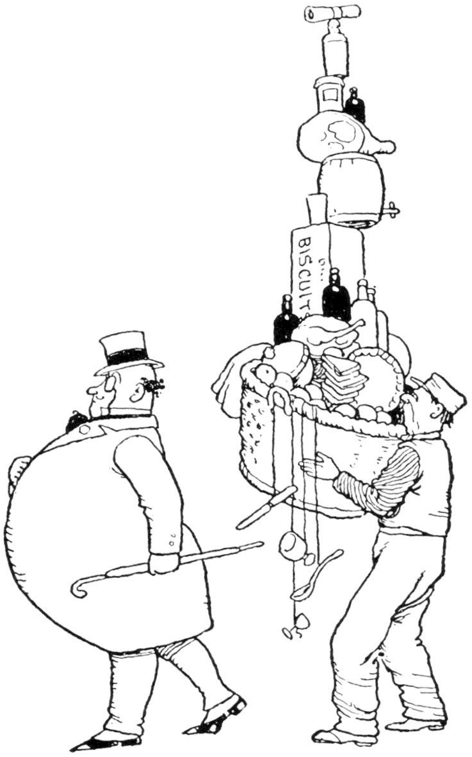

EXHIBITIONS OF ORIGINAL WORK BY WILLIAM HEATH ROBINSON

1904 Dickenson and Foster, London:
Illustrations to Rabelais by W. Heath Robinson.

1905 Royal Academy, London:
A Decorative Panel (no. 1473).

1908 Brook Street Gallery, London:
Illustrations to Twelfth Night by W. Heath Robinson.

1924 The Fine Art Society, London:
Humorous Drawings by W. Heath Robinson (84 works).

1928 Sunderland Public Art Gallery:
Original Humorous and Other Drawings by W. Heath Robinson (78 works. Cat. intro. by Percy Bradshaw).

1930 *Empress of Britain*, Canadian Pacific liner (launched 1930; sunk by enemy action 1940):
Decorations to Knickerbocker Bar and First Class Children's Room.

1933 British Hospitals Air Pageant:
Decorated aeroplane performing flying displays.

1934 Olympia, London:
Ideal Home Exhibition: The Gadgets.

1935 Chelsea Arts Ball, Albert Hall, London:
Backdrop design *Looking Back to the Stone Age.*

1945 The Fine Art Society, London:
Memorial Exhibition (127 works. Appreciation by A. C. R. Carter).

1971 The Cookham Festival:
The Cookham Family Robinson (2 works, in an exhibition devoted to painting, drawing, book illustration and sculpture by 21 members of the Robinson family, from five generations).

1973 Science Museum Loan Circulation Exhibition:
Heath Robinson (photographs, drawings and models). [This exhibition toured Britain for at least 15 years.]

1972 Medici Gallery, London:
W. Heath Robinson Centenary Exhibition (69 works).

1975 Portsmouth City Museum and Art Gallery:
William Heath Robinson (95 works. Cat. intro. by Andrew Greg) Also shown at Winchester City Museum, Southampton Art Gallery and Wolverhampton Art Gallery.

1977 Mappin Art Gallery, Sheffield:
William Heath Robinson (50 works. Cat. intro. by James Hamilton).

1983 Haringey Library, Crouch End Arts Festival:
William Heath Robinson (Cat. intro. by Geoffrey Beare).

1984 Chris Beetles Gallery, London:
The Illustrators: The British Art of Illustration 1800–1984 (8 works).

1987 Chris Beetles Gallery, London:
W. Heath Robinson: The Inventive Comic Genius of our Age (330 works. Cat. essays by Geoffrey Beare, Dr Robert Buckman and Oliver Robinson).

Chris Beetles Gallery, London:
The Illustrators: The British Art of Illustration 1800–1987 (27 works).

1988 Chris Beetles Gallery, London:
The Illustrators: The British Art of Illustration 1800–1988 (9 works)

1989 Chris Beetles Gallery, London:
The Illustrators: The British Art of Illustration 1800–1989 (17 works).

Maas Gallery, London:
Masters of British Illustration (1 work).

Bearne's Fine Art Auctioneers, Torquay:
Other Worlds (3 works).

1990 Chris Beetles Gallery, London:
The Illustrators: The British Art of Illustration 1800–1990 (4 works).

1991 Chris Beetles Gallery, London:
The Illustrators: The British Art of Illustration 1800–1991 (7 works).

1992 Chris Beetles Gallery, London:
The Brothers Robinson. (393 works)

Royal Festival Hall, London:
William Heath Robinson: Machines and Inventions. (62 works)

CONTENT TO BE ORDINARY

THE SOURCES OF WILLIAM HEATH ROBINSON

LANGSTON DAY REMARKS on how in adult life Will looked back on his boyhood, remembering many small incidents which 'had helped to sharpen his imagination and shape his peculiar sense of humour'.[1] Though Will himself recalls specific events in *My Line of Life*, such as the spectacle of Uncle George Heath in his dark green Volunteer's uniform being prepared for the Easter Review on the Brighton Downs, or the gloomy state occasions of family funerals, other incidents of the kind that fed his imagination occurred around him every day. It is a particular characteristic of his art that, however bizarre the situation created, there is enough observation of life to give a disturbing edge of reality to Will's subjects.

Speaking in 1908, Will admitted that his humour had been subject to literary rather than artistic influences, and singled out Lewis Carroll and W. S. Gilbert as sources.[2] As Will was an artist dealing with the interpretation of English writing through images, this is probably inevitable. English humour is so overwhelmingly literary, because the language is so rich, so widely understood, and has been blessed with so many great writers who have been incomparably funny in it. Greek, Dutch or Danish humour probably has a more limited appeal. Bright stars like Edward Lear or Max Beerbohm, whose

Has brought her breakfast

genius tripped backwards and forwards across the boundaries of art and literature, are exceptions that probably prove the rule, as, indeed, in his deadpan telling of the stories of *Uncle Lubin* and *Bill the Minder*, is Will Heath Robinson himself. Will's sources were not, however, limited to such classic writers as Cervantes, Carroll and Gilbert. It is likely that his inspiration came from a much wider range of written sources, some as close to home as his own local newspaper.

The headlines of the local paper of his youth, *The Islington Gazette*, reveal the same whimsicality that Will later captured in the titles and situations of his own drawings. In stories published during his youth, presumably true, the paper reported, for example, on 'The Disputed Ownership of a Vest',[3] on the difficulties of the incredibly-named Oscar A. Junck, 'A Sculptor in Trouble',[4] and on 'A Bicyclist Charged with Furious Riding' three times around Thornhill Square in four minutes. The defendant's only reported plea in this case, heard at Clerkenwell Police Court, was that 'he was not going nearly so fast as he could.'[5] Between regular reports of sermons preached locally, of people being brought to trial for adulterating milk, and many accounts of a 'Shocking Suicide', these tales of local life were the staple of the paper's information.

In a letter to the Editor of the *Gazette*, an anonymous correspondent records an incident he had witnessed in Upper Street, Islington, in 1884 which, thirty or more years later, could be a description of a Heath Robinson drawing:

> I saw an elderly man wearing a long skirted coat stop for an instant to look at some painter's work. At that moment a tramcar going northwards was met by an Archway omnibus going Citywards. The driver of the latter came close to the kerbstone, the overhanging wheels caught in the old man's coat, turning him completely round.... A narrower escape ... I never saw.[6]

This event contains all the ingredients of an incident in a Heath Robinson drawing in which opposites come together to generate a climax: the old fashioned and the new; slowness and speed; pedestrians and public transport; dignity and impudence. The incident has a Pickwickian ring, too, in that, apart from a few bruises and splashed mud, only pride is hurt, and life goes on as normal.

Whether picked up literally from local newspapers or gleaned from his unhurried observations of everyday life in the street or amongst his own family, Will found depths of inspiration in the ordinary. In an evocative passage in *My Line of Life*, in which he lets his mask slip momentarily, he writes of his morning walks as an older man in Waterlow Park, Highgate:

> A few old retired men meet daily as at a Club and chat and nod and argue. A young man studies a newspaper in search of a job. A lonely and pathetic old lady has brought her breakfast in a paper parcel to eat in the shade of the trees ... [T]hey are all unconscious that they are bravely supporting the fabric of social life. Without their aid it would fall. They are not original. They are content to be ordinary.[7]

Charles Dickens, a far greater chronicler of the ordinary, was read widely by Will, and here, too, he found more sources for his inspiration. *Sketches by Boz*, for example, is full of episodes that prefigure his work. One, 'The Full Report of the Second Meeting of the Mudfog Association for the Advancement of Everything', discusses 'a most delicate and beautiful machine, of little larger size than an ordinary snuff-box ... composed exclusively

Chat and nod and argue

How a fallen crumb may be the means of destroying the reputation of a reputable citizen
Pen and ink and wash, 1924
From *Hutchinsons Magazine*
Private Collection

of steel,' with which 'more pockets could be picked in one hour than by the present slow and tedious process in four-and-twenty.'[8]

The Mudfog Association goes on to consider 'Practical suggestions on the necessity of providing some harmless and wholesome relaxation for the young noblemen of England', in which a space of ground not less than forty square miles be enclosed by a brick wall and laid out with roads, turnpikes, bridges and villages, so that Four-in-hand Clubs can indulge in riotous living without interfering with others. Automaton policemen and magistrates would parody the maintenance of law and order, and extra large door-knockers and bell handles, constructed so that they could easily be wrenched off at night, would be fitted to doors. Attendants would be provided to screw them on again daily. This absurd idea is also Heath Robinson country, but one with a crucial difference. While Dickens was satirizing contemporary life to prompt social change, Heath Robinson, one of the millions of beneficiaries of Dickens's campaigns, was able to create comic situations that amused rather than angered his audience because the battle had largely been won.

Dickens was the great popular campaigner for social improvement through adequate investment in the new technology of the middle decades of the nineteenth century. His weekly magazine *Household Words* spoke directly to millions as they travelled to work or as they sat at home or read in their clubs. One of the most

In search of a job

The New Humane Cow-Catcher (left) and Pulling the communication cord
Pen and ink, 1935
From *Railway Ribaldry*

important of his campaigns in *Household Words* centred on two inventions designed to improve safety on the railway. In 'Need Railway Travellers be Smashed?'[9] he inveighed against railway companies who delayed the implementation of an invention to safeguard signals and points. Two years later, in 1853, he returned to the subject in support of the introduction of 'Crowley's Safety Switch and Self-Acting Railway Signals' following two railway accidents with heavy loss of life at Brighton and Redhill.[10] Dickens mocked the Railway Board's introduction of a dangling bell in the footplate connected to the guard's cabin by a long wire, their only attempt to improve matters, as being done 'with an eye to failure ... for the bell did nothing but jingle the whole way with the motion of the train and the driver never could be sure whether or not the guard was ringing it.' What the Railway Board introduced in 1853 as a deliberate, if laughable, attempt to improve public safety, is mirrored by Heath Robinson's laughable, if deliberate, solution to the same problem in *Railway Ribaldry* (1935), a celebration of the centenary of the Great Western Railway.

The adventures of modern life which most vividly fed Will's imagination concerned flying. Balloons, airships and aeroplanes of ever more complex and inventive construction filled his drawings throughout his career, and indeed, one of his earliest surviving works, *'The great white eagle flew down again ...'* (1898) concerns the magical effects of flight. The high ground of Alexandra Palace in Wood Green, four miles north of Islington, was the setting of regular demonstrations of ballooning and flying in the 1880s and 90s. One incident in particular was reported by *The Islington Gazette* in 1889, and once again its ingredients of technical breakdown, incompetence, rudeness, pride and muddled authority make it a typically Heath Robinson occasion.

The *Gazette* reported how 'Professor Williams, the American aeronaut and parachutist' made a hot air balloon ascent from Alexandra Palace, intending to descend by parachute in front of the crowd. Something, however, went badly wrong, and Williams became unable to detach the parachute from the balloon. Hanging from the basket by his hands, Williams drifted helplessly for two miles, gradually descending until he landed on the

The great white eagle flew down again
Pen and ink and wash, 1898
From *The Quiver*
Victoria and Albert Museum, London

roof of the offices of the Hornsey Local Board, damaging telegraph wires in the process. Up came the caretaker, who confiscated the parachute and demanded £5 to repair the damage. Williams refused to pay; the manager of the Alexandra Palace arrived out of breath and handed over the money; the caretaker gave a receipt; and Williams returned a hero to the stage of the Central Hall of 'Ally Pally', where he 'met with an enthusiastic reception'.[11]

Will may not have known of this particular incident, but he did watch other aeronauts parachuting over the grounds of Alexandra Palace,[12] and would have been as aware as everybody else of the realities of flying at the close of the nineteenth century. The dangers and humours of flying provided vivid source material for both realist and fantasist visionary writers, and were widely reflected in contemporary fiction. Jules Verne's *The Clipper of the Clouds*, published in England in 1887, contains dramatic descriptions of a voyage across the world in *The Albatross*, a flying machine with the hull of a ship which was lifted into the air by a set of 37 rotor blades.

For all the detail Verne gives of the appearance of *The Albatross*, he is remarkably slippery when telling of how it is made. 'Unsized paper,' he writes, 'with the sheets impregnated with dextrin and starch and squeezed in hydraulic presses, will form a material as hard as steel ... And it was this lightness and solidity which Robur availed himself of in building his aerial locomotive.'[13] As for how *The Albatross* was powered: 'He employed electricity, that agent which one day will be the soul of the industrial world. But [Robur] required no electro-motor

Uncle Lubin aloft in his balloon
Pen and ink, 1902
From *The Adventures of Uncle Lubin*

to produce it. All he trusted to was piles and accumulators. What were the elements of these piles, and what were the acids he used, only Robur knew.'[14] With remarkable sang-froid, Jules Verne describes *The Albatross*'s world voyage. 'The pass at last was traversed,' he writes of the crossing of the Himalayas. '*The Albatross* began to descend. Coming from the hills out of the forest region there was now beneath them an immense plain stretching far and wide. Then Robur stepped up to his guests, and in a pleasant voice remarked: "India, gentlemen."'[15]

The ballooning exploits of Thomas Monck Mason, a nineteenth-century pioneer of flight, are less well remembered than those of Jules Verne's heroes, but they did nevertheless provide direct inspiration for the writings of Verne's forebear, Edgar Allan Poe. In turn, they are a possible source for the appearance of the balloon that carries Heath Robinson's Uncle Lubin to the moon. Mason had made a 500-mile balloon flight from London to Weiberg in Germany in 1836, and in 1843 he exhibited his improved motor-driven dirigible balloon at the Royal Adelaide Gallery in London.[16] Poe's short story *The Balloon Hoax*, published in America in 1844, and widely available in England in collected editions of Poe's work by 1883, parodies Mason's account, and tells of how eight Englishmen set off to fly from North Wales to Paris, but changed course during the voyage and flew across the Atlantic to America in three days.[17]

Poe describes the balloon, which he based on Mason's description of his own craft, as 'composed of silk, varnished with the liquid gum caoutchouc. It is of vast dimensions, containing more than 40,000 cubic feet of [coal] gas.' The luggage that the eight men brought with them included

> ... cordage, barometers, telescopes, barrels containing provisions for a fortnight, water casks, carpet-bags, and various other indispensable matters, including a coffee-warmer, contrived for warming coffee by means of slacklime, so as to dispense altogether with fire.... All these articles were suspended from the hood overhead.

The balloon had a four foot deep wicker car, a rudder, a screw, a guide rope and an anchor.[18] Mason's craft, with its cordage, carpet-bag, rudder and screw, is uncannily close to the airship which Uncle Lubin built 'in a few days' to carry him to the moon in search of his nephew, Little Peter.

A moon voyage was, in 1902 when *The Adventures of Uncle Lubin* was published, hardly more fantastic a proposition for balloon passengers than was an Atlantic crossing in 1844. We can be fairly certain that Will was as well acquainted with *The Balloon Hoax* and other Poe stories as he was with Poe's *Poems*, which he illustrated in 1900. Writing of Will's work in 1916, A. E. Johnson maintained that:

> Poe's mystic vision and the vague but vast imagery which he employs made a strong appeal to [Heath Robinson's] temperament. [He] found himself at work upon a subject with which he felt himself in sympathy – a subject so congenial to his own imaginative instincts as to relieve his mind of that concern with the artist's *literary* motive and idea ...[19]

The illustrators of 'Penny Dreadfuls' and other nineteenth-century science fiction comics and magazines devised yet more fantastic machines and dramatic situations, and these, too, are possible sources, or prompts, for Will's imagination. A particularly popular character in the American magazines published in England by Aldine Publishing Co. from 1894 was Frank Reade, an inventor with a precociously inventive son, Frank Reade Junior.[20] In the stories, which proclaimed themselves with three exclamation marks to be 'Jules Verne Out-

A matter of time
Pen and ink, 1919
From *Flypapers*
Private Collection

'Let us hope,' Will writes, 'that at any rate the two noble gentlemen were able, at least, to mitigate the fall of their captain, though I fear that this is as much as we may hope for.'

done', the Readeses invented the Steam Man, a coal-burning, steam-driven metal robot with smoke pouring out of its topper, a Steam Horse, an electric Air Ship and an Electric Bird, which was able to hang motionless in the air, its vast wings lazily flapping, despite the weight of its searchlight, its dynamite gun, customs house-style superstructure and heavy webbed feet and tail. The illustrations in these magazines suggest how much Will's work belongs to a wide genre, and how isolated it has since become, the magazines being largely forgotten.

The last two decades of the nineteenth century saw a rapid growth in the patenting of inventions as the prosperity and wealth of Britain grew. During the five years from 1901 to 1905, over 140,000 British patents were granted to a wide range of highly imaginative inventors.[21] They ranged from an extraordinarily simple device for testing the state of one's breath,[22] to largely forlorn inventions such as Turnbull's Self Emptying Spittoon for the Floors of Railway Carriages[23] and Ryan's Improved Wicket for the Game of Cricket, in which an electrical bell rang when the cricket ball struck the wicket.[24] If Hawkins' Improvement for Aerial or Flying Machines (also applicable to submarines)[25] failed to find the success that its inventor dreamed of, a device patented in Britain a few months later in 1904, Wright Brothers' Improved Aeronautical Machine,[26] changed the world.

One of the many pioneers of flying who failed where the Wright Brothers succeeded was Sir Hiram Maxim (1840–1916), the American-born inventor of the Maxim Gun. Maxim described himself as a 'chronic inventor', and Heath Robinson was widely held to rival him in the role.[27] Throughout his career, Maxim filed a multitude of patents including a mouse trap, an inhaler for bronchitis sufferers, a merry-go-round and an automatic sprinkler. One of his least successful inventions was the steam driven flying machine, on which he worked from 1889 to 1894. This consisted of a large central plane with two side frames, and engines and boilers weighing 600 lbs and 1,200 lbs respectively. The water it required to produce sufficient steam for an hour's trip weighed an additional 6,000 lbs. In tests at Bexley, Kent, in 1894, this beast did, technically, fly, as its runner wheels were seen to lift off the railway track momentarily.[28] The steam-driven flying machine stands for a generation of seriously

The Haroplane
Pen and ink, 1919
From *Flypapers*
University of Birmingham Library

Will's caption for this drawing reads: 'The Haroplane is considered by the some to be . . . the last word to be said on aeroplanes.'

considered inventions that inspired such well-known Heath Robinson fantasies as *The Haroplane*, before themselves being consigned to oblivion.

The titles of Will's inventions read like a list of forlorn patents, themselves the result of the desperate ingenuity and persistence of Victorian and Edwardian inventors such as Maxim. When Alice asks the White Knight in *Through the Looking Glass* what his horse's anklets are for, he replies, modestly, 'To guard against the bites of sharks. It's an invention of my own.'[29] Even the hyperactive Major-General in Gilbert and Sullivan's *Pirates of Penzance*, who claims to be very good at integral and differential calculus, and who knows the scientific names of beings animalculus, is a forerunner of Heath Robinson's pompous officials and suited businessmen who have fully equipped themselves to survive the scientific revolution of the twentieth century.

Will's sources were not, however, solely drawn from living memory or contemporary literature, and two historical classics in particular caught his imagination and fed his work as strongly as any work of fiction. These were Sir James Frazer's study of magic and religion *The Golden Bough*, passages from which he had memorized, and William H. Prescott's *History of the Conquest of Mexico*.[30] Prescott writes vividly in his earlier

chapters about the achievements of the Aztecs, their social structure, their scientific and astronomical discoveries and their works of art and architecture. One passage, on the multifarious uses the Aztecs made of the Mexican Aloe, pays tribute to the ingenuity of the civilization in making the maximum possible use of one cultivated plant. The passage also parallels Will's many drawings of industrial processes in which raw materials are fully exploited, one by-product after another being manufactured with minimal waste, and each part of the process leading inexorably on to the next:

[The Mexican Aloe's] bruised leaves afforded a paste from which paper was manufactured; its juice fermented into an intoxicating beverage, *pulque*, of which the natives, to this day, are excessively fond; its leaves further supplied an impenetrable thatch for the more humble dwellings; thread, of which coarse stuffs were made, and strong cords, were drawn from its tough and twisted fibres; pins and needles were made of the thorns at the extremities of its leaves; and the root, when properly cooked, was converted into a palatable and nutritious food. The [plant], in short, was meat, drink, clothing and writing materials for the Aztec! Surely never did Nature enclose in so compact a form so many of the elements of human comfort and civilization![31]

What Will's industrial drawings have in common with the Aztecs as described by Prescott is that there is no shortage of labour. The Aztecs in their teeming thousands could manhandle a fifty-ton porphyry Calendar Stone over broken country without the aid of cattle, suggesting 'no mean ideas of their mechanical skill and of their machinery'.[32] In his own case, when Will needed more men to work his Match Tipping Machine, for example, he could just draw them in, wages no object.

James Frazer in *The Golden Bough* writes of the origins and practice of ancient customs, with a scholarly detail and a strength of narrative that scrupulously avoids anecdote and gives his book its enduring power. That Will could quote passages by heart is evidence not only of the quality of the book's prose, but also of the fascination that Frazer's words held for him. If Frazer was the recorder and thus a preserver of ancient customs, Heath Robinson was a creator of no less bizarre new ones, such as *Inspecting Stockings on Christmas Eve* or *Testing a Fiancée*.

A writer whose life represents, even defines, the professionalization of science, was H. G. Wells. Where the strength of Poe's or Verne's writing lay in its feats of imagination, Wells was coolly prosaic. His description in *Marriage* of a monoplane preparing to crash-land, has a calm, unexcitable sophistication: '... the monster came sliding up the sky over the trees beside the church to the east, already near enough to look big, a great stiff shape, big buff sails stayed with glittering wire, and with two odd little wheels beneath its body. It drove up the sky, rising with a sort of upward heaving ...'[33]

Paradoxically, many of Jules Verne's inventions have, in time, materialized, while Wells's imaginings remain, broadly, as unattainable now as when he wrote.[34] Wells himself paid tribute to Verne in the preface to a collected edition of Wells's scientific romances:

[Verne's] work dealt almost always with actual possibilities of invention and discovery, and he made some remarkable forecasts. The interest he provoked was a practical one; he wrote and believed and told that this or that thing could be done, which was not at that time done. He helped his reader to imagine it done and to realize what fun, excitement or mischief would ensue. Most of his inventions have 'come true'. But these stories of mine collected here do not pretend to deal with possible things; they are exercises of the imagination in a quite different field. They belong to a class of writing which includes *The Golden Ass of Apuleius* ... and the story of *Frankenstein*.[35]

William Heath Robinson falls properly into the Wells camp. If H. G. Wells' fantasies provoked panic or outrage,[36] Heath Robinson's generate a more domesticated mirth. The very use of his name as a descriptive tool suggests that by giving it to an unruly or complicated machine, the machine is somehow controlled. Adam named the animals for a like purpose,[37] and in doing so he helped to defuse man's fear of the unknown. In *An Airman's Outings*, Captain Alan John Bott described the appalling mechanics of the gun in his aeroplane in the First World War, and, by so doing, controlled it: 'The moveable mounting for the observer's gun in the rear cockpit ... we called it the Christmas Tree, the Heath Robinson, the Jabberwock, the Ruddy Limit, and names unprintable.'[38]

The complicated pieces of machinery that took Heath Robinson's name were, by a curious, circular, ramshackle route, the same sort of equipment that gave him his earliest inspiration. His fascination with the apparatus of the school science laboratory has been remarked upon, as has his love of theatrical machinery. It was these, with their ropes, wires, springs, trapdoors, and their room for elaborate improvisation, that captivated Will at an early age, and provided the first test bed for his invention.

NOTES

1 DAY, p. 59.

2 Anon: 'Mr. W. Heath Robinson and His Work'; *The Strand Magazine*, Vol. 36, July 1908, p. 45.

3 *Islington Gazette*, 26.6.1888.

4 *Ibid.*, 25.5.88.

5 *Ibid.*, 25.6.88.

6 'Upper Street Perils'; *Islington Gazette*, 25.6.84.

7 MLOL, pp. 192 and 194.

8 Charles Dickens: *Sketches by Boz*; Hazell, Watson & Viney edition [n.d.], p. 481.

9 *Household Words*, Vol. 4, 29.11.51, pp. 216ff.

10 'Self Acting Railway Signals'; *Household Words*, Vol. 7, 5.3.53, pp. 43–5.

11 'Sensational Balloon Affair at the Alexandra Palace'; *Islington Gazette*, 7.6.89.

12 MLOL, pp. 16–17.

13 Jules Verne: *The Clipper of the Clouds*; London, Sampson Low, Marston & Co. Ltd., 1887, p. 54.

14 *Ibid.*, p. 52.

15 *Ibid.*, p. 86.

16 Harold Beaver (ed.): *The Science Fiction of Edgar Allan Poe*; Harmondsworth, Penguin, 1976, p. 370. Thomas Monck Mason published an account of his voyage in *Aeronautica: or Sketches Illustrative of the Theory and Practice of Aerostation...*; F. C. Westley, 1838.

17 The story was first published in *The New York Sun*, 13.4.1844. It later appeared in collections of Poe's work published in Britain, including A. & C. Black's 3-vol. edition (Edinburgh, 1883), Vol. I, p. 94ff; and J. Shiells and Co.'s 8-vol. edition (London, 1895), Vol. III, p. 239ff.

18 Edgar Allan Poe: 'The Balloon Hoax', *The Works of Edgar Allan Poe*; 3 vols, Edinburgh, A. & C. Black, 1883, Vol. I, p. 99.

19 A. E. Johnson: 'The Line Drawings of W. Heath Robinson'; *The Studio*, Vol. 67, 1916, p. 227.

20 Bethnal Green Museum of Childhood: *Penny Dreadfuls and Comics*; London, Victoria and Albert Museum, 1983, pp. 36 and 38.

21 Rodney Dale and Joan Gray: *Edwardian Inventions 1901–05*; W. H. Allen, 1979, p. 2.

22 Leder's Foul Breath Indicator. Patent no. 16011/1902. Patentee: Xavier Henry Leder, Seaman, London.

23 Patent no. 8429/1904. Patentee: J. H. Turnbull, Railway Fitter, Gateshead.

24 Patent no. 3618/1904. Patentee: James Ryan, St Bride's Institute, London.

25 Patent no. 1534/1904. Patentee: Edward Caesar Hawkins, Long Stratton, Norfolk.

26 Patent no. 6732/1904. Patentees: Orville and Wilbur Wright, Manufacturers, 1127 West Third Street, Dayton, Ohio.

27 Percy V. Bradshaw: *The Art of the Illustrator – W. Heath Robinson and his Work*; London, The Press Art School, n.d. [1918], p. 5.

28 *D.N.B.*; Sir Hiram Maxim: *My Life*; 1915.

29 Lewis Carroll: *Alice Through the Looking Glass*, Ch. VIII.

30 Conversation with Dom Basil Robinson, 1990.

31 William H. Prescott: *History of the Conquest of Mexico*; London, Swan Sonnenschein, Le Bas and Lowery, 1886, pp. 65–6. See also Charlotte Du Cann: 'Green Cows'; *Independent Magazine*, 13.7.1991, p. 28ff.

32 *Ibid.*, p. 68.

33 H. G. Wells: *Marriage*; Macmillan, 1912, p. 93/4.

34 Bernard Bergonzi: *The Early H. G. Wells – A Study of the Scientific Romances*; University of Manchester Press, 1961, p. 18.

35 H. G. Wells: *The Scientific Romances of H. G. Wells*; Gollancz, 1933. Quoted Bergonzi, *op. cit.*

36 Ref. panic over Orson Welles's broadcast of *The War of the Worlds* [1938] and the protest mounted by Indians at Wells's *A Short History of the World*, 1923. See David C. Smith: *H. G. Wells – Desperately Mortal: A Biography*; Yale University Press, 1986, pl. 23 (f. p. 253).

37 *Genesis*, Ch. 2, vv. 19–20.

38 Contact [Capt. Alan John Bott]: *An Airman's Outings*; i, 12. Toronto, McClelland, Goodchild and Stewart, 1917. Quoted *O.E.D.*, Vol. VII, p. 77.

THE LAST WORD FOR WILLIAM HEATH ROBINSON, WHO WRITES ABOUT HIS WORK

'I REALLY HAVE A SECRET SATISFACTION IN BEING CONSIDERED RATHER MAD.'

SHORTLY AFTER HEATH ROBINSON moved to Cranleigh in 1918, he was invited by the artist and publisher Percy Bradshaw to contribute to the series of publications *The Art of the Illustrator*. Bradshaw was the owner of the Press Art School, a highly successful Correspondence College he founded shortly before the First World War. With leading illustrators such as Bert Thomas, Harry Rountree, H. M. Bateman and William Heath Robinson as teachers and advisers, the school developed the talents of a new generation of men and women who came to supply illustrations and cartoons to newspapers and magazines. In 1913 over six hundred new pupils had enrolled, and by the end of the war Bradshaw was enrolling more than three thousand a year. Bradshaw employed twenty-two assistants on his teaching and clerical staff at Tudor Hall, Forest Hill, London. He wrote in his autobiography *Drawn from Memory* that 'letters and drawings which formerly came through my letter-box now arrived in sacks, postal vans collected my outgoing mail, and the Press Art School was in touch with nearly every part of the world. Many drawings arrived with the mud of the trenches on them; others, stained and matted together with sea-water, bore the official label "Damaged by Enemy Action".'[1] Among the artists who received their early training through Bradshaw's correspondence courses were Kenneth Bird ('Fougasse'), Leo Cheney, Will Houghton and Bertram Prance.

In *The Art of the Illustrator*, Bradshaw invited twenty artists, including Frank Reynolds, C. E. Brock, Russell Flint and William Heath Robinson, each to make an illustration which would be photographed at six different stages during its creation and published in a folio in six photogravure plates with a commentary on the artist's working method. The series gave a unique insight into the variety of ways an illustration grows on its artist's drawing board, and into twenty artists' different working methods.

In the Introduction to his folio, which followed the creation of his ink and watercolour drawing The Young Pan, *Heath Robinson wrote:*

Needless to say, the most important thing is the Subject of these drawings – I mean, the ridiculous plot, the absurd combination of circumstances, or whatever the main idea of the picture happens to be. The particular character of this class of humour, however, is not due to the subject alone, but to a combination of other elements acting with it.

First of these, is the stone-blindness of the persons involved to the humour of the situation, though this is staring them in the face. By a sort of negative process, this utter unconsciousness greatly increases the humour; indeed the success of the drawing largely depends on the interacting of these two elements acting one upon another.

It will be seen that it is not enough so to contradict the laws of gravity, or any other law of Nature, as to be merely incongruous; the main idea must be *ridiculously* humorous to give adequate point to the lack of humour in the characters involved; in fact, the combination should be a demonstration of the fund of humour provided by those lacking any sense of it.

There is, however, a third element which is of great importance, and that is the execution or Technique. To complete the scheme, this technique should argue, in the artist who draws the picture, a lack of humour quite equal to that of the characters he represents.

The Artist, therefore, has to act a part; and, in this connection, I would like to admit how gratified I am at

The Young Pan
Pen and ink, 1918

being confounded with my part – like the villain who triumphs at being hissed when leaving the stage. I really have a secret satisfaction in being considered rather mad, when, actually, I am playing the part of an Artist who strains, with all his powers, to suggest the absolute conviction, logic and solid reality of the things he portrays.

I consider that my technique, for this purpose, *must* be *naïve*, and have all the appearance of absolute conscientiousness. But it should not be merely conscientious. The vital thing is to express, by means of a certain technique, the determined *effort* to attain accuracy; and it is this effort alone which should be manifest.

After many experiments, I feel that this effect is best expressed, first of all, by a hard, obviously painstaking, uncompromising outline, with an evident anxiety to leave nothing out, and proving, by its unpreferential treatment of everything, its absence of any desire to go out of its slow, solemn way to improve the humour of the situation. Every object should then be modelled with the most apparent effort to express its solidity and reality, leaving nothing to the imagination, and dispelling the slightest tendency to mystery.

Yet another element, the consideration of which may be of use to the student, is the Composition of the picture. This should be dictated solely by the requirements of the theme, to which, while it unfolds itself, the attention should be completely held. With this end in view, the utmost advantage should be taken of the space at your disposal, and a most economical selection be made of the humorous material to be included. Remember that, once included, everything has to stand therein very substantially, and that reliance on mystery or other veil to hide it, or diminish its importance, is out of the question.

In order to explain the technical aspect of these humorous drawings of mine, in such a manner that the explanation shall be of use to the student, it has been necessary to analyse the humour rather carefully, as, in work of this nature, it is so intimately associated with the technique or execution....

I don't know what else there is to say, except to observe once again that the technique of such work should not be merely conscientious. It is not, for instance, enough to emulate the scientific accuracy of the camera, for success in this would obviously destroy all possibility of humour and that special sense of *effort* which I have already insisted upon.

It will be realized that a more masterly and sophisticated style than mine – though very easily attained – might at once destroy the special character I aim at in these drawings. A pure Line method would suggest itself as suitable for such subjects, but somehow I have found that the results are never so successful as those attained with Line and Wash combined.

I would add one remark with regard to the Six Stages. I would not like it to be thought that I deprecate or belittle the value and use of models. I merely find that, for my own purpose, it is better not to use them *directly*. As a matter of fact, in the Sixth Stage, I *have* endeavoured to improve the drawing by reference to models.

1 Percy V. Bradshaw: *Drawn from Memory: Adventures in the Arts*; Chapman and Hall, 1943, pp. 47ff.

BOOKS AND ARTICLES ABOUT HEATH ROBINSON

Anon.: 'Mr. W. Heath Robinson and his Work'; *The Strand Magazine*, Jul. 1908, pp. 41–9.

Anon.: 'A Maker of Absurdities'; *London Magazine*, Aug. 1908, p. 626.

Anon.: 'Photographic Interviews No. V – A Famous "Sketch" Artist: Mr. W. Heath Robinson'; *The Sketch*, 4.1.11, pp. 399–400 [Photographs of WHR also appeared as a headpiece to *The Bitter Bite*; *The Sketch*, 19.6.07, p. 307.]

Anon.: 'Christmas Leaves from the Publishers'; *Illustrated London News*, 7.12.12, p. 852.

Anon.: 'The Heath Robinson "Ideal Home" at Olympia'; *Decoration*, Apr. 1934, pp. 77–9.

Anon.: 'Mr. Heath Robinson – Humorous Artist' [Obituary]; *The Times*, 14.9.44.

Anon.: 'Heath Robinson's Contraptions'; *Illustrated London News*, May 1972, p. 35ff.

A. L. Baldry: 'The Art of Mr. Heath Robinson'; *The Studio*, May 1925, pp. 242–9.

Geoffrey Beare: *The Illustrations of W. Heath Robinson*; Werner Shaw, 1983. Intro. by Oliver Robinson.

Geoffrey Beare: *The Brothers Robinson*; Chris Beetles Ltd, 1992.

Geoffrey Beare: *Heath Robinson Advertising*; Bellew, 1992.

Chris Beetles Ltd: *W. Heath Robinson (1872–1944) – The Inventive Comic Genius of Our Age*; Chris Beetles Ltd, 1987. Contains essays by Geoffrey Beare, Dr Robert Buckman and Oliver Robinson.

Percy V. Bradshaw: *The Art of the Illustrator: W. Heath Robinson and his Work*; The Press Art School, n.d. [1918]

Cookham Festival: *The Cookham Family Robinson*; Cookham, Berks., 1971.

Ian Coster: *London Opinion*, August 1940. [Interview with WHR]

G. W. Langston Day: 'The Gadget King'; *Everybody's Weekly*, 31.3.45, pp. 8–9.

Langston Day: *The Life and Art of W. Heath Robinson*; Herbert Joseph, 1947.

Lesley Garner: 'Magic in his Madness'; *The Sunday Times Magazine*, 4.6.72. Cover and pp. 14–22.

Andrew Greg: *William Heath Robinson*; exhibition catalogue introduction; Portsmouth City Museums, 1975.

Herbert B. Grimsditch: 'William Heath Robinson'; *Dictionary of National Biography 1941–1950*, p. 729–30.

James Hamilton: *William Heath Robinson*; exhibition catalogue introduction; Sheffield, Mappin Art Gallery, 1977.

Melvyn Horder: 'The World of Heath Robinson'; *Times Saturday Review*; 21.7.73.

A. E. Johnson: *W. Heath Robinson*; Adam and Charles Black, 'Brush, Pen and Pencil' Series, 1913. [Reviewed *The Athenaeum*, 7.6.13, p. 629.]

A. E. Johnson: 'The Line Drawings of W. Heath Robinson'; *The Studio*, May 1916, pp. 223–38.

R. Furneaux Jordan (intro.): *The Penguin Heath Robinson*; Penguin Books, 1966.

David Larkin (ed.): *Charles and William Heath Robinson*; Constable, 1976. Intro. by Leo de Freitas.

John Lewis: *Heath Robinson – Artist and Comic Genius*; Constable, 1973.

Christopher Mann: 'Heath Robinson as Advertisement Designer'; *Commercial Art*, Jun. 1927, pp. 256–9.

W. Heath Robinson: 'How I Spend Christmas'; *The Bookman*, Dec. 1909, p. 138.

W. Heath Robinson: 'In the Days of My Youth'; *T.P.'s and Cassell's Weekly*, 18.4.25, pp. 956, 964, 966.

W. Heath Robinson: *My Line of Life*; Blackie, 1938. Reissued by E. P. Publishing, Wakefield, 1974.

Ian Rogerson: *The Robinson Brothers: An Exhibition of Book Illustration by Thomas Heath, Charles and William Heath Robinson*; Manchester Polytechnic Library, 1987.
[This book contains an excellent catalogue of the collection of books by the Robinson brothers in Manchestesr Polytechnic Library.]

Fenn Sherie: 'Joking Apart'; *Pearson's Magazine*, Dec. 1930, pp. 579–85.

Maurice Sly: 'How They Make You Laugh'; *The Sunday Statesman Magazine Section*; Calcutta, 11.8.38, p. 18.

GENERAL BOOKS AND ARTICLES

Thomas Balston: 'English Book Illustration 1880–1900'; *New Paths in Book Collecting* (ed. John Carter); Constable, 1934.

Geraldine Beare: *Index to The Strand Magazine 1891–1950*; Greenwood Press, 1982.

Percy V. Bradshaw: *Drawn from Memory*; Chapman and Hall, 1943.

John Christian (ed.): *The Last Romantics*; Lund Humphries, Barbican Art Gallery, 1989.

Walter Churcher: 'The London Sketch Club'; *The Studio*, Vol. 63, 1915, pp. 243–55.

David Cuppleditch: *The London Sketch Club*; Dilke Press, 1978.

Marion Hepworth Dixon: 'The Delicacy of Humour'; *The Ladies Realm*, Dec. 1907, pp. 231–8.

David Driver (ed.): *The Art of Radio Times – The First Sixty Years*; BBC, 1981.

William Feaver: *When We Were Young – Two Centuries of Children's Book Illustration*; Thames & Hudson, 1977.

Michael Felmingham: *The Illustrated Gift Book 1880–1930*; Scolar Press, 1988.

Charles Harris: *Islington*; Hamish Hamilton, 1974.

John Harthan: *The History of the Illustrated Book – The Western Tradition*; Thames & Hudson, 1981.

Edward Hodnett: *Five Centuries of English Book Illustration*; Scolar Press, 1988.

C. Geoffrey Holme and Ernest G. Halton (eds.): *Modern Book Illustrators and Their Work*; Studio Special Number, 1914.

Geoffrey Holme (ed.): *Caricature of Today*; intro. by Randall Davies, Studio Special Number, 1928.

Simon Houfe: *The Dictionary of British Book Illustrators and Caricaturists; 1800–1914*; Antique Collectors Club, 1978.

Cecil Hunt: *Author-Biography*; Hutchinson, 1935.

Cecil Hunt: *Ink in My Veins – Literary Reminiscences*; Robert Hale, 1948.

Diana L. Johnson: *Fantastic Illustration and Design in Britain 1850–1950*; Rhode Island Museum of Art, 1979.

John Lewis: *The Twentieth Century Book*; Herbert Press, 1984.

Lord Mackintosh: *By Faith and Work*; Hutchinson, 1966.

Bertha E. Mahoney, Louise Payson Latimer and Beulah Folmsbee (eds.): *Illustrators of Children's Books 1744–1945*; The Horn Book, Boston, 1947.

F. A. Mercer and W. Gaunt (eds.): *Modern Publicity and Commercial Art Annual, 13*; The Studio, 1936–7.

Percy Muir: *Victorian Illustrated Books*; Batsford, 1971.

Brigid Peppin: *Fantasy: Book Illustration 1860–1920*; Studio Vista, 1975.

Brigid Peppin and Lucy Micklethwait: *Dictionary of British Book Illustrators: The Twentieth Century*; John Murray, 1983.

Gordon N. Ray: *The Illustrator and the Book in England from 1790–1914*; Pierpont Morgan Library and OUP, 1976.

Malcolm Salaman: *British Book Illustration Yesterday and Today*; The Studio, 1923.

R. E. D. Sketchley: *English Book Illustrators of Today; Appreciation of the Work of Living English Illustrators with Lists of their Work*; Kegan Paul, Trench, Tuibner & Co., 1903.

John Russell Taylor: *The Art Nouveau Book in Britain*; Methuen, 1966.

Joyce Irene Whalley and Tessa Rose Chester: *A History of Children's Book Illustration*; John Murray, Victoria and Albert Museum, 1988.

One inch of joy surmounts of grief a span,
Because to laugh is proper to the man.

FRANÇOIS RABELAIS,
translated by Sir Thomas Urquhart, 1653

INDEX

PICTURE SOURCES

The author and publisher are grateful to the trustees of the Estate of Mrs J. C. Robinson for permission to reproduce the work of William Heath Robinson.

Windsor Castle, Royal Library © 1992 by gracious permission of Her Majesty the Queen: 57.
Bonhams: 96.
British Library: 52.
British Library, Newspaper Library: 12, 16, 28, 36, 54, 56, 76, 100, 116.
Canadian Pacific Archives A–9996, Musk coll.: 99.
Christies: 9, 11, 89.
Connolly Brothers (Curriers) Ltd.: 80, 82.
Harry Ransom Humanities Research Center, The University of Texas at Austin: 117.
Ian Jefferies, Buntingford Civic Society: 62.
Imperial War Museum: 65.
The Joan Brinsmead Trust: 3, 17, 24, 25, 26, 30, 44, 47, 56, 58, 62, 73, 74, 86, 87, 91, 93, 97, 98, 103, 109, 117.
Mary Evans Picture Library: 40.
The National Gallery of Canada, Ottawa: 45.
National Portrait Gallery: 98.
Prinknash Abbey: 95.
Department of Archives and Manuscripts, Reading University: 14, 20, 30, 31.
By permission of the Trustees of the Science Museum: 94.
Sheffield City Art Galleries: 49, 53, 81, 113, 118.
Société des Produits Nestlé S.A., Vevey, Switzerland: 78.
Courtesy of the Board of Trustees of the Victoria & Albert Museum: 2, 19, 64, 69, 107, 137.

Picture research by the author, assisted by Karin Hills